W9-BRQ-342

Information and American Democracy

Technology in the Evolution of Political Power

This book assesses the consequences of new information technologies for American democracy in a way that is theoretical and also historically grounded. The author argues that new technologies have produced the fourth in a series of "information revolutions" in the United States, stretching back to the founding. Each of these, he argues, led to important structural changes in politics. After reinterpreting historical American political development from the perspective of evolving characteristics of information and political communication, the author evaluates effects of the Internet and related new media. The analysis shows that the use of new technologies is contributing to "postbureaucratic" political organization and fundamental changes in the structure of political interests. The author's conclusions tie together scholarship on parties, interest groups, bureaucracy, collective action, and political behavior with new theory and evidence about politics in the information age.

Bruce Bimber is Associate Professor of Political Science and Director of the Center for Information Technology and Society at the University of California in Santa Barbara. He formerly held positions at RAND and Hewlett-Packard. He is author of *The Politics of Expertise in Congress* and numerous articles dealing with technology and politics. He holds a Ph.D. in political science from MIT and a B.S. in electrical engineering from Stanford.

ANNENBERG
LIBRARY

COMMUNICATION, SOCIETY AND POLITICS

Editors

W. Lance Bennett, *University of Washington*

Robert M. Entman, *North Carolina State University*

Editorial Advisory Board

Larry M. Bartels, *Woodrow Wilson School of Public and International Affairs, Princeton University*

Jay G. Blumer, Emeritus, *University of Leeds* and *University of Maryland*

Daniel Dayan, *Centre National de la Recherche Scientifique, Paris,* and *Department of Media & Communications, University of Oslo*

Doris A. Graber, *Department of Political Science, University of Illinois at Chicago*

Paolo Mancini, *Istituto di Studi Sociali, Facoltà di Scienze Politiche, Università di Perugia* and *Scuola di Giornalismo Radiotelevisiv, Perugia*

Pippa Norris, *Shorenstein Center on the Press, Politics, and Public Policy, Kennedy School of Government, Harvard University*

Barbara Pfetsch, *Wissenschaftszentrum Berlin für Socialforschung*

Philip Schlesinger, *Film and Media Studies, University of Stirling*

David L. Swanson, *Department of Speech Communication, University of Illinois at Urbana-Champaign*

Gadi Wolfsfeld, *Department of Political Science and Department of Communication and Journalism, The Hebrew University of Jerusalem*

John Zaller, *University of California, Los Angeles*

Politics and relations among individuals in societies across the world are being transformed by new technologies for targeting individuals and sophisticated methods for shaping personalized messages. The new technologies challenge boundaries of many kinds – between news, information, entertainment, and advertising; between media, with the arrival of the World Wide Web; and even between nations. *Communication, Society and Politics* probes the political and social impacts of these new communication systems in national, comparative, and global perspective.

Information and American Democracy

TECHNOLOGY IN THE EVOLUTION OF POLITICAL POWER

Bruce Bimber

University of California, Santa Barbara

WITHDRAWN
FROM
UNIVERSITY OF PENNSYLVANIA
LIBRARIES

 CAMBRIDGE
UNIVERSITY PRESS

CAMBRIDGE UNIVERSITY PRESS
Cambridge, New York, Melbourne, Madrid, Cape Town, Singapore, São Paulo, Delhi

Cambridge University Press
32 Avenue of the Americas, New York, NY 10013-2473, USA

www.cambridge.org
Information on this title: www.cambridge.org/9780521804929

© Bruce Bimber 2003

This publication is in copyright. Subject to statutory exception
and to the provisions of relevant collective licensing agreements,
no reproduction of any part may take place without the written
permission of Cambridge University Press.

First published 2003
Reprinted 2008

Printed in the United States of America

A catalog record for this publication is available from the British Library.

Library of Congress Cataloging in Publication Data

Bimber, Bruce A. (Bruce Allen), 1961–
Information and American democracy : technology in the evolution of
political power / Bruce Bimber.
p. cm. – (Communication, society, and politics)
Includes bibliographical references and index.
ISBN 0-521-80067-6 (hb.) – ISBN 0-521-80492-2 (pb.)
1. Information society – Political aspects – United States. 2. Information technology –
Political aspects – United States. 3. Internet – Political aspects – United States.
4. Political participation – United States – Computer network resources.
5. Democracy – United States. 6. Communication – Political aspects – United States.
I. Title. II. Series.
JK468.A8 B56   2002
320.973–dc21   2002067675

ISBN 978-0-521-80067-9 hardback
ISBN 978-0-521-80492-9 paperback

Cambridge University Press has no responsibility for the persistence or
accuracy of URLs for external or third-party Internet Web sites referred to in
this publication and does not guarantee that any content on such Web sites is,
or will remain, accurate or appropriate. Information regarding prices, travel
timetables, and other factual information given in this work are correct at
the time of first printing, but Cambridge University Press does not guarantee
the accuracy of such information thereafter.

For Laura

Contents

Figures and Tables

FIGURES

TABLES

Acknowledgments

The origins of this volume lie in the interplay between research and teaching that constitutes the central theory of the modern university. Several years ago, a student in my course on technology and politics prepared an exceptionally good term paper about a new subject, the Internet and political equality. When I had designed the course earlier that year, 1995, the Internet had struck me as no more than one of several potentially important sociotechnical phenomena relevant to politics and social issues, along with genetic engineering, industrial competitiveness, and defense conversion following the end of the Cold War. Although the student's paper did not venture far from material that I had covered in the course, it prompted me to think further about the subject and eventually to launch my own inquiry into theoretical aspects of technology and information in American democracy. This book is one result. I have since lost track of the student who wrote that paper, but I acknowledge here her contribution to the direction of my research.

Students of business history will recall that 1995 was the year when Netscape Communications Corporation announced it would become a publicly held firm. That stock offering remains perhaps the most powerful symbol of the evolution of the Internet from a limited, government-sponsored, academically oriented enterprise into an economic and social phenomenon of vast scale. I managed to turn a tiny investment into a somewhat larger one on the first day of the Netscape public offering, but I do not write as a technology booster. My orientation toward technology as a force for social and political change, as well as for the production of wealth, rests on only a skeptical optimism. I grew up in what came during my youth to be called "Silicon Valley" and I picked up the local trade by earning a bachelor's degree in electrical engineering after high school. Having learned to design semiconductor circuits in the early 1980s is something akin to knowing Latin. It is hardly irrelevant to contemporary discourse and language but is far from sufficient for getting by on the street. I bring from that experience an abiding interest in technology as a motor for social and political change of all kinds. My study of information technology in recent years has been motivated in large part by an interest in the linkages between technological development and political change.

In academic volumes such as this one, recognition of assistance from others typically follows a particular order, beginning with professional colleagues, then moving on to students and assistants, and then finally family. I depart from that tradition. My greatest debt in the preparation of this work, as in all my undertakings, is to my partner and wife, Laura Mancuso. Her support was not simply in the manner of wifely forbearance during my hours at the computer. It combined professional wisdom and intellectual advice, as well as being a true life partner – that *and* putting up with my writing and the trying procedures of academia, such as pursuing tenure. My gratitude to her is deepest and comes first.

I am also indebted to my parents for launching me originally on my career as an engineer and then showing unconditional support when I became a social scientist in graduate school. Many friends provided support and encouragement as I wrote and researched, especially Arnold Schildhaus and Judith Mustard and the entire Broyles-González family: Yolanda, Esmeralda, Francisco the elder, and Francisco the younger.

Within the profession, my two greatest intellectual debts are to W. Russell Neuman, of the University of Michigan, and Jessica Korn, now of the Gallup Organization. Russ encouraged me in 1999 to get on with things and begin the book that had been gestating and that others had warned me against rushing. He then provided invaluable advice and encouragement at many points along the way. Jessica collaborated with me on a related writing project and helped me work through many of the ideas that form Chapter 2, especially the material on Federalist theory.

Several people worked with me as research assistants on projects connected with this book, some of whom have since moved on and are now researchers, teachers, or other professionals. Former UC Santa Barbara students involved in the project early on whom I thank are: Robin Datta, Kaushik Ghosh, Margrethe Kamp, Kendra Pappas, Robin Volpe, and Gary Wang. Current graduate students also assisted ably at various points, including Robert Hinckley and Lia Roberts, who did expert jobs at helping to prepare some of the quantitative analyses. Most especially, I thank three first-rate doctoral students who conducted the bulk of the case study interviews reported in Chapter 4: Joe Gardner, Diane Johnson, and Eric Patterson. They formed a great team and made development of the case studies enjoyable.

The cases are based on approximately eight dozen interviews with lobbyists, campaign staff, activists and political entrepreneurs, public officials, interest group staff and executives, and other political professionals. Most of these informants agreed to be interviewed on the record, and they are cited in the narrative. Those who were uncomfortable with attribution are not identified but were nonetheless helpful with background material. I am grateful to all who gave their time during busy professional schedules to talk with me or the members of my research team, either in person or by telephone.

In a class all her own is another professional research assistant, Florence Sanchez, of the Department of Political Science at UC Santa Barbara. She read and copyedited the entire volume – *closely*. The quality and professionalism of her work is beyond all expectations. She improved every page.

I have benefited immensely from conversations with others, many of whom are likely not aware that their comments at various meetings and workshops or in the hallways were influencing the direction of my research and writing. Among these are Scott Althaus, W. Lance Bennett, Ann Crigler, Richard Davis, Michael X. Delli Carpini, Andrew Flanagin, Doris Graber, Chuck House, M. Kent Jennings, Deborah Johnson, Alan Liu, Helen Nissenbaum, Pippa Norris, Tom Schrock, Rebecca Fairley Raney, David Swanson, Michael Walzer, John Woolley, and the late Steve Chaffee.

Financial support for the research in this book was provided by two grants from the National Science Foundation and also grants from the Carnegie Corporation and the Pew Charitable Trusts. Intramural funding came from the Regents of the University of California. I am most grateful to all of these financial supporters.

Bruce Bimber
Santa Barbara, California
May 2002

Information and Political Change

This book is an inquiry into the evolution of American democracy. It explores an aspect of democratic politics in the United States about which surprisingly little is known: the relationship between characteristics of political information in society and broad properties of democratic power and practice. My inquiry is motivated in part by the dramatic revolution in information technology taking place at the beginning of the twenty-first century. Over the space of about five years, we have witnessed the adoption of new means for communication and management of information by virtually every political organization and institution of consequence in the country. At no time in the history of American democracy has a new set of communication and information-handling capacities been assimilated so rapidly by the political system.

The pace of these changes has precipitated much speculation about political change and transformation, from visions of direct democracy and erosion of processes of representation and institutional deliberation because of new technology to enhancement or degradation of the "public sphere" and the state of citizens' civic engagement. Such speculations resonate strongly in a period when democracy in America is enervated by many problems: low voter turnout, the distortions of money and campaign finance arrangements, low public trust, a political culture dominated by marketing and polling, and the profound influences of one particular technology, television. What the new capacities for communication and the management of information portend for such problems, and indeed whether they portend anything at all, is one focus of this book.

The year 1999 was in many ways a milestone for the revolution that was taking place in information technology, in part because an unusual form of political behavior appeared. This activity involved peripheral organizations and ad hoc groups using information infrastructure to undertake the kind of political advocacy that traditionally has been the province of organizations with far greater resources and a more central position in the political system. A good example comes from very early in the year, when the Federal Deposit Insurance Corporation (FDIC) and other agencies proposed new regulations under the friendly euphemism "Know Your Customer." The Know Your Customer rules included requirements that banks report certain customer financial transactions to the government in order to assist authorities with the identification of money laundering and other illegal activities.

The FDIC, which insures private deposits in banks and provides other regulatory functions in the financial sector, is typically not the source of controversy or high-profile political conflict. The agency's activities fall into one of those corners of public policy where little citizen attention illuminates details of the relationship between an industry and its regulators. When the FDIC published its proposed rules late in 1998 with the agreement of the banking industry and Congress, and in coordination with allied agencies – the Office of Thrift Supervision, the Office of the Comptroller of the Currency, and the Federal Reserve – "Know Your Customer" seemed a routine change in banking regulations.

Yet by February of 1999, just two months after the agency's Notice of Proposed Rulemaking formally initiated the public phase of regulatory proceedings, everything about the politics of Know Your Customer had changed. Vehement public objections poured into the agency at an unprecedented rate, complaining about threats to privacy and government intrusion into citizen affairs. Congressional support dried up as legislators backed away, and the banking industry itself announced that it, too, opposed the rule. By early March, when the comment period ended, the FDIC had accumulated about 250,000 public comments, all but a hundred or so opposed. In the face of strident public opposition and the about-face by other political actors, the agency had found itself politically isolated. Drawn up short by the magnitude and vehemence of the objections, the FDIC along with its sister agencies withdrew the regulations and issued public statements bordering on contrition.

What lay behind this unexpected collective action on behalf of financial privacy and the remarkable back-tracking by an agency? A good deal of social science research suggests that we should find a powerful organization or coalition of organizations behind such a large effort. Political scientist Jack Walker has described the practical requirements of citizen-based policy advocacy in the following way: "Political mobilization is seldom spontaneous. Before any large element of the population can become a part of the American political process, organizations must be formed, advocates must be trained, and the material resources needed to gain the attention of national policy-makers must be gathered."[1] Some scholars have likened this process to the requirements of formal business enterprise, observing that internal features of groups as organizations are typically the strongest predictors of their success at recruiting and mobilizing citizens behind issues and succeeding with political demands.[2]

Yet in the FDIC case, as in others that took place in 1999, little such organizational infrastructure is found. No powerful interest group or public lobby with hundreds of thousands of members had mobilized citizens. No deep pockets had funded the effort. No political consultants or media advisors had orchestrated public relations and the media angles. No candidate or public official had drawn attention to the regulatory proposal. Neither the Republican nor Democratic party organizations had worked the issue. Virtually none of the ingredients of collective action that social science theory suggests should lie behind citizen-based policy advocacy was present.

Instead, a peripheral group in American politics, the Libertarian Party, initiated the protest against the FDIC's regulations – a group never before able to marshal national-level resources for an advocacy effort of this size. Like most American "third parties," the Libertarians are habitually constrained by the interdependent limitations of a small membership, few financial resources, and a system of electoral rules oriented toward two-party competition. Instead of using traditional organizational infrastructure, which it sorely lacks, the party relied almost exclusively on information infrastructure. Its leaders used the Internet to identify interested citizens, distribute information, and solicit participation in the protest. Starting with a small list of active party members, the initiators of the effort began a process of information exchange and communication about the pending policy change. That flow of information expanded geometrically, spreading quickly far beyond the party's membership and sphere of influence. The aggressiveness and extent of the Internet-based campaign – not the clout of the Libertarians themselves – successfully signaled to agency officials as well as to legislators that banking privacy

[1] Jack L. Walker, *Mobilizing Interest Groups in America: Patrons, Professions, and Social Movements* (Ann Arbor: University of Michigan Press, 1991), p. 94.
[2] Paul E. Johnson, "Interest Group Recruiting: Finding Members and Keeping Them," in Allan J. Cigler and Burdett A. Loomis, eds., *Interest Group Politics*, 5th ed. (Washington, D.C.: CQ Press, 1998), pp. 35–62; Terry M. Moe, *The Organization of Interests* (Chicago: University of Chicago Press, 1980).

could be a significant electoral issue. In the end, this was the story of how an industrial-era government institution created during the New Deal responded to collective action during the information era.

That this story does not appear to square with standard theories of policy advocacy and collective action is intriguing for several reasons, not the least of which is that many other political organizations and groups are attempting to repeat the Libertarians' success with issues of their own. Across the spectrum of interest groups, new information infrastructure appears to be affecting strategies of recruitment, advocacy, and mobilization. Electoral campaign organizations have also embraced new technology-based modes of internal organization and communication, as well as external communication with voters. The first major legislative effort of George W. Bush in 2001 revealed how new means of communication had become a routine part of the political scene. While trying to sell his tax cut in the states of swing Democratic senators, Bush told an audience in Atlanta, "If you find a member that you have some influence with, or know an e-mail address, or can figure out where to write a letter . . . just drop them a line."[3]

Researchers observing such developments have already amassed a sizable catalogue of contemporary uses of information technology by political actors, including new forms of mobilization, descriptions of how campaigns make use of new technology, and portrayals of how information technology is employed by government institutions themselves.[4] Much of this research, which we consider throughout this book, has supported one or more of three main findings. The first is a largely null finding of participation effects. This finding emerges from attempts to discover a stimulus effect from new technology on political engagement

---

[3] The speech was March 4, 2001, reported in Frank Bruni and Alison Mitchell, "Bush Pushes Hard to Woo Democrats Over to Tax Plan," *New York Times*, March 5, 2001, p. A1.

[4] E.g., see: Lori A. Brainard and Patricia D. Siplon, "Activism for the Future: Using the Internet to Reshape Grassroots Victims Organizations" (paper presented at the annual meeting of the American Political Science Association, Boston, Sept. 4–7, 1998); Laura Gurak, *Persuasion and Privacy in Cyberspace* (New Haven: Yale University Press, 1997); Karen James and Jeffrey D. Sadow, "Utilization of the World Wide Web as a Communicator of Campaign Information" (paper presented at the annual meeting of the American Political Science Association, Washington, D.C., Aug. 27–31, 1997); Anthony Corrado and Charles M. Firestone, eds., *Elections in Cyberspace: Toward a New Era in American Politics* (Washington, D.C.: Aspen Institute, 1996); Christopher Weare, Juliet A. Musso, and Matthew L. Hale, "The Political Economy of Electronic Democratic Forums: The Design of California Municipal Web Sites" (paper presented at the annual meeting of the American Political Science Association, Atlanta, Ga., Sept. 2–5, 1999).

or learning at the individual level. It does not appear, at least so far, that new technology leads to higher aggregate levels of political engagement. The failure to identify major effects has a great deal in common with the "limited effects" tradition in media studies dating back to the work of Paul Lazersfeld in the 1940s. That literature sought and failed to find substantial direct effects of mass media on public opinion and other dependent variables common in the study of political behavior. Its failure to account for processes such as agenda setting and framing was key, and this provides clues in the search for effects of contemporary information technology. It seems clear so far that information technology does not exert large direct effects on traditional participation and public opinion, but it is far from clear what other effects might exist.

The second finding in scholarship on information technology and politics is the existence of the so-called digital divide, a gap between those "on line" and "off line" that falls along socioeconomic, racial, and gender lines. The claim is that access to the new information environment is decidedly unequal, and moreover, it is unequal in ways that exacerbate traditional divisions and inequalities in society. The evidence for this effect is now substantial and unequivocal. However, viewed in light of the limited participation effects finding, the implications of the digital divide are less than certain.

The third finding from research so far is the presence of novel forms of collective action. A number of descriptive case studies – the earliest dating to the mid-1990s – have documented instances of unusual groupings of citizens organizing and using information technology in pursuit of political objectives. The emphasis in these studies is the capacity of political entrepreneurs to overcome resource barriers by using comparatively inexpensive information technology. These events suggest interesting developments in the nature of collective action, the limited participation effects and digital divide notwithstanding, and the case of the Libertarians and the FDIC falls into this category.

This book begins where these three strands of literature leave off, in an effort both to advance our understanding of their findings and to integrate them into a larger picture. The book addresses the following questions: What do stories such as the Know Your Customer protest mean? Will similar developments lead to political transition as well as technical change? What do the possibilities portend for how scholars theorize about politics? Increasingly, the important intellectual tasks associated with information technology and democracy involve synthesizing a larger causal picture across events and cases in order to assess what theoretical connections might link contemporary developments with important historical episodes, such as the emergence of interest group politics a century ago and the development of party politics a century before that. In what ways might the history of American political development shed light on current changes in American politics, and vice versa?

The process of synthesizing a larger, theoretical framework for understanding information technology and politics has proven divisive as scholars attempt to capture various developments in technology under the rubrics of political scale, equality, deliberation, community, social association, and the like. One theorist is Benjamin Barber, who in *Strong Democracy* advocates the use of information and communication technologies for enhancing citizen engagement with democratic affairs.[5] In that work, published while the revolution in information technology was in its infancy, Barber addresses the possibility of telecommunication technology serving as a means for overcoming problems of scale in large democracies and for creating communicative forums such as "town halls," which would not be limited by physical proximity. Similar views are suggested by other political theorists not widely known for their conceptions of information technology. The best example is Robert Dahl, who argues that democracy is threatened more by inequalities associated with information and knowledge than by inequalities in wealth or economic position. Dahl writes in *Democracy and Its Critics* that information technologies may provide important remedies for political inequality by making political information more universally accessible.[6] Communitarian theorist Amitai Etzioni makes a similar argument, claiming that technological improvements in the flow of information may both enhance equality and contribute to the construction of stronger community.[7]

On the other hand, a number of scholars have come to more pessimistic conclusions, among them empirical researchers who bring a vital calibration to purely deductive analysis. Some of these researchers have argued that the politically decentralizing capacities of information technology, like those demonstrated in the story of the Libertarians and the FDIC, will be overcome by traditional organizational interests. Some suggest that traditional media firms will successfully colonize new technology,

[5] Benjamin R. Barber, *Strong Democracy* (Berkeley: University of California Press, 1984).
[6] Robert A. Dahl, *Democracy and Its Critics* (New Haven: Yale University Press, 1989).
[7] Amitai Etzioni, *The Spirit of Community: Rights, Responsibilities, and the Communitarian Agenda* (New York: Crown Publishers, 1993).

preserving patterns of power established in the era of broadcasting.[8] Similarly, traditional advocacy organizations and parties are moving to extend their dominance to the new realm of information technology. Their success might relegate events like the FDIC protest back to the political periphery. Several recent empirical studies have suggested that intensive use of information technology may diminish social capital, counteracting whatever gains in participatory equality might flow from it.[9] Some scholars are concerned that the information revolution might advance the speed of politics, thus undermining deliberation and consolidating the trend toward government-by-public-opinion-poll.[10]

Concerns about fragmentation and the loss of the common public sphere now comprise an important undercurrent of critique of information technology by many scholars, one to which we return in the following chapters of this book.[11] Among those concerned is Benjamin Barber, who eventually shifted away from his earlier enthusiasm, expressing the reservation that contemporary information technology may undermine the quality of political deliberation and the nature of social interaction.[12] The most authoritative theoretical claim so far in this vein comes from constitutional scholar Cass Sunstein. He interprets the information revolution in terms of the decline of the "general interest intermediary" and the failure of the public common(s), and the replacement of these by a political communication system that fosters fragmentation and polarization.[13]

These possibilities pose some of the central empirical questions that this book addresses: How is technology affecting society and politics? Was the Libertarian Party's success in 1999 merely an outlier, the kind of counterexample one occasionally tolerates in social science theory? Or

[8] Richard Davis, *The Web of Politics* (London: Oxford University Press, 1998); Richard Davis and Diana Owen, *New Media in American Politics* (London: Oxford University Press, 1998).

[9] E.g., see Norman Nie and Lutz Ebring, "Internet and Society: A Preliminary Report," Feb. 17, 2000, http://www.stanford.edu/group/siqss/Press_Release/Preliminary_Report.pdf. For a different view, see "The Internet Life Report," The Pew Internet and American Life Project, Pew Charitable Trusts, May 10, 2000, http://www.pewinternet.org.

[10] Jeffrey B. Abramson, F. Christopher Arterton, and Gary R. Orren, *The Electronic Commonwealth* (Cambridge, Mass.: Harvard University Press, 1988).

[11] For a useful summary grounded in political theory, see Anthony G. Wilhelm, *Democracy in the Digital Age: Challenges to Political Life in Cyberspace* (New York: Routledge, 2000).

[12] Benjamin R. Barber, "The New Telecommunications Technology: Endless Frontier or End of Democracy," in Roger G. Noll and Monroe E. Price, eds., *A Communications Cornucopia* (Washington, D.C.: Brookings Institution, 1998), pp. 72–98.

[13] Cass Sunstein, *Republic.com* (Princeton, N.J.: Princeton University Press, 2001).

might the Know Your Customer protest represent a new phenomenon of lasting consequence for American democracy – collective action increasingly dissociated from traditional political resources and infrastructure?

In addition to the empirical matters, this book also seeks to address a set of deeper theoretical issues and social science questions. The premises behind these questions are that information technology is relevant to politics because information *itself* is relevant, and that the revolution in information technology that burst on the American landscape in the mid-1990s is fundamentally a revolution in information – in what it costs, how it flows, and the nature of its distribution. Within the concept of "information" may lie links that connect historical episodes of American development with contemporary politics and technology.

For the purposes of exploring theoretical issues in this book, I often depart from discussing technology and instead discuss information, which I define very broadly. There are several reasons for doing so, some pragmatic and some conceptual. First, because of the continuous change and integration of technologies, there is danger in constructing explanations of social and political phenomena framed around period-specific instantiations of technology. The set of technologies known throughout most of the 1990s as "the Internet" is steadily merging with other technologies, such as broadcast television and radio, recorded music, cellular telephony, and handheld electronic devices. As these technologies evolve, what is actually "the Internet" will become less clear and less important. The fundamental modes of communication that various technologies enable will become more crucial than the machinery involved.

A second reason for conceptualizing the revolution in information technology in terms of information itself concerns the interdependence of old and new forms of communication. During the 1990s, a good deal of the literature on the social and political impacts of technology implicitly or explicitly differentiated between the "on line" and "off line" worlds, comparing Internet-based politics with traditional politics or "virtual" communities with "real" ones.[14] Yet new information technologies continue to operate alongside and complement traditional media and older

---

[14] For examples of the terminology of "cyberpolitics," "digital democracy," and the like, see: Barry N. Hague and Brian D. Loader, eds., *Digital Democracy: Discourse and Decision Making in the Information Age* (London: Routledge, 1999); Cynthia J. Alexander and Leslie A. Pal, *Digital Democracy: Policy and Politics in the Modern World* (New York: Oxford University Press, 1998); Steven G. Jones, ed., *Cybersociety: Computer-Mediated Communication and Community* (Thousand Oaks, Calif.: Sage Publications, 1995); Graeme Browning, *Electronic Democracy: Using the Internet to Influence American Politics* (Wilton, Conn.: Pemberton Press, 1996); Kevin A. Hill and John E. Hughes,

modes of communication. Electoral campaigns use web sites and tele-vision commercials, e-mail and the postal service, wireless devices and fax machines. A campaign might use broadcast news coverage to steer citizens to a web site for making donations, which are then used to pur-chase campaign advertising on television. Often it makes more sense to speak of a single "world" with on-line and off-line features than attempt-ing to maintain a distinction between an on-line world and an off-line world, categories that are largely artifacts of historical transition. The revolution in information technology means that democracy is growing increasingly information-rich and communication-intensive, not sim-ply that democracy is now characterized by the use of one particular technology or another.

Just what constitutes "information" for the purposes of this analy-sis? Information has lovely literary and scientific histories that on rare occasions intersect.[15] It is beyond the scope of this book to trace those histories, but I hope it is sufficient to observe that in English literature and philosophy, the word "information" makes occasional appearances as far back as Chaucer's Canterbury Tales, prior even to the printing of the Gutenberg Bible.[16] Shakespeare animated the word memorably in *Coriolanus*, when Menenius asks forgiveness for the bearer of bad news: "But reason with the fellow, before you punish him, where he heard this, lest you shall chance to whip your information and beat the messenger who bids beware of what is to be dreaded."[17] Among philoso-phers, John Locke's invocation of information in *An Essay Concerning Human Understanding* is striking because of its foreshadowing of Claude Shannon's later creation of the modern scientific theory of information: "From whence commonly proceeds noise, and wrangling, without im-provement or information."[18] Differentiating information and noise in a

---

Cyberpolitics: Citizen Activism in the Age of the Internet (New York: Rowman and Littlefield, 1998).

[15] For a thorough analysis of the modern meaning of information from a humanistic perspective, see Albert Borgmann, *Holding on to Reality: The Nature of Information at the Turn of the Millennium* (Chicago: University of Chicago Press, 1999).

[16] Geoffrey Chaucer, "Tale of Melibeus," in *The Canterbury Tales*, ed. Paul G. Ruggiers (Norman: University of Oklahoma Press, 1979), p. 933, line 1486.

[17] William Shakespeare, *Coriolanus*, ed. Lee Bliss (Cambridge, Eng.: Cambridge Univer-sity Press, 2000), p. 234.

[18] John Locke, *An Essay Concerning Human Understanding*, Book 3, Ch. 10, Section 22. VI. Public domain version 1995 [1690], available at http://www.ilt.columbia.edu/ Projects/digitexts/locke/understanding/chapter0310.html. In 1948, Claude Shannon published a mathematical model of the communication of information that re-mains the foundation of information theory in engineering. See C. E. Shannon,

mathematical way would indeed prove a centerpiece of twentieth-century digital theory, 250 years after Locke.

For the purposes of the present inquiry, I begin with a modern definition of information, based on the *Oxford English Dictionary*: "knowledge communicated concerning some particular fact, subject, or event." Knowledge about facts, subjects, or events is inextricably bound to virtually every aspect of democracy. Such knowledge may concern the interests, concerns, preferences, or intentions of citizens as individuals or collectives. It may also concern the economic or social state of communities or society, or the actions and intentions of government officials and candidates for office. In what follows, political information constitutes any knowledge relevant to the working of democratic processes.

In his classic *The Nature and Origins of Mass Opinion*, John Zaller observes that the content of elite discourse, such as claims about the state of the world from party leaders and editorial positions of newspapers, contains information, but it is not "just information."[19] Because political discourse is the product of values and selectivity as much as verifiably "objective" observations, it comprises a mix of information and other factors. For my purposes this definition too narrowly constrains the concept of information by associating it with "truth" and "objectivity." I assume that when a political actor communicates a personal statement about the world containing a mix of facts and values, that actor is simply communicating a package of information, some of it dealing with "facts" and some of it with his or her values and predispositions. Some "facts" may even be wrong, but they can be communicated nonetheless and they constitute information.[20]

"A Mathematical Theory of Communication," *Bell System Technical Journal* 27 (July 1948): 379–423, and (October 1948): 623–656.

[19] John Zaller, *The Nature and Origins of Mass Opinion* (Cambridge, Eng.: Cambridge University Press, 1991), p. 13.

[20] That a recipient of communication may have difficulty distinguishing the facts and values in a message or may be unable to verify truth claims does not change the fact that information in a broad sense has been transmitted, perhaps with a high level of uncertainty associated with it. How much "true" information recipients extract from a message is a function of their own sophistication and their knowledge of the person communicating. Imagine, for instance, a situation where a candidate for office broadcasts a factually false message that his opponent is a communist, or an opponent of civil rights, or an adulterer. If a voter, believing the message, abandons her support for the accused candidate and votes instead for the accuser, there can be no doubt that communication has occurred and that information – albeit containing a false claim – has been transmitted. Whether the information in a message is "true" or "objective," and whether in this case the accuser sincerely believes his propaganda, is a separate question from the existence of information and communication.

"Information" need not stand in opposition to opinions, stories, rhetoric, or signals about value structures. Information might be a "fact" about the rate of inflation published by the Bureau of Economic Analysis just as well as a political official's statement about the need to control inflation. A candidate's promise on a web site or broadcast advertisement "to protect Social Security" conveys certain political information, just as a Congressional Budget Office report on Social Security fund solvency conveys other information of a different and perhaps more satisfyingly "objective" sort. Information is simply something that can be known or communicated.

To avoid epistemological and ontological concerns that fall outside the scope of this book, it is useful not to bind the definition of information too tightly to the human acts of perception and knowing. I assume that information can exist independently of its perception and understanding by any particular political actor. It is important, however, to observe the intimacy of the connection between "communication" and "information," as implied in the Oxford definition. Throughout this book, I use "communication" to mean simply the transfer or exchange of information. Certainly, different forms of communication may convey different quantities of information in different ways, but I do not attempt to isolate the two concepts.

My definition of information therefore extends well beyond facts, and my definition of communication well beyond a quantitative transmission model. My conception of information is consistent with Inguun Hagen's interpretation of the process of television news-watching by citizens, which may involve not only becoming informed in a narrow sense, but also diversion, habit or ritual, and fulfillment of a sense of duty or obligation.[21] Information defined this way permeates human activity, and in principle the complete range of human meaning can be conveyed by communication.

Defined this broadly, information becomes vital to democracy in myriad ways: in the processes by which citizen preferences are formed and aggregated, in the behaviors of citizens and elites, in formal procedures of representation, in acts of governmental decision making, in the administration of laws and regulations, and in the mechanisms of accountability that freshen democracy and sustain its legitimacy. None of these elements of the democratic process can operate apart from the exchange and flow

---

[21] Inguun Hagen, "Communicating to an Ideal Audience: News and the Notion of an 'Informed Citizen,'" *Political Communication* 14, no. 4 (1997): 405–419.

of information among citizens and their associations and organizations, among citizens and government, and within government itself.

More to the point, the *structure* of information in America at the outset of the twenty-first century is very different from that at the outset of the twentieth century, just as its structure then differed from that in the age of Jefferson. Not only the volume of political information available in society, but also its distribution and cost, have varied from one age to another. This important observation introduces the central theoretical problems that this book addresses. How do historically changing properties of political information affect the evolution of democracy? What patterns might exist in the evolving nature of information and its relationship to politics? To what extent can the character of democracy be traced to causes rooted in the informational characteristics of a particular age? To pose these questions is to situate modern technology and applied questions about the contemporary information revolution in the larger sweep of American political development.

OVERVIEW OF THE THEORY

Surprisingly, information and political development have been understood far better in isolation than in relation to one another. Scholars of democratic politics typically do not explore the possibilities of information serving as a motive force or an independent variable. For most researchers who attempt to find cause-effect relationships for political outcomes, information at best constitutes context rather than a cause, a factor that remains on the sidelines. As a result, ideas about information and democracy typically achieve no better than a skeletal existence, as in Francis Bacon's aphorism in *The Great Instauration* about knowledge and power being synonymous. His famous observation provides little insight into the real relationship between knowledge and power, and in any case was intended as a reflection not on politics but on science and human agency in the natural world.

How can the relationship between information and political change be approached theoretically? My perspective is based on the observation that many features of social and economic structure were derived from the characteristics of information during the period in which they arose. Throughout most of the twentieth century, for example, the information necessary for economic transactions, education, social interaction, and many other facets of modernity had certain properties. It was hierarchically organized, costly to obtain and difficult to manage, and in most settings asymmetrically distributed. French social theorist Pierre Levy refers to these properties as a "communications ecology," the basic features of information and communication to which human institutions and organizations are adapted.[22] Vertically integrated firms, retail stores, administrative organizations, and even universities are in part adaptations to a communications ecology in which information is costly and asymmetric.

From this perspective, the contemporary information revolution involves deep changes in the communications ecology, with potential consequences for institutions and processes whose structures are in substantial ways adapted to older communications arrangements. This revolution is not simply an increase in the volume of information, or what philosopher Albert Borgmann calls "the roar of information."[23] It is also qualitative, as information of all kinds becomes cheaper, its structure ever more complex and nonlinear, and its distribution far more symmetric than at any time in the past.

In principle, such developments could have structural consequences that are far-reaching. Indeed, it is already apparent that economic structure is sensitive to such changes, as economic transactions are transformed on a large scale, new methods of retailing visibly overtake the commercial world, and old business relationships and structures give way to new, information-intensive arrangements. Perhaps less abruptly but no less profoundly, other institutions sensitive to features of information and communication may change as well. Education may be altered for better or worse (or both) as printed matter grows less central to the transmission of knowledge, meaningful engagement with others at a distance becomes more readily possible, and the kinds of skills relevant to economic and personal well-being change. The fabrics of social association, cultures, even private lives may be rewoven, insofar as these depend upon the nature and accessibility of information. And so it may be for democracy, to the extent that its structures represent adaptations to particular informational circumstances.

I argue that this perspective can illuminate contemporary political developments as well as some critical moments of historical change in the United States. Reexamining founding-era debates, the early history of parties, and the industrial revolution in the United States suggests that an informational perspective can shed new light on important junctions

---

[22] Pierre Levy, *Collective Intelligence: Mankind's Emerging World in Cyberspace* (Cambridge, Mass.: Perseus, 1997).
[23] Borgman, *Holding on to Reality*, p. 3.

in American political development. A remarkable and widely overlooked element of the Federalist–Anti-Federalist debate involves informational complexity and institutional arrangements. Considering this debate sets the stage for evaluating the properties of information and their influence on U.S. political development from the founding era on. In the transition from an elitist political system with highly circumscribed citizen engagement in the early nineteenth century to a majoritarian democracy where power was wielded through large coalitions based on broad citizen involvement among white men, I suggest, is evidence of the first major reconstitution of political information. Another is associated with the evolution of the modern, group-based, pluralistic political system.

Transitions are revealing because they expose important underlying causal mechanisms that may be obscured in times of stasis. History will undoubtedly record the late twentieth and early twenty-first centuries as a period of marked transition fueled by new communication and information capacities. One theme of this book is how the revolution in information technology provides an opportunity to explore contemporary *and* historical connections between information and features of democracy. We have the Internet to thank for directing our attention to an old and fundamental phenomenon, one as old as Madisonian ideas about the extended republic and the advantages of a federal nation over a confederation of small states.

This perspective is broadly akin to scholarship in economics dealing with information and organizational structure, although I do not employ the formal assumptions of the economics of organization or the tenets of rationalism. Rather, it is sufficient to assume simply that organizations and institutions matter, that they tend to respond over time to changes in opportunities and constraints, and that opportunities and constraints are powerfully shaped by the nature of information and communication. Commentators on American politics frequently identify democratic failings in the world of political communication – in the ways that mass media present news, in the ways that candidates and government officials communicate with the public, in the privileged treatment accorded the messages of certain groups, in citizens' habits of political learning and attention to public affairs. Critiques of the state of political communication tacitly accept a fundamental assumption that the evolution of systems of communication exerts forces on the evolution of democracy. This book explores that assumption.

The theoretical relationship between information and political transition that I seek to describe has been overlooked by most scholars who attempt to explain political development from an empirical perspective. Up to a point, scholars have been safe in paying little attention to matters of information. The status of who possessed or managed political information and who did not, as well as the accessibility of information generally, have changed slowly during many eras of American political development, with the exception of four periods that I refer to as "information revolutions."[24]

One finds only hints about a possible connection between information and political change in the work of scholars dealing with various episodes of American politics. It is customary in histories of the interest group system, for instance, to observe the importance of communication technologies in facilitating what groups do.[25] Consequently, telephone banks, fax machines, and the ability to manage mailing lists electronically are mentioned in the story of modern pluralism but given little importance, as in David Truman's classic *The Governmental Process*. In a tantalizing but largely overlooked passage, the father of modern empirical research on pluralism writes that "the revolution in the means of communication" is a precondition of the development of the interest group system.[26] To say that one factor is a "precondition" for another is to use a strong term. It invokes a linkage that is necessary but not necessarily sufficient – half of a causal claim, so to speak.

Truman goes so far as to remark that "the revolution in communications has indeed largely rendered obsolete . . . Madison's confidence in the dispersion of the population as an obstacle to the formation of interest groups."[27] This is a subtly provocative suggestion about the role

---

[24] Communication researcher Irving Fang also employs the term "information revolution," but applies the concept to the entire history of communication in the West. He identifies six information revolutions: the Writing Revolution, beginning in the eighth century B.C.; the Printing Revolution, beginning in the fifteenth century; the Mass Media Revolution, beginning in middle of the nineteenth century and encompassing mass newspapers, the telegraph, and photography; the Entertainment Revolution, beginning in the late nineteenth and early twentieth century and including recorded sound and images; the Communication Toolshed Revolution, beginning in the mid-twentieth century and encompassing the home as the locus of entertainment communication; and the contemporary Information Highway Revolution. See Irving Fang, *A History of Mass Communication: Six Information Revolutions* (Boston: Focal Press, 1997).

[25] Allan J. Cigler and Burdett A. Loomis, eds., *Interest Group Politics*, 5th ed. (Washington, D.C.: CQ Press, 1998); Mark Petracca, *The Politics of Interests* (Boulder: Westview, 1992); Jeffrey M. Berry, *The Interest Group Society* (Boston: Little, Brown, 1984).

[26] David Truman, *The Governmental Process: Political Interest and Public Opinion* (New York: Alfred E. Knopf, 1965), p. 55.

[27] Ibid.

of information and communication in maintaining a just democratic order according to Madisonian terms. It reminds us that present developments are not the first revolution in communications and information, and it echoes observations of the original student of pluralism, Alexis de Tocqueville, who identified the connection between information and the rate of formation of civic groups. More than a century before Truman and not long before the death of Madison, Tocqueville observed the information–faction connection in the relationship between newspapers and associations. As we see in the next chapter, Tocqueville's idea, which can be summarized in his quip that "newspapers make associations, and associations make newspapers," is probably the first social scientific claim that collective action requires the solving of information problems.[28]

Contemporary analysis occasionally echoes Truman and Tocqueville on communication. One subtext in the recent literature is that modern organized interests play a game of information at least as much as they play a game of money or organization.[29] A few scholars have even suggested that interest group influence rests *primarily* on the flow of information, rather than on money, organization, or other features of organizational infrastructure. Unfortunately, given that democracies are now in the grip of an information revolution, this theory has not significantly influenced larger models of contemporary political structure or change in the United States.

The study of political parties has treated information similarly. Researchers analyzing the origins of the party system in the United States sometimes note the relevance of communication technology to party development, but typically leave things at that. Historian William Shade, for instance, notes that "the development of communications technology which made possible not only statewide but nationwide networks" was the "key" to the success of early parties in the United States during the first half of the nineteenth century, but he does not elaborate.[30] In his synthetic theoretical work on parties, political scientist John Aldrich observes that communication technology is one of the major features of the historical setting that shapes the party system, but he does not

---

[28] Alexis de Tocqueville, *Democracy in America*, vol. 2 (1840; rpt., New York: Vintage Books,1945), p. 120.

[29] Frank R. Baumgartner and Beth L. Leech, *Basic Interests: The Importance of Groups in Politics and Political Science* (Princeton: Princeton University Press, 1998); Cigler and Loomis, eds., *Interest Group Politics*.

[30] William G. Shade, "Political Pluralism and Party Development: The Creation of a Modern Party System, 1815–1852," in Paul Kleppner et al., eds., *The Evolution of American Electoral Systems* (Westport, Conn.: Greenwood, 1981), p. 105.

treat technological change as a relevant variable.[31] A central but often forgotten obstacle to the emergence of parties in the United States was the need to solve communication problems associated with organizing the electorate. The formation of civic associations in the same period required the solution of similar problems, as did the formation of interest groups a century later. In these and other ways, information and communication technology have appeared as bit players in scholars' explanations of some crucial crossroads in American political development, but they have rarely held the intellectual spotlight.

One of the few theorists to interpret the evolution of democracy in more explicitly informational terms is Dahl, who understands the historical development of modern political institutions as driven by information problems embedded in demands for policy. He writes in *Democracy and Its Critics* that a central feature of modern "polyarchy" was the creation of "new institutions in order to adopt democracy to the growing need for the mobilization of specialized knowledge."[32] Dahl understands that a central dynamic of the modern state is the development and exercise of power associated with asymmetrically distributed information, and that the organization of democratic power in response to public as well as elite demands for public policy is regulated by the need for information. Accounts of state building and public policy that focus exclusively on public demands and on policy responses miss a vital fact that was well known to the American founders: The state is more than an allocator of services and values; it is an apparatus for assembling and managing the political information associated with expressions of public will and with public policy.

In what follows, I attempt to integrate Dahl's premise with the hints and clues about information left by Tocqueville, Truman, and others, including James Madison and Max Weber. I believe that there are good but underappreciated reasons that scholars have noticed the relevance of information technology at what are arguably the two most important historical turning points in American political development: the rise of party-based majoritarian politics and the evolution of group-based political pluralism. My aim is to explore what integration might be possible between those two developmental milestones and the present, using information as the nexus. I should add that in so doing, it is not

---

[31] John Aldrich, *Why Parties? The Origin and Transformation of Political Parties in America* (Chicago: University of Chicago Press, 1995).

[32] Dahl, *Democracy and Its Critics*, p. 338.

my primary aim to predict the *future* of the information revolution and American politics, a risky temptation to which a number of writers have succumbed. I restrict myself instead to analyzing the nature and causes of changes under way in American democracy *at present*. I intend this book to be an argument for conceptualizing the evolution of information as an important contributor to political change at the largest scale – not information defined narrowly as the quantifiable messages exchanged by rational agents in signaling games and the like, but as a universally important ingredient in political processes.

Much of my thesis is based on the observation that elites exercise a powerful influence on the organization of democracy, through their capacity to influence public opinion, set agendas, mobilize citizens into collective action, make decisions, and implement policies. The identity and structure of elites is neither fixed across time nor random in its changes. Many factors affect the identity and structure of elites, and the state of information is one of them. Exogenous changes in the accessibility or structure of information cause changes in the structure of elite organizations that dominate political activity, and these in turn affect the broad character of democracy.

I develop this theoretical claim in two steps, one historical and one contemporary. First, I reinterpret parts of American political history in informational terms. I argue that information regimes exist in American political history as periods of stable relationships among information, organizations, and democratic structure. The features of an information regime are: (1) a set of dominant properties of political information, such as high cost; (2) a set of opportunities and constraints on the management of political information that these properties create; and (3) the appearance of characteristic political organizations and structures adapted to those opportunities and constraints. Information regimes in the United States have been interrupted by information revolutions, which involve changes in the structure or accessibility of information. These revolutions may be initiated by technological developments, institutional change, or economic outcomes. An information revolution disrupts a prior information regime by creating new opportunities for political communication and the organization of collective action. These changes create advantages for some forms of organization and structure and disadvantages for others, leading to adaptations and change in the world of political organizations and intermediaries. This is to say that democratic power tends to be biased toward those with the best command of political information at any particular stage in history.

The first information regime in the United States emerged from an information revolution during the Jacksonian democratization. It was facilitated by the creation of the first national-scale system for communicating political information, namely, the remarkable U.S. Postal Service and the equally remarkable American newspaper industry, which Tocqueville himself believed to be the most vibrant in the world by the 1830s. National flow of political information was largely impossible in the decades after the founding. Its absence had blocked the development of new parties prior to the 1830s. Those parties that arose in the mid-nineteenth century were the final component of this information regime, an adaptation in part to the opportunities and constraints for the flow of information created by the postal service and newspaper systems. Beneath America's majoritarian politics of the nineteenth century was a distinguishing set of arrangements for the distribution of political information. These arrangements would eventually be superceded by others; but for a half to three-quarters of a century, they defined the majority of possibilities for large-scale political communication and civic engagement in the United States.

The second American information revolution led to an information regime that lasted into the middle of the twentieth century. That revolution was a product of the industrial revolution and the growing American state, which transformed the landscape of political information requisite to politics. Information became enormously complex and highly differentiated between about 1880 and 1920 because the number of policy issues on the national agenda multiplied, as did the number of private and public actors engaged in the exchange of information. Such complexity favored a new form of organization adapted to the management and flow of specialized and increasingly costly information: the organized interest group. Though this new form of organization would eventually rise to prominence after the New Deal, interest-group politics of the twentieth century reflected and rested upon the new set of informational characteristics that emerged at the turn of the century. Interest groups can be understood as information specialists that prevailed over generalists (the parties) in some of the central communication functions in politics.

The pluralism connected with the second information regime persisted throughout the twentieth century, but was affected by a third, transitional revolution during the period of the 1950s–1970s involving broadcasting. The broadcast information revolution had two distinct phases. In the first, the mass audience for communication tended to weaken party organizations as central players in campaigning and at the same time create new possibilities for mass politics – a trend counter to the group-based politics of the second information regime. However, in the later stage of this information revolution, the rise of cable television and the multiplication of channels began a process of fragmentation and division of communication and information. These developments set the stage for the contemporary information revolution involving the Internet and associated technologies.

It should be clear that an information revolution is not simply an abrupt change in the technology of communication. A set of technological changes becomes revolutionary when new opportunities or constraints associated with political intermediation make possible altered distributions of power. These new capacities and possibilities are a function of the political and social context in which technology evolves. Moreover, an information revolution need not necessarily be driven by communication technology at all. My approach to analyzing political history has not been to draw up a list of technologies – telegraph, steamboat, railroad, telephone, radio, television, and so on – and ask how each affected politics. I have approached the problem orthogonally, by asking when, if ever, the properties of information and communication have changed abruptly, and then inquiring how such changes influenced politics. This approach implicates some technological innovations in abrupt information revolutions but not others. It identifies sources of informational change that would not make most lists of interesting technologies, such as the postal service. It also includes socioeconomic developments involving technologies but which are not, strictly speaking, technologies at all, such as the industrial revolution.

To argue that some very important features of American democracy have roots in informational phenomena is not to suggest that other factors have been unimportant in influencing change. Social science has at its disposal a well-stocked tool kit of explanatory structures that can be used to account for political change in the United States. The tools in this kit include models of the strategic choices through which instrumental people pursue goals, features of institutions and the ways that they shape behavior, the power of ideas to effect change, the often intangible elements of culture, the machinations of economic interest and power, the influence of social movements and identity, and even the contingency and idiosyncrasy of history. Rather than suggesting that these factors be set aside in favor of a causal explanation dealing exclusively with information, I claim that informational phenomena must be added to the picture for a complete account. This book explores how characteristics of information might find a more prominent place in the social science tool kit.

The second large step in my theory of information and democracy deals with contemporary political change, and involves applying lessons from the history of information in American politics to the present situation. The information-regime model of American politics and insights from the study of interest groups and political participation provide the means to investigate how contemporary information technology affects democracy. In the current period, as in the Jacksonian age and era of industrialization, the properties of information are again changing. Technology is increasing the complexity and specialization of information while at the same time decreasing its cost, thereby making abundant political information and communication available to anyone with the motivation to acquire it, provided they have access to information technology. In a general sense, the information regime model predicts that such a large-scale change in the cost of information should lead to political change, through its effects on the identity and structure of political intermediaries.

As we see in Chapters 3 and 4, among the most important trends predicted from theory are a decreasing association between the distribution of traditional political resources and the capacity to organize political action, like the Know Your Customer protest at the FDIC. This phenomenon involves the substitution of information infrastructure for organizational infrastructure. It suggests the rise of new ad hoc political associations and groups, as well as altered strategies and commitments of resources on the part of traditional organizations. It entails increasing attention in the policy process toward "outside" lobbying and public opinion, as well as increasing orientation toward issues and events, rather than more stable interests and long-term political agendas.

My main thesis about contemporary political developments is that *technological change in the contemporary period should contribute toward information abundance, which in turn contributes toward postbureaucratic forms of politics.* This process involves chiefly private political institutions and organizations such as civic associations, as well as interest groups, rather than formal governmental institutions rooted in law or the Constitution. To the extent that the central functions of these private institutions involve the collection, management, or distribution of information under circumstances where information has been costly and asymmetrically distributed, the contemporary information revolution has the capacity to alter organizational structures. The result is a diminished role on many fronts for traditional organizations in politics. The pluralism of the 1950s and 1960s was a politics of bargaining among institutionalized interests. That changed in the 1970s and 1980s to a pluralism of more atomistic issue groups, less inclined and able at elite bargaining and more tightly focused on so-called single issues. The accelerated pluralism of the 1990s and 2000s increasingly involves situations in which the structure of group politics is organized around not interests or issues, but rather events and the intensive flow of information surrounding them.

This progression from interest groups to issue groups to event groups does not imply that the former organizational form is displaced entirely. It should involve, rather, the loosening of certain organizational boundaries and structures and an increasing heterogeneity of forms working alongside one another, as we see in Chapter 4. As in previous information regimes, political influence in the fourth regime should remain biased toward those with the best command of political information. The contemporary information revolution should make traditional, bureaucratically structured organizations of all kinds less able to dominate political information – this is the central motor of political change.

In this way, it is possible to array contemporary developments with historical ones. The first information revolution made national-scale political information available for the first time, which contributed to centralized, hierarchical organizations serving as the basis for collective action in politics. In the second information revolution, national-scale political information grew complex and costly, which led to the rise of decentralized, specialized, and bureaucratized organizations as the basis for collective action. The third information revolution created a modern tension between mass politics and pluralism, but left major, highly institutionalized organizational forms in a position of dominance. In the contemporary revolution, national-scale information is growing abundant, but no less complex than ever. The result should be a weakening of the organizational structures of the previous regimes. This sequence is summarized in Figure 1.1.

One of the major problems facing social scientists concerned with American democracy is the state of citizenship and levels of civic engagement. By many traditional measures, these are in decline, as the literatures on social capital, public opinion, voting participation, and the public sphere indicate. On the other hand, critics of declinist arguments have posited alternative interpretations of the data, based on new forms of engagement and changes in the meaning of citizenship. Many have

---

FIRST INFORMATION REVOLUTION: 1820s-1830s

Technological and institutional developments lead to:
The first possibilities for mass flows of political information.

These contribute to an information regime with:
A centralized, simple system of political organizations (parties) serving as the dominant influence on policy-making and collective action.

↓

SECOND INFORMATION REVOLUTION: 1880s-1910s

Socio-economic development leads to:
National-scale political information growing costly, specialized, and complex.

This contributes to an information regime with:
A decentralized, complex system of specialized and resource-dependent organizations (interest groups) serving as the dominant influence on policy-making and collective action.

↓

THIRD INFORMATION REVOLUTION: 1950s-1970s

Technological development leads to:
Possibilities for commanding the attention of a national-scale mass audience.

This contributes to an information regime with:
A centralized, extremely resource-dependent system of market-driven organizations capable of influencing policy-making and some forms of collective action, along with the specialized political organizations of the previous information regime.

↓

FOURTH INFORMATION REVOLUTION: 1990s-present

Technological development leads to:
A condition of information abundance.

This contributes to possibilities for an information regime with:
Post-bureaucratic political organizations as the basis for policy-making and collective action.

Figure 1.1. Summary of the four political information revolutions in the United States.

suggested that participation in affinity groups, youth soccer leagues, support groups, interest organizations, and other novel associations may be replacing memberships in venerable but outdated groups such as Elks Clubs, Rotaries, and Boy Scouts. If so, the research indicating a decline in social capital may be due to a combination of inadequate conceptualization and measurement of the wrong activities.[33] Likewise, in influencing explicitly political engagement, new forms of "lifestyle" politics, political consumerism, and other novel ways of being "political" may be displacing the traditional political actions that scholars have measured.[34] Therefore, to the extent that political and civic identity and modes of action are changing, civic engagement may also simply be changing shape rather than decaying.

This debate will benefit substantially from the passage of time, as historical perspective sharpens assessments of stability and change and as new survey evidence differentiates long-term from short-term trends. The debate is relevant here, nonetheless, because of the possible role of information technology in it. One of the most persistent speculations about "the Internet and politics" has been that cheap, ubiquitous information and communication will expand possibilities for engagement and fuel a rise in overall levels of citizen involvement with their communities and political system. It is clear that the contemporary information revolution is making the individual's political *environment* far more information-rich. It is also clear from research on political behavior and public opinion that political knowledge – information that has been assimilated by individuals – is connected with political action. In other words, more knowledgeable citizens are indeed more engaged. But the link between changes in citizens' informational environment and changes in their internal political knowledge is far less clear. It seems intuitive that exposure to more information should lead to the internalization of more information and to changes in behavior. Some rational theories of political behavior formalize that link, interpreting the cost of information as an important regulator of its "consumption" and of the action that follows. Decrease the cost of a desired good, such as information, and more will

---

[33] Theda Skocpol, "Unravelling from Above," in Robert Kuttner, ed., *Ticking Time Bombs: The New Conservative Assault on Democracy* (New York: New Press, 1996), pp. 292–301; Michael Schudson, "What If Civic Life Didn't Die?" in Kuttner, ed., *Ticking Time Bombs*, pp. 286–291; Nicholas Lemann, "Kicking in Groups," *The Atlantic Monthly* 277, no. 4 (1996): 22–26.

[34] For a discussion, see W. Lance Bennett, "The UnCivic Culture: Communication, Identity, and the Rise of Lifestyle Politics," *PS: Political Science and Politics* 31, no. 4 (1998): 741–761.

be acquired by citizens, up until the point where marginal costs match marginal value. Empirical verification of this apparently straightforward model has been highly problematic, however, especially when it is framed in terms of longitudinal variation in citizens' information environments.

It is important that a theoretical account of information and political change take up this problem as a counterpart to organizational-level matters. My approach involves a psychological perspective on political information that stands in contrast to instrumental conceptions of information as a rationally consumed good. Following work in political psychology, I posit that the informed citizen in the age of the Internet is not a rational actor, nor necessarily even one who pursues short-cuts and satisficing strategies in lieu of exhaustive and thorough information-gathering. Instead, informed citizenship involves the information-rich growing even richer as the cost of information falls, while those poor in information remain so. In practice, people should acquire information in so-called biased ways that support existing beliefs rather than reducing uncertainty. Most important, their consumption of information should occur in ways that are highly contingent on context and the stimulus provided by elites and organizations.

This view leads to the hypothesis that in the cycle of information revolutions and regimes, including contemporary developments, changes in the nature of political information should typically exert little direct influence on levels of citizen engagement. As a force in democracy, therefore, information should work somewhat differently at the level of organizations and the level of individuals. Information revolutions, including the present one, should have profound and direct consequences for organizations and political structure, but only indirect, less tangible consequences for politics at the level of individual political engagement. The effects of changes in information, I argue, are concentrated on *political form* through an increasing independence of political structure from traditional economic and social structures.

THE EMPIRICAL PICTURE

To explore this model empirically, I draw on evidence from several research projects. This evidence is both quantitative and qualitative in nature. The quantitative evidence comes from survey research oriented toward issues of individual-level behavior. It includes data from the American National Election Studies and several proprietary surveys of my own based on national probability samples. The survey data allow statistical modeling of the diffusion of information technology and the relationship between use of information technology and various forms of political behavior. I use this analysis to explore the psychological approach to explaining individual-level effects of information.

The qualitative evidence deals mainly with elite behavior and the organization-level effects of information. It begins with the reinterpretation of American political development sketched above, drawing on secondary literature and selected primary materials extending back to *The Federalist* and *The Anti-Federalist Papers*. This historical review and analysis provides the foundation for the concept of information regimes. For the contemporary period, the qualitative evidence takes the form of case studies based on documentary evidence, public records, and about eight dozen interviews conducted by telephone and in person in San Francisco, St. Louis, Santa Barbara, and Washington, D.C. These case studies deal with political organizations of diverse kinds. They include ad hoc political groups formed in the absence of virtually all of the traditional organizational infrastructure typically associated with collective action, as well as mainstream political organizations with offices, paid staff, memberships, and other resources. These cases examine how traditional interest groups and campaign organizations use information infrastructure and adopt new strategies in response to new communication and information-management possibilities. They evaluate the relationship between traditional, bureaucratic forms of political organization and contemporary organizational forms that can be called 'postbureaucratic.'

While I adapt some of the theoretical apparatus from the study of economic organizations, the implications of the contemporary information revolution for politics are different from its implications for economics. In politics, no direct analogue exists to the manufacture of physical goods; therefore, the ascendancy in the economy of services and "knowledge work" over industrial-era production does not quite have a parallel in politics. In addition, the process of competition, birth, death, and restructuring among private firms has only a partial analogue in politics. Within comparatively few constraints, economic organizations come and go, or merge and reorganize in response to market conditions and the strategic efforts of economic actors. Only certain types of political organizations operate in a similarly liberal marketplace, namely, media businesses, interest groups, civic associations, and other nongovernmental organizations. On the other hand, formal government institutions are rooted in the Constitution or in laws that are not readily changed, and so they do not respond directly and autonomously to changing conditions in the political "market," technological or otherwise. Political parties fall somewhere between these two categories in that they are private competitive organizations with autonomy over internal organization and strategy but highly institutionalized in law and electoral rules. The contemporary information revolution plays out differently in the realms of economics and politics – not only more slowly, but also in qualitatively different ways.

Of course, these processes have important normative implications. While this book is not oriented toward the interpretation or analysis of philosophical problems associated with information and democracy, it does summarize links from the empirical and theoretical problems to normative matters. For instance, a central normative problem concerns the possibility of tradeoffs within democratic systems between equality and a coherent, integrated public sphere, tradeoffs that are mediated by the cost and degree of institutionalization of information. To the extent that changes in the cost and accessibility of information tend to deinstitutionalize certain features of politics, they contribute toward the goal of political equality. As Robert Dahl argues, telecommunication technology makes possible a more equitable distribution of political information about a broad array of subjects.[35] While the future state of the so-called digital divide is unclear, as we see in Chapter 5, evidence from the contemporary information revolution supports Dahl's claim.

On the other hand, as political structure becomes flexible and in many cases unpredictable, and as citizens are exposed to a greater variety of competing elite views and demands as a result of the information abundance, the formation of coherent and stable public opinion may grow more difficult rather than less so. One effect of the constraints on information that institutions create is more integrated, coherent public agenda and opportunities for stable preferences that can, in principle, command broad support. As information becomes more abundant and less well institutionalized, possibilities for unstable cycling of agendas and preferences may arise. The possibility that political equality and the achievement of a deliberative public good may be linked through control over information is one of the most consequential normative problems raised by the information regimes model.

PLAN OF THE BOOK

To advance claims about the role of information in democracy is to tackle a subject of sobering proportions. In framing this analysis, I have

---

[35] Dahl, *Democracy and Its Critics.*

27

made a number of decisions about where to focus my efforts. I do *not* pursue in depth the causes and consequences of technology in general. The questions that this book explores are motivated by the fact that new information technology is influencing the character of politics in the United States; yet I am not concerned to any great extent with cataloging and describing information technology. I often gloss over distinctions between kinds of information technology, for example, between wireless and cable technology, bulletin boards and chat rooms, and so on. Occasionally, such distinctions may be important. For instance, those interested in how web sites can affect the campaign process may find it very important to distinguish one-way information delivery systems (from candidates to voters) from interactive techniques that permit voters or would-be voters to express themselves and become actively engaged with a campaign. Indeed, "interactivity" is currently a hot topic among political consultants helping candidates use new technology.

Instead of attending closely to technological matters and details of this kind, I concentrate on the broad sweep of technological development. In particular, I focus on the fact that various contemporary technologies are in many different ways creating a more information-rich and communication-intensive society and polity. Terms such as "communication abundance" and "media abundance" are often used to describe this phenomenon.[36] Understanding the consequences and historical context for media abundance is more important here than drawing connections between any particular technology and political outcome.

Focusing on the forest rather than the trees has an important advantage. From a technological perspective, it avoids the consequences of dwelling on specific technologies that are subject to frequent change or obsolescence. Certainly, the meaning of "information technology" has evolved rapidly. Thirty years ago, state-of-the-art information technology entailed large, centralized data processing machines, which permitted rapid tabulation of polling data, generation of "computerized" mailing lists and databases, and other centralized political functions. Up-to-date communication technology meant fax machines, telephones, broadcast television, and the like. Twenty years ago, interconnected computer systems had just became practical, but information technology still mainly meant stand-alone data processing equipment, smaller computers, and nascent computer networks, as well as telecommunication equipment of

---

[36] E.g., see Jay G. Blumler and Dennis Kavanaugh, "The Third Age of Political Communication: Influences and Features," *Political Communication* 16 (1999): 209–230.

all kinds, including satellite systems, telephones, faxes, and cable. In the political realm, these technologies facilitated targeted grassroots political organizing and new kinds of campaigning. It had become apparent twenty years ago that communication and information technology would one day merge, but that day was still largely in the future.

Ten years ago that merger began, as the Internet took its place as the central technological and conceptual feature of the information age. As the center of an orbiting system of technologies, the Internet embodies the vast pool of information now available by technological means, the flexible ways that this information can be put to use, the many decentralized forms of communication that are possible, and the merger of media from distinct forms such as television and publishing into a flexible, multifeatured, linked system.

Ten or twenty years from now, the specific technological meaning of "information technology" will have evolved even further in ways that are difficult to predict. With some information handling and communication freed from physical cables and connections, the traditional "computer" will yield its monopoly over "computing" and information processing to a wealth of new appliances and devices that communicate, make decisions, and process information.

Despite uncertainty about the state of specific technologies in the future, one fact is clear: Technological evolution is moving in the direction of more information-richness and communication-intensiveness. Whatever the details of specific technologies at a particular moment, the large-scale trend has been and will be toward information abundance. In the methodologist's terminology, this is the independent variable of interest.

In focusing on this major trend, rather than analyzing the details of the web or chat rooms or e-mail, I proceed something like a biologist interested in theorizing about mammals, who in particular seeks to explain what the presence of mammals means for earth's ecosystems, or how mammals affect their environment differently than birds. Such a biologist might reasonably be excused for failing to address differences between coyotes and wolves, or bobcats and lynx. In this book, especially in the case studies, I occasionally discuss specifics of web sites in campaigns, their differences from electronic mail, and other particulars. But these specifics are always discussed as they relate to the larger theme of the evolution toward information abundance and its implications for democracy.

Many observers have sought to divine *the* effect of the Internet, as if its consequences for any particular realm of activity must be consistent or even singular. This premise has fueled speculation about whether the Internet will advance or undermine political equality – as if it must strictly do one or the other. Historically, this kind of thinking about technology has often been colored strongly with optimism. The development of powered flight, for instance, was met with expectations of increased world peace due to intensified contact between nations.[37] The development of broadcast technology led many to expect increased citizen knowledge and the advancement of "high" culture.[38] We now know that powered flight did indeed intensify the peaceful links between certain distant nations, just as it simultaneously extended the possibilities for war among others. Broadcast telecommunication can indeed serve to inform, to disseminate ideas and art, and on occasion to educate, just as it also serves as a medium of entertainment, diversion, and reduction of culture to the simple and the lurid.

Like flight and broadcasting, information technology may have many effects at once. It may advance political equality in certain ways and undermine it in others, or enhance the power of states in some respects and diminish it in others. It may increase opportunities for superficial, thoughtless, democratically hollow speech as well as opportunities for meaningful deliberation and public speech. It is best to assume that information technology might both strengthen and weaken democracy, as well as exert little influence at all on some democratic processes.

In approaching the explanatory task this way, I do not invoke the standard theories used by social scientists to explain the influence of technology on society, especially technological determinism and its theoretical opposite, social construction. The fundamental claim of technological determinism is twofold. First, the evolution of technology is not random or happenstance but follows an ordered sequence in the direction of greater complexity. This is to say that human agency and influence are not important to the direction of technological development: The Internet was bound to be developed because of the laws of nature, as were the internal combustion engine and the nuclear bomb, regardless of the economic or social circumstances that happened in practice to attend their emergence in history. Second, technological determinism holds that the technologies present in the human environment at each particular historical moment "determine" the character of societies. That is, the nature of

[37] Sven Lindqvist, *A History of Bombing* (New York: New Press, 2001).
[38] Lawrence K. Grossman, *The Electronic Republic: Reshaping Democracy in the Information Age* (New York: Viking, 1995).

technology drives economics and political arrangements, not the other way around.[39]

I neither advocate nor attempt to refute technological determinism here. In the first place, I do not try to explain where information technology comes from and what the determinants of its evolution are. I am agnostic about whether information technology represents a human destiny of some kind and also about the extent to which human agency can shape its development. It is sufficient for my argument simply to take the technology roughly as I find it. My strongest claim in this regard is about the evolution of politics in the direction of information abundance, but I do not propose a technologically deterministic accounting of why that is.

The claims of social constructionism are richer but less bold. Their roots lie in the series of classic studies published in the mid-1960s by Jacques Ellul, Leo Marx, Lewis Mumford, Herbert Marcuse, and others.[40] These helped establish an intellectual tradition tracing the influence of culture, economic interests, and politics on technological design, and they positioned technology as a battleground over values and power. Jacques Ellul's *The Technological Society* contended that technological determinists were subtly wrong. Advancing technology was indeed influencing the human condition in profound ways, but not because of properties inherent in technology. A collapse of deliberation regarding the public good had led to failure of democratic control over technology. In the place of public consideration and choice over technology was a set of normative standards centered on efficiency and productivity. New technology, Ellul and others argued, was now being accepted and adopted by publics wherever it promised gains in economic efficiency, as if that one goal was itself constitutive of a good society. The result was a technological enterprise virtually autonomous of meaningful political control.

Contemporary scholars in economics, history, political science, sociology, and the humanities have elaborated the work of Ellul and others into

---

[39] The classic statement of this theory is found in Robert Heilbroner, "Do Machines Make History?" *Technology and Culture* 8, no. 3 (1967): 333–345. For a discussion and overview of the literature, see Merritt Roe Smith and Leo Marx, eds., *Does Technology Drive History? The Dilemma of Technological Determinism* (Cambridge, Mass.: MIT Press, 1994).

[40] Jacques Ellul, *The Technological Society* (New York: Vintage, 1964); Leo Marx, *The Machine in the Garden: Technology and the Pastoral Idea in America* (London: Oxford University Press, 1964); Lewis Mumford, *The Myth of the Machine*, vol. 2: *The Pentagon of Power* (New York: Harcourt, Brace, Jovanovich, 1970); Herbert Marcuse, *One Dimensional Man* (New York: Beacon, 1964).

the modern theory of the social construction of technology.[41] In place of the concept of autonomous technology is now a set of claims that technologies embody and advance political interests and agendas – such as industrial efficiency – and are the product of social structure, culture, values, and politics as much as the result of objective scientific discovery.

Information technology is a ripe subject for analysis from this perspective, because of the collaboration of the U.S. government, private corporations, and universities that went into the development of the Internet. That is a story of Cold War military spending and strategy, the effect of institutions on policy, and how a public good once rejected by the market and subsidized by the government evolved into a mixed public-private good driven almost purely by private enterprise and increasingly contested between industries. Nonetheless, it will not be my purpose to explain the political origins of the Internet or other information technology, and for that topic I refer readers to other sources.[42] The Internet is indeed a "social construction," but I do not explore that issue here.

Technology can be understood as political in the following ways without invoking either technological determinism or social constructionism. By definition, technological development produces tools that permit novel forms of action, novel behaviors, and in some cases novel forms of value. When people engage in new acts with their new tools, their behavior sometimes falls outside the boundaries of extant rules and institutions. Governing institutions are rarely able to anticipate new forms of action that will be made possible by technology, such as cloning of life forms, mass distribution of pornography, or the collection and sale of personal information about citizens by businesses. When such acts first emerge, they are often ungoverned or undergoverned by existing

---

[41] A good single-volume introduction and overview of this literature is Sheila Jasanoff et al., eds., *Handbook of Science and Technology Studies* (Thousand Oaks, Calif.: Sage Publications, 1995).

[42] For works presenting historical essays relevant to the history of the Internet, see: Thomas P. Hughes, *Rescuing Prometheus* (New York: Pantheon, 1998); Michael Margolis and David Resnick, *Politics as Usual: The Cyberspace "Revolution"* (Thousand Oaks, Calif.: Sage Publications, 2000); Bruce L. R. Smith, *American Science Policy since World War II* (Washington, D.C.: Brookings Institution, 1990); David C. Mowrey and Nathan Rosenberg, *Paths of Innovation: Technological Change in 20th Century America* (Cambridge, Eng.: Cambridge University Press, 1998); David M. Hart, *Forged Consensus: Science, Technology and Economic Policy in the United States, 1921–1953* (Princeton: Princeton University Press, 1998); Katie Hafner and Mathew Lyon, *Where Wizards Stay Up Late: The Origins of the Internet* (New York: Simon and Schuster, 1996).

legal and political structures. They lead as a result to demands for policy change and a cycle of political action. The more flexible and malleable a technology is, the broader the range of these "policy vacuums" and political cycles it is likely to precipitate.[43] At the same time, new actions made possible by technologies can affect social and economic structures as well as values. Where such changes persist, they alter the identity and organization of political actors and interests. In these ways technologies are political, and I explore here patterns in such processes.

My argument is organized as follows. In the next chapter, I establish the idea of information revolutions and regimes. This chapter is organized historically, because my interest lies in tracing the evolution of information and the ways that the structure of organizations in politics follows changes in the character of information. It begins, like American democracy itself, with *The Federalist*, from which I extract ideas about information, institutions, and power. It then traces developments in the information landscape of American politics throughout the nineteenth and twentieth centuries and suggests what these meant for the structure of democracy.

Chapter 3 applies the information regime model to contemporary American politics. It discusses the nature of informational change under way at present, and identifies the properties and limitations of postbureaucratic political organization. Chapter 4 explores the information regime concept empirically in the contemporary period. It contains the case studies of information technology and political organization. Chapter 5 takes up the individual-level component of information revolutions and regimes using survey evidence. Chapter 6, the final chapter, provides a summary of the argument, draws comparisons with other countries, and concludes with a normative discussion of information, political equality, and the public sphere.

---

[43] Philosopher James Moor and others apply the term "policy vacuum" to this situation precipitated by technology.

2

Information Revolutions in American Political Development

THE INFORMATION THEORY OF *THE FEDERALIST*

In December of 1787, Alexander Hamilton broke new ground in the public-relations campaign to persuade the American states of the merits of the proposed Constitution. His defense of federal power that we now know as *Federalist 23* landed in four newspapers in two days: in the *New York Packet* and the *New York Journal* on the 18th, and the next day in the *Independent Journal* and the *Daily Advertiser*.[1] It was the first essay in the Federalist series to appear in that many newspapers, and it presumably reached the largest audience since Madison, Hamilton, and Jay began their media blitz in October. That kind of multioutlet exposure would even please a modern political communications director, although Hamilton's demands on the reader would hardly pass muster against modern standards of political rhetoric.

In his essay, Hamilton used a remarkable phrase to describe the proposed government. The new government was to be *the center of information* for the new nation.[2] Hamilton had in mind a far-sighted idea: that the distribution of political information is important to the health of democracies, and that one of the several advantages of a large, federal republic over a system of confederated states was its superior informational properties. Hamilton believed that the U.S. government would elicit a healthier flow of information than the system under the Articles of Confederation, and would better wed that information to representation and policy making. With Madison, Hamilton was sketching out a striking set of ideas about information and democracy, the foundation

---

[1] Jacob E. Cooke, ed., *The Federalist* (Middletown, Conn.: Wesleyan University Press, 1961). All subsequent references to *The Federalist* are to the Cooke edition.
[2] Ibid., p. 149.

of a political theory of information. Those ideas are a good place to begin an exploration of information and American political development.

Remarkably, the term "information" appears about three dozen times in *The Federalist*, within nineteen of the eighty-five essays. The term "communication" appears another dozen. In a passage in *21* dealing with taxation, for instance, Hamilton addresses the problem of assessing the comparative wealth of states or nations. He attacks the quota system for funding war under the Articles, which specified that states be charged for the collective defense in proportion to their land area. Hamilton argues for the rejection of land area or population as measures of states' position in the union. The wealth of a state or society, he argues, is a function of many properties beyond size, especially the state of economic commerce. That observation comes as no surprise from the pen of Hamilton, who would argue four years later in the *Report on Manufactures* for the virtues of division of labor, improvements in worker skills and expertise, organizational specialization and diversification, and other features of industrialization.[3] More striking are additional properties in Hamilton's list: "the genius of its citizens" and "the degree of information they possess."[4] He could hardly have conceived of the modern information economy, yet he clearly understands information and knowledge to be resources, and he recognizes that their distribution varies across states and societies. Hamilton proposes that possession of information can be a measure of a society's development, and that one might compare Russia with Germany as to their information-richness, or North Carolina with Pennsylvania, or Kings County with Montgomery County.

Hamilton's ideas about information continue their modern relevance on more directly political matters. As "Publius," Hamilton and his collaborators invoke information in their arguments about two of the major principles for which their essays are known: the issue of distance or remoteness of the central government from the people, and the famous defense of the extended republic as a solution to the problem of faction. Although widely overlooked, their use of information as a political concept connected to problems of remoteness and faction constitutes a latent Federalist theory of information. This theory shows how one might conceive of the federal government as the nation's "center of information" in more than a passing way.

[3] Samuel McKee, Jr., ed., *Alexander Hamilton's Papers on Public Credit, Commerce, and Finance* (New York: Liberal Arts Press, 1957).
[4] *The Federalist*, p. 133.

INFORMATION AND DISTANCE

The problem of situating more power in a government remote from the local problems of the states was a central objection to the Constitution proposed in 1787. This objection appears throughout Anti-Federalist thought, and it presented an important strategic concern for Publius in the battle over ratification. As a body of political claims, Anti-Federalist writing is far better for illuminating the nature of popular political rhetoric in the founding period than for establishing a coherent theory. Anti-Federalist authors were many in number, some of whose identities remain unknown, and unlike Publius, they were not engaged in a project of coordinated analysis. Their articles are far less analytic than rhetorical, and do not shy from personal attacks. Samuel Bryan, for instance, writing as "Centinel" in January of 1788, labels Publius "deranged" and calls him a fear-monger. In a derisive passage that might unfortunately strike a chord with many college students first confronting Madison, Bryan chastises him for his "accumulated myriads of unmeaning sentences" and wishes Publius "might have spared his readers the fatigue of wading through his long-winded disquisitions."[5]

In their arguments about distance and the remoteness of the proposed government from the problems of the people, Bryan and other Anti-Federalists posited an information problem. They observed that democratic policy making requires thorough information. Specifically, it requires a government to assemble a coherent body of knowledge comprising all information about local conditions and issues across a polity. They conceived of national public interest as the sum of local political interests across all citizens, and therefore believed national-scale political information should entail the sum of all local information.

These conceptions contributed for the Anti-Federalists to limits on how large a democracy could be. The size problem is generally recognized as their chief defense of state governments, and is understood to encompass several issues, including uniformity of administration, the fostering of a sense of citizenship, and accountability of government to the people.[6] Running throughout their objections to the large republic is a strong concern with information and communication that has generally gone unrecognized by scholars. Anti-Federalists feared that as the scale of a republic grows, political information eventually becomes too

[5] John D. Lewis, *Anti-Federalists versus Federalists: Selected Documents* (San Francisco: Chandler Publishing, 1967), p. 150.
[6] For an overview, see Joseph M. Bessette, ed., *Toward a More Perfect Union: Writings of Herbert J. Storing* (Washington, D.C.: American Enterprise Institute, 1995).

complex for both citizens and government officials. In small democracies, they believed, governments can be well informed about the detailed and specific wants of their citizens. In large republics, government faces an unattractive dilemma: settling for an incomplete and even vague impression of public and private interests, or collapsing under the complexity of too much information by attempting to assemble a complete picture of the public's circumstances and wants.

The first horn of this information dilemma was posed by Richard Henry Lee, the most widely read of the Anti-Federalists and among the most politically distinguished. A Virginia Burgess, delegate and briefly president of the Continental Congress, signer of the Declaration, and U.S. Senator from 1789 to 1792, Lee observed that representation cannot succeed on generalized information, but requires specific knowledge of the circumstances of all citizens. Writing as "The Federal Farmer," Lee observes that states vary in "opinions, customs, and views," and that "these differences are not so perceivable among the members of Congress, and men of general information in the states, as among the men who would properly form the democratic branch." Representative legitimacy, Lee believes, can rest only on the basis of specific rather than general political information. Regarding Congress, he continues: "I have no idea that the interests, feelings, and opinions of three or four millions of people, especially touching internal taxation, can be collected in such a house."[7] There is simply too much information to be gathered, and so legislation is destined to rest on inadequate information.

The other horn of the dilemma is described by George Clinton, also a delegate to the Continental Congress, a general in the Continental Army, later first governor of New York, and Vice President under Jefferson and Madison. In the third "Cato" letter, issued in October of 1787, Clinton addresses the possibility that the information problem in a large state might be solved by increasing the size and elaboration of government, especially the number of representatives in the legislature. He argues against that strategy as leading to unworkable complexity in government: "Where, from the vast extent of your territory, and the complication of interests, the science of government will become intricate and perplexed, and too mysterious for you to understand and observe."[8] That is, government cannot simply be scaled up in size to accommodate more interests and information, because complexity presents limits,

---

[7] Morton Borden, ed., *The Antifederalist Papers* (N.p.: Michigan State University Press, 1965), p. 97.

[8] John D. Lewis, *Anti-Federalists versus Federalists*, pp. 190–191.

especially on the capacity of the public to observe and understand government, and to assimilate adequate information to assert democratic control.

Samuel Bryan pursues the idea that information problems infect the public as well as elected officials. Multiplying representatives in a national-scale legislature undermines the transparency of government for citizens, he believes, creating complexity that will overwhelm citizens and render their efforts at participation and accountability ineffective. In one of the more far-sighted Anti-Federalist documents, Bryan anticipates certain twentieth-century thought on accountability and divided control:

> The highest responsibility is to be attained in a simple structure of government, for the great body of the people never steadily attend to the operations of government, and for want of due information are liable to be imposed upon. If you complicate the plan by various orders, the people will be perplexed and divided in their sentiment about the source of abuses or misconduct; some will impute it to the senate, others to the house of representatives, and so on, that the interposition of the people may be rendered imperfect or perhaps wholly abortive.[9]

Simpler, unitary government, Bryan believes, facilitates the acquisition of "due information" on the part of the public, and therefore improves accountability. If the information associated with government is less complex and more straightforward, then "whenever the people feel a grievance, they cannot mistake the authors, and will apply the remedy with certainty and effect, discarding them at the next election."[10] For Anti-Federalists such as Bryan, Lee, and Clinton, representation succeeds in proportion to the particularity and specificity of information linking citizens with government; in other words, the need to avoid intractable complexity in political information helps set upper bounds on the manageable size of democratic government. Madisonian multiplication of interests at the societal level, they believe, creates insuperable information problems at the level of the state and in the relationship between state and civil society.

Publius has answers for this challenge, although they are not organized in a single place in *The Federalist*. Like the Anti-Federalist recourse to matters of information, the Federalist understanding of information

---

[9] Ibid., p. 141.   [10] Ibid.

and communication has largely escaped notice. An important part of the response to the size objection comes from Hamilton in *84*, who observes that in the smallest democracies of just the sort that Montesquieu and the Anti-Federalists advocate, important obstacles still exist to the kind of direct, mutual observation between citizens and government that Cato and Centinel presuppose. In neither small nor large democracies, Hamilton notes, can citizens and government officials exchange information directly and fully. Choosing Montgomery County as an example, he points out that even in a jurisdiction of this size, the flow of political information requires informed citizens to rely upon "the public prints," correspondence, and communication with others if they are to attend to the affairs of government. Less-informed citizens must in turn rely upon the better-informed. Therefore, political communication and the flow of information will always be mediated, even in the smallest of states. Establishing the principle of mediated information flow, regardless of the size of government, lays the foundation for overcoming the problem of scale.

For Hamilton, the mediation of political information is more than a technical necessity. It is politically desirable because it permits the filtering and aggregation of local communication, as well as the building of larger views and a synthetic body of national-scale political information. The informational tasks of central government are to aggregate information in such a way that a useful synthesis results, in which the informational whole is greater and wiser than the sum of the individual facts about local problems. In the construction of a national view of problems, it is useful that some local details recede into the background – a point of view that was an anathema to Anti-Federalists.

One step in the process of mediating and synthesizing information involves elected officials learning about problems outside their own constituencies. Here Madison takes up the argument: "Whilst a few representatives, therefore, from each State, may bring with them a due knowledge of their own state, every representative will have much information to acquire concerning all the other States."[11] Hamilton claims that the state governments have an important role to play in the flow of information because they can serve as information aggregators, standing between local problems and the larger national view. In the proposed system of government, local information is to be assembled into state-level information in the state governments. The state governments would then bring to the

---

[11] *The Federalist*, p. 381.

federal government a body of information already aggregated at a first level. In the Capitol, a second level of aggregation would occur as legislators inform themselves about the problems and interests of other states, melding these into a national conception. The result is to be a balance of local, state, and federal perspectives and information, rather than a simplistic summation of all local political facts and knowledge. In this view, the federal structure is crucial both for parsing public policy into state and national problems and for feeding appropriate information into the process of national-level decision making. The mechanism works in reverse as well, facilitating the monitoring of government actions for citizens. Hamilton believes the state governments will employ a "regular and effectual system of intelligence" about the national councils on behalf of constituents.[12] Citizens need not therefore bear responsibility for directly observing all actions of a distant federal government. They may read about government, observe the effects of decisions upon them, and rely upon their state officials for information regarding national affairs.

Claims about information aggregation and synthesis in response to complexity also appear in Madison's defense in *53* of the two-year House term, which he acknowledges is at odds with the norm of one-year service in the state houses. The "great theatre" of national legislation calls for a double-length term, he claims, because of the heterogeneity of national information problems.[13] The laws and circumstances of the states are not uniform, creating a burden for legislators of acquiring "extensive information" about subjects outside their own states and districts.[14] In *35*, Hamilton explains further that institutional arrangements should produce elected officials who are "acquainted with the general genius, habits and modes of thinking of the people at large and with the resources of the country."[15] Publius does not deny the existence of complexity in the national government, but sees elected officials in a Burkean light, acting on behalf of constituents from a political perspective that is national in scope. He rejects the premise of the Anti-Federalist question about how enough local information can reach a remote and distant central government. The question, instead, is, How can information be synthesized into a national composite?

The message of Madison and Hamilton is that large republics do more than simply guard against majority faction; they communicate and aggregate political information better than do small republics. Michael Schudson is correct when he observes in *The Good Citizen*, "[Publius]

---

[12] Ibid., p. 582.   [13] Ibid., p. 362.   [14] Ibid., p. 363.   [15] Ibid., p. 222.

is developing a political theory here that places communication at its center."[16] The ways that institutional arrangements affect the flow of information is central to the operation of democracy, Publius believes, and is vital to understanding how governments in large polities can succeed. His view of state governments as central information intermediaries we now see as off-base, since state governments have grown to be more important as intermediaries for the flow of money, rather than information, from the national government to the citizen. Yet his recognition of the importance of mediation and aggregation is not only correct but remarkable, because no national system of mass newspapers yet existed to provide an example, as we see below.

INFORMATION AND FACTION

For Madison and Hamilton, the role of information in solving the problem of faction is related to the problem of size and distance. A light reading of Publius on the problem of faction sometimes leads no further than the well-known argument taught to introductory students of American politics: that the multiplication and diversification of interests in the extended republic protects against tyranny by placing obstacles in the way of majorities. Minority factions take care of themselves, as it were, because majority-rule institutions prevent them from tyrannizing, while the problem of majority factions is diminished through dilution and fragmentation. Yet there is a good deal more to the problem of factions than this reading suggests, and in a fuller exploration of Publius, the dynamics of information come into play.

Factions, Madison writes, are those groups whose pursuits are adverse to the rights of others or to the common good. Not all groups necessarily pursue unjust aims, so some groups are factious and some are not. The typology of possible political groups implicit in the *Federalist 10* argument, therefore, is fourfold: factious minority groups, nonfactious minority groups, factious majority groups, and nonfactious majority groups.[17] With minority groups of any kind kept from tyranny by majoritarian institutional arrangements, the problem of controlling factions is reduced to permitting nonfactious majorities to govern while simultaneously blocking the action of factious majorities. George Carey describes this task as "the filter problem" in the Federalist theory of the

---

[16] Michael Schudson, *The Good Citizen: A History of American Civic Life* (New York: Martin Kessler, 1998), p. 85.

[17] James Yoho, "Madison on the Beneficial Effects of Interest Groups: What Was Left Unsaid in *Federalist 10*," *Polity* 27, no. 4 (1995): 587–605.

extended republic; that is, filtering out the bad majorities while permitting good ones to govern.[18]

Some influential observers claim that Publius offers no adequate solution to the filter problem. This is a grave charge, because if the government is to govern democratically, majorities with just aims must form and be permitted to act.[19] The idea that the Federalist design cannot discriminate between factious and nonfactious majorities once fueled acceptance of the Beardian interpretation of the Constitution, namely, that by indiscriminately frustrating majorities, the framers locked in place a system of elite privilege. In his 1956 *A Preface to Democratic Theory,* Robert Dahl saw the problem as insuperable and argued that by failing to filter, the government vested an elite minority with a vast veto power over proposals both inimical to and supportive of the larger public good.[20] For Gary Wills, it is simply a matter of Publius's failure to define factiousness.[21]

That approach to the filter problem short-changes Publius. Certainly, he was cognizant of the objection. In the well-known passage in *51* that "a coalition of a majority of the whole society could seldom take place on any other principles than those of justice and the general good," Madison asks readers to trust that majorities will form in his system, and that when they do, those majorities will tend to form on the basis of agreeable principles.[22] It is not the case, Madison would have us believe, that the extended republic dilutes and divides interests so as to make majorities unworkable. The extended republic somehow biases majority politics in the direction of the common good. But how is this to happen?

Part of the answer, Carey observes, is that national representatives come from heterogeneous districts, each containing multiple interests, so that no representative is entirely beholden to a particular faction.[23] District interests do not necessarily constrain lawmakers; therefore, each representative must reflect upon and compromise among contending

---

[18] George W. Carey, *The Federalist: Design for a Constitutional Republic* (Urbana: University of Illinois Press, 1989).

[19] James Allen Smith, *The Spirit of American Government* (New York: Macmillan, 1907); Charles A. Beard, *An Economic Interpretation of the Constitution* (New York: Macmillan, 1913).

[20] Robert A. Dahl, *A Preface to Democratic Theory* (Chicago: University of Chicago Press, 1956).

[21] Gary Wills, *Explaining America: The Federalist* (Garden City, N.Y.: Doubleday and Company, 1981).

[22] *The Federalist*, p. 353.

[23] George W. Carey, *The Federalist: Design for a Constitutional Republic.*

interests. This weakens the tendency for factiousness in the national legislature.

More important, informational dynamics help solve the filter problem, and Publius is more explicit about this effect. He assumes that policy making in the context of multiple, contending interests has different requirements than policy making among small, homogenous groups, including the exchange of extensive political information and the intensive vetting of ideas. Publius realizes that before a majority can be formed in a large, heterogeneous democracy, a thorough process of political communication must take place in which contending ideas are voiced, and arguments and counterarguments are forwarded. On the other hand, smaller, homogeneous states can more easily assemble poorly informed, nondeliberative majorities that tend to factiousness. The deliberations of the dissimilar parties to a potential majority in a heterogeneous system reveal political information about interests and intentions. In other words, assembling majorities among diverse interests is possible, but commits politicians to the disclosure and exchange of information.

The question then becomes, Why is the justness of democratic outcomes related to the extent of information associated with them? The answer lies in Publius's faith in the latent reason of political elites. He believes that humans possess simultaneously the capacity for both good and bad actions, and the design of governments should serve to facilitate the good. The passions, that great threat to justice, he believes, thrive in information-poor environments. They are more likely to be subdued by reason and better judgment where information is rich. In *64*, Madison notes that it is the "*secret* wishes of an unjust and interested majority" (emphasis added) against which precautions are needed. Factious majorities differ from nonfactious majorities in that the former are rooted in seduction of the public, secrecy, appeals to the passions, and demagoguery. Their politics depends on an environment where information is circumscribed and where alternatives, rival possibilities, and the other ingredients of deliberation are absent.

This connection between information and deliberation appears throughout *The Federalist*. For instance, Hamilton writes in *68* that the electoral college will succeed because electors are likely to "possess the information and discernment" requisite to choosing the national leader.[24] In defense of the qualifications for the Senate in *62*, Madison observes the need for "greater extent of information and stability of character" on

---

[24] *The Federalist*, p. 458.

the part of senators. Information and good judgment again go hand in hand. In 35, Madison writes: "If we take into the account the momentary humors or dispositions which may happen to prevail in particular parts of the society, and to which a wise administration will never be inattentive, is the man whose situation leads to extensive inquiry and information less likely to be a competent judge of their nature, extent, and foundation than one whose observation does not travel beyond the circle of his neighbors and acquaintances?"[25] A national government, writes Hamilton in 27, would be "better administered" than the state governments, in part because the circumstances of the national government "promise greater knowledge and more extensive information in the national councils." In 58, Madison continues that the "eloquence and address of a few" – demagoguery – is most likely to act on people "of limited information and of weak capacities."[26] In 64, Jay nicely summarizes the premise of his partners: "[D]iscretion and discernment" are to be found in government in proportion to "the means of extensive and accurate information."[27]

Publius recognizes that human reason and judgment are fallible even in the presence of adequate information, and thus he also understands that the public as well as elites may be possessed of a mixture of motives that are not always just.[28] So while he rejects the idea that democracy depends on the good will of public actors, he nonetheless believes that given adequate information as an antidote to demagoguery, enough people will be inclined toward justice and reason for democracy to succeed.[29] In this argument, Publius resolves the filter problem. The extended republic does not obstruct all majorities indiscriminately, but biases politics toward the disclosure of greater amounts of information than do smaller, simpler democracies. That informational tendency exerts a filtering effect, since prudence and good judgment are facilitated by information.

One need not accept the formal view of Benjamin Page and Robert Shapiro, who have argued the *entire* problem of the passions is one of "incomplete information," to be persuaded by Publius that information matters in the success of democracy, and that institutional arrangements matter in the state of information. On this point, the authors of *The*

---

[25] Ibid., p. 221.   [26] Ibid., p. 396.   [27] Ibid., p. 433.

[28] Edward J. Millican, *One United People: The Federalist Papers and the National Idea* (Lexington: University of Kentucky Press, 1990).

[29] David F. Epstein, *The Political Theory of "The Federalist"* (Chicago: University of Chicago Press, 1984).

Federalist and their Anti-Federalist opponents could agree. They parted company on the question of precisely how institutional structure affects the state of democratic information. The Federalists saw connections between heterogeneity and the disclosure of information that the Anti-Federalists did not, and they anticipated that the flow of political information would be mediated and aggregated.

The issue of complexity and the most appropriate institutional arrangements for dealing with it therefore emerges as one of the major themes in this debate about political information. It appeared to the Anti-Federalists that the informational tasks of governing could quickly grow complex – too complex, they felt, for a large state to succeed. Publius's emphasis on aggregation and mediation, on the other hand, reflects his quite different understanding of the problem. Not only can complexity be managed, but it should also be embraced because broader patterns and perspectives may emerge from it.

This central Federalist conception can be summarized in the thesis that the state of democracy is partly a function of the ways that political structure affects the disclosure, mediation, and aggregation of political information. From the perspective of the twenty-first century, this idea perhaps gives the impression of being self-evident. But like much of what Publius wrote, it was hardly so in an age before the rise of mass media, political parties, and interest groups, and before the creation of the First Amendment protections for information. The Federalists could not foresee how this relationship would play out over time. The structure and mediation of information would one day be dominated by private political organizations as well as formal institutions of government; the identities of information aggregators would themselves change as the complexity and cost of information changed; and the mass public itself would one day become involved intimately in the flow of information. But the Federalist thesis serves as a useful foundation for evaluating the coevolution of information and political structure from the founding period on. It also reminds us that important contemporary developments in information and politics driven by technology have conceptual roots in early American political thought. Most important, in theoretical terms, this proposition suggests the possibility of a causal relationship between properties of information and features or qualities of democracy. Going a step further than Publius, one can posit that features of information – such as degree of complexity or level of accessibility and extent of its distribution – might vary over time, and that this variation might be connected in some way with political structure and with the state of democracy in general. Here are the roots of a theory of information and American democracy.

When and under what circumstances have features of political information varied across American history? Prior to the contemporary period, three eras of transformation in information since the founding stand out as candidates. The first of these occurred in the early nineteenth century, when national-scale transmission of information became possible for the first time in the United States. In the age of Jefferson, virtually no arrangements for the communication of national political information existed in the United States. Indeed, the process of information aggregation and communication envisioned by Publius had all but failed to materialize by the 1810s, and the effects of that failure were enormous. Yet by 1841, when Tyler took over the presidency after Harrison's death, a new national political communication and information system existed. This system was both qualitatively and quantitatively different from what had existed before, in ways that the Federalists would have recognized.

The second period of major change occurred between the 1880s and approximately 1920. Whereas the developments of 1820 to 1840 made national communication possible for the first time, events between 1880 and 1920 expanded dramatically the volume and cost of political information attendant to public life. It was what sociologist James Beniger calls a "control revolution" and its central issue was complexity – a Federalist theme playing out a century after the founding.[30] The third period of change was the 1950s to the late 1970s, when television became so potent a force in American culture and politics. The many influences of television on the evolution of politics are important in two ways here. Up until the late 1980s, the development of television is the story of the rise of the mass audience for political communication – the acceleration of high-cost political communication and the institutionalization of a limited set of gatekeepers on the flow of political information – the rise of a particularly potent form of informational mediation. From the early 1990s on, with the spread of cable and satellite television, the development of television becomes the story of a tension between the mass audience and the narrower audience, between mass communication and selective, targeted communication that exploits an abundance of "channels" and falling costs for communication.

---

[30] James R. Beniger, *The Control Revolution: Technological and Economic Origins of the Information Society* (Cambridge, Mass.: Harvard University Press, 1986).

These three periods — 1820s–30s, 1880s–1910s, and 1950s–70s — are not the only eras in which communication and the character of information changed in the United States, but they are the most important, more so than the emergence of the telegraph, of railroads, and even telephones, all of which did more to contribute to dominant features of information in society than to change them. What then were the dynamics of informational change in these periods, and how might that change have affected politics? Consider each in turn.

THE FIRST INFORMATION REVOLUTION AND THE RISE OF MAJORITARIANISM

It is useful to establish a picture of the state of political information throughout American society at the end of the founding era. The central feature of the period 1789–1820 was the absence of an effective system for the national-scale flow of political information. Before the 1820s, communication and the exchange of information were constrained by the limits of face-to-face contact and slow human travel. No electronic or electrical communication medium would operate until the telegraph at mid-century, and no true system of national news existed to assemble and distribute information. Postal service was rudimentary, with the distribution of mail unreliable and often unavailable in many places. The number of roads or rivers used for the conveyance of messages was insufficient to move information around the country in a functional way.

Simply put, no workable method existed for the public to communicate reliably or thoroughly outside their immediate communities. In informational terms, not much of "a public" can be said to have existed; rather, the nation consisted of a patchwork of largely isolated local publics. Not only were states such as Vermont and South Carolina isolated informationally from each other, but even within a state, one region was typically cut off from the next. Citizens of Philadelphia enjoyed no more exchange of information with people living in the Pennsylvania interior than with those in Boston — perhaps even less, since ships could at least pass news along the seaboard.

The lack of effective communication meant that government was cut off from citizens, since public officials had no better means to communicate with their constituents than did the general public with each other. A representative elected to the House was hard pressed to identify the needs of all members of his district, and for senators the problem was even larger. One can imagine, for instance, the difficulties faced by Senator John Armstrong, Jr., of New York, who served 1800 to 1804.[31] A native Pennsylvanian who had settled in Dutchess County, New York, at the age of thirty-six, how could he as senator follow the concerns of his constituents hundreds of miles away in the frontier town of Buffalo, for example? How could he even identify in common with them an ideology or meaningful party attachment? Obstacles to communication were exacerbated for officials actually located in the capital city, since the possibility of consultation with constituents was largely out of the question, and the flow of news from the state or district spotty at best. In a sense, Presidents faced the greatest communication problem, since they were chosen by electors representing a public about whom they could know little, and whom they could not address. Historian James Sterling Young labels the lack of communication in the early republic a "quarantine" of government from society; indeed, a government official at the outset of the nineteenth century acknowledged that he and his colleagues amounted to "monks in a monastery."[32]

The political consequences of this monastic isolation and absence of national-scale communication can scarcely be exaggerated. Representation rested on only the sketchiest of foundations, since public officials had no systematic way of knowing more than a little about their constituents. By the same token, the capacity of voters to assign responsibility for outcomes and hold officials accountable was limited, since even the most attentive elites found it hard to form a clear picture of the details of policy making. The concerns of citizens in one community could not be readily communicated to those in another, and conversations about the national interests did not take place outside of individual communities and councils of elites. The impoverishment of information and communication stunted the evolution of political identities, since identity formation requires the exchange of ideas and values among citizens and the perception of self in relation to others. Needless to say, given all this, the limited flow of information obstructed the formation of coalitions and coordinated political action, thus retarding the development of a system of political parties. Protoparties had emerged by the 1790s, but

---

[31] He served from 1800 to 1802 and 1803 to 1804, due to a series of resignations, appointments, and elections. U.S. Senate, Biographical Directory of the United States Congress, 1774-Present, 2001. http://bioguide.congress.gov.

[32] George Gibbs, *Memoirs of the Administrations of Washington and John Adams*, vol. 2 (New York: William van Norden, 1846), cited in James Sterling Young, *The Washington Community 1800–1828* (New York: Columbia University Press, 1966), p. 32.

through the 1810s and into the '20s, their weakly coupled networks and alliances kept them from nationalizing or institutionalizing themselves.[33] The "Republican" in Vermont in 1796 would have had little connection with a "Republican" in South Carolina, and sharing party labels did not necessarily dispose citizens toward the same presidential candidates or political ideas. Despite the efforts of party-builders, the nascent parties simply could not gain national traction so long as it was largely impossible to communicate systematically on a national scale. This failure of national political integration formed a continuing basis for the highly sectional voting that lasted until the contests of 1836, 1840, and 1844, even as the parties began to solidify.[34]

The communication problems affecting everything from representation to party development thrust the country into what Paul Goodman calls a "crisis of integration." Democratic action rooted in the public interest and resting on the legitimacy of majority sentiment was for the most part impossible, since "no one could authoritatively know or interpret the majority's wishes because the people themselves often had no opinion, and when they did, it was hopelessly divided or fragmented."[35] Elected officials maneuvering for influence had little chance to appeal to the demands of the public or to invoke a public mandate. In the arena of public opinion, these conditions created "the politics of assent," whereby the many fragmented publics largely assented to decisions made on their behalf by the American political gentry.[36] Isolation and the resulting political enervation were distinguishing characteristics of democracy in the Jeffersonian period.[37] In the near absence of the flow of even simple political information, no important political intermediaries could arise to organize the public, initiate collective action, or

---

[33] Paul Goodman, "The First American Party System," in William Nisbet Chambers and Walter Dean Burnham, eds., *The American Party Systems: Stages of Political Development* (New York: Oxford University Press, 1967), p. 86; Richard P. McCormick, "Political Development and the Second Party System," in William Nisbet Chambers and Walter Dean Burnham, eds., *The American Party Systems*; Richard P. McCormick, *The Second American Party System: Party Formation in the Jacksonian Era* (Chapel Hill: University of North Carolina Press, 1966).

[34] Ronald P. Formisano, "Federalists and Republicans: Parties, Yes – System, No," in Paul Kleppner et al., eds., *The Evolution of American Electoral Systems* (Westport, Conn.: Greenwood, 1981), pp. 33–76; McCormick, "Political Development and the Second Party System."

[35] Goodman, "The First American Party System," p. 61.

[36] Schudson, *The Good Citizen.*

[37] James Sterling Young, *The Washington Community 1800–1828* (New York: Columbia University Press, 1966).

aggregate demands. In other words, a society with a highly constrained flow of political information was not one in which democratic power could readily accumulate.[38]

As late as the 1820s, it appeared as though the Anti-Federalists may have been right in their assessments of information and communication. Due to inadequacy of information, neither government nor public could properly understand one another, and the remoteness of government from the people exacerbated other communication problems due to the remoteness of communities from each other across the large republic. By the end of the Jeffersonian era, the faith of Madison and Hamilton in state governments as informational intermediaries appeared to have been misplaced.

Against this backdrop, events of the 1820s and '30s in the realm of communication constitute nothing less than a revolution. This revolution created a system of national-scale political information that fed democratic development across the spectrum: the emergence of ideology and identity, the creation of a national political agenda and public will, the explosion in participation among white males, the energizing of a government previously adrift in its own nation, and the creation of political intermediaries situated at the center of these processes.

As historian Richard John has shown, the central component of this revolution was the postal service.[39] Elementary postal services had existed in the prerevolutionary period and in the early years of the new republic, but they did not constitute a functional national mail system. In 1790, the nation had just seventy-five post offices, handling about 300,000 letters that year. This meant the United States had one post office for every 43,000 people, and these offices carried about 0.1 letters per capita per year. The vast majority of Americans simply did not have access to regular mail. Without the kind of telecommunication systems that would develop later, the absence of good mail service meant that

---

[38] This enervation of the American political system in the Jeffersonian age is consistent with W. Russell Neuman's model of the relationship between the volume of political communication in a society and the degree of political centralization or decentralization. Neuman argues that the nature of power in societies with a high volume of political communication can vary between hyperpluralistic faction and instability or totalitarianism, as a function of the degree of political centralization. But societies with a very low flow of political communication converge on conditions of entropy and political decay. See W. Russell Neuman, *The Future of the Mass Audience* (Cambridge, Eng.: Cambridge University Press, 1991); see fig. 1.2.

[39] Richard R. John, *Spreading the News: The American Postal System from Franklin to Morse* (Cambridge, Mass.: Harvard University Press, 1995).

many Americans, especially those outside cities, had no way to send and receive messages regularly, aside from word of mouth and the hand delivery of letters, and therefore no systematic way to receive news or political information.

In the half-century after the founding, all this would change as a result of a massive project of institution building in connection with the mail – a kind of Manhattan Project of communication. By 1840, the United States had created more than 13,000 new post offices, one for every thousand people, and these handled 40 million letters annually. The postal service had grown by two orders of magnitude in half a century, and was now substantially larger and more sophisticated than that of any other nation.[40] It was the first American governmental institution to surpass unequivocally those of the major European powers in scope and capability, and it meant that information of all kinds could move reliably around the country in new ways.

At roughly the same time, an organizational transformation was under way in the news media. The American newspaper business changed dramatically in the 1830s, just as the postal service was coming into its own, and for reasons that are not unconnected, as Richard John has shown. One important change involved the content of the news, which through the 1820s had been very circumscribed. What papers existed had been a mix of mercantile and political papers, but most catered chiefly to the interests of merchants and other elites. They were, in Michael Schudson's words, "bulletin boards for the business community."[41] The average paper of the postcolonial period resembled more closely a brief modern trade journal than a contemporary newspaper. Schudson describes:

> The typical daily was four pages long. Its front page was almost exclusively devoted to advertising, and the fourth page likewise was strictly advertising. These outside pages were like the cover of a book or magazine – one turned to the inside to find the content of the paper. Page two carried editorial columns. Much of page two and page three detailed the arrival of ships in the harbor and the contents of their cargoes, as well as other marine news.[42]

[40] All figures reported by Richard R. John, *Spreading the News*, from various sources.

[41] Michael Schudson, *Discovering the News: A Social History of American Newspapers* (New York: Basic Books, 1978), p. 16. This excellent volume provides a very useful account of the emergence of the newspaper business in the United States, and I rely heavily on Schudson's interpretation and data.

[42] Ibid., p. 14.

No journalistic news ethic yet existed, and the content reflected this and the circumscribed subscribership. Postcolonial papers paid little attention to public information and the sort of news necessary to creating and sustaining a public sphere. In Irving Fang's words, the colonial and postcolonial newspaper in the United States was "so dear [expensive] that the average person did not see a copy of a newspaper and possibly might not have even been aware of the existence of such a thing as a newspaper."[43]

These "Dark Ages" of journalism, as one observer puts it, were to change dramatically in the 1820s and '30s with the rise of the "penny papers," a new breed of newspaper aimed at a mass readership and costing one-sixth the going rate of six cents for traditional papers.[44] These new papers carried information about societal affairs and community activities as well as crime and other matters of popular interest. Moreover, they addressed political affairs, carrying reporting mixed with opinion about issues and public matters. Many established a new brand of political coverage by assigning correspondents to Washington. For the first time in the history of the United States, citizens with access to a newspaper could regularly obtain information about politics. They could read the text of a presidential address, a congressional speech, or a government document; in addition, they could follow first-hand coverage of political affairs or be apprised of party notices and bulletins.[45] To be sure, the revolution of the penny press did not kill off the party paper, which remained viable at least through the Civil War; nor did it mean that the press abruptly became politically neutral. By mid-century, many papers were still partisan. But the content and role of the paper in American life had been fundamentally changed.

These changes in content were accompanied by an explosion in the number of media businesses and the total circulation of newspapers. A number of estimates are available for this growth, and while these vary somewhat, all indicate a very rapid expansion. Irving Fang finds that the number of newspaper businesses grew from 37 weeklies and no dailies at the time of the revolution to 650 weeklies and 65 dailies by 1830,

---

[43] Irving Fang, *A History of Mass Communication: Six Information Revolutions* (Boston: Focal Press, 1997), p. 52.

[44] Frank Luther Mott, *American Journalism – A History of Newspapers in the United States through 260 Years: 1690 to 1950* (New York: Macmillan, 1950).

[45] Fang, *A History of Mass Communication*, p. 52.

and that it then doubled again by 1840.[46] Frank Luther Mott estimates there were 200 newspapers in business in 1801 and 1,200 by 1833, and Michael Schudsen reports that newspaper circulation itself quadrupled between 1830 and 1840 – a time when the total population of the nation grew by one-third.[47] Mott cites an enthusiastic article in an 1836 issue of the *Philadelphia Public Ledger,* a penny paper, about the presence of newspapers in American life by the mid-1830s:

> In the cities of New York and Brooklyn, containing a population of 300,000, the daily circulation of the penny papers is not less than 70,000. This is nearly sufficient to place a newspaper in the hands of every man in the two cities, and even of every boy old enough to read. These papers are to be found in every street, lane, and alley; in every hotel, tavern, counting-house, shop, etc. Almost every porter and dray-man, while not engaged in his occupation, may be seen with a paper in his hands.[48]

The scale and reach of American news, like that of mail, was revolutionized in the years leading up to 1840.

These developments in infrastructure were linked, since a central function of the newly muscular post office was the distribution of newspapers. In fact, as Tim Cook observes, the post office was "geared more for the prompt, widespread delivery of news than for individual correspondence."[49] During this period of transformation, the post office carried roughly as many newspapers as letters, and in some years more. In 1830, the nation's post offices handled 16 million newspapers and a little under 14 million letters.[50] In the cities, newspaper delivery was conducted chiefly by hand carriers, but in the rural areas where most people lived, it depended on mail service.

Existing public policy nourished the newspaper business and its connection to the postal service. In 1792, the U.S. Congress passed what might be called the first "information infrastructure policy," the Post Office Act, linking together what would now be called "content providers" with the sole national "service provider." The act provided for the free exchange of

[46] S. D. N. North, *The Newspaper and Periodical Press* (Washington, D.C.: U.S. Government Printing Office, 1884), cited in Fang, *A History of Mass Communication.*
[47] Mott, *American Journalism*; Schudson, *Discovering the News.*
[48] Mott, *American Journalism*, p. 241.
[49] Timothy E. Cook, *Governing with the News: The News Media as a Political Institution* (Chicago: University of Chicago Press, 1998).
[50] All figures on postal service capacity from John, *Spreading the News.*

content among newspaper businesses, permitting each business to mail a free copy of each issue to every other news business of its choice. By Richard John's estimate, these exchanged papers constituted between a third and half of the weight of all the postal service's mail in 1820.[51] This remarkably farsighted provision expanded an older colonial era practice of "printers exchanges" and contributed directly and forcefully to the creation of the national news media system.[52]

The Post Office Act went further as information infrastructure policy.[53] Postal rates on newspapers were set so low that the postal service lost money on them, which it made back on letters. This meant that the law arranged for the subsidization of the newspaper-based public sphere by the private letter business.[54] An even more important provision of the law dealing with postal rates entailed the question of setting the charge for carrying a paper or letter proportionate to the distance traveled. Since the labor required to deliver a letter or paper across the country was vastly different from that required for delivery across town, during the debate, some proponents had argued for a graduated system in which senders would pay in accordance with the distance the letter or paper was to travel. Legislators finally rejected that scheme in favor of the flat rate system, specifically in order to encourage the flow of information and to reduce the relevance of physical proximity to communication.[55]

By the 1840s, the post office and press together constituted a new political communication system in the United States, with capacities far beyond anything that had existed in the first decades of the century. Together they gave citizens information about one another, informed them about government, and created a way for government to learn about citizens and communicate to them – the three fundamental information tasks in democracy. News from around the nation was available to citizens in one place, the local newspaper. The speed of information to the most distant parts of the country could typically be measured in days or weeks, rather than months, and its arrival was sufficiently reliable that the public could stay abreast of economic and social affairs and monitor political developments. Government officials

---

[51] Ibid.   [52] Cook, *Governing with the News*.
[53] I rely on John, *Spreading the News* for an excellent interpretation of the pretelegraph postal service as information infrastructure, and for the Post Office Act as the nation's first information infrastructure policy. On this subject, also see Cook, *Governing with the News*.
[54] John, *Spreading the News*.   [55] Schudson, *The Good Citizen*.

could follow the affairs of the nation as a whole, signal their intentions, claim credit for policy and outcomes, and appeal for the public authority to institute change. Contemporaries had the sense that the vast distances of the nation were being overcome or even rendered unimportant, and some even spoke of the creation of national community.[56] By about the end of Madison's life in 1836, a sweeping change in the movement of political information had occurred in the United States, creating a system of the general sort that he had claimed vital to the health of democracy.

It is important to note that these changes are attributable only partly to "technology," defined narrowly as artifacts, though rapid changes in techniques of printing were indeed part of the story. In the two and half centuries following the invention of printing, comparatively few technological improvements were made. Then in the early eighteenth century, mass printing was facilitated by a variety of developments, especially the mass production of paper in continuous sheets and the iron printing press, which was followed quickly by the steam-driven rotary press. The hand-powered screw presses in use at the time of the American founding could produce at best about 150 sheets per hour; however, by 1827, mechanized state-of-the-art presses could print 7,000 sheets in an hour.[57] By the end of the nineteenth century, this figure would grow by another factor of ten. While these technological developments fueled the dramatic change in information infrastructure, the information revolution depended more importantly on the development of two organizations: the postal bureaucracy and the political party.

The contributions of this information revolution to the Jacksonian democratization and broader political development were pervasive. With the fall of voting qualifications, which were largely gone by 1840, came new political divisions and an explosion in voting participation, which rose from around 10 percent in 1820 to 80 percent in 1840. This flood of citizens into the democratic process outpaced even the entry of women after 1920 and African Americans in the South in the middle of the twentieth century.[58] At the same time, states were instituting popular elections for presidential electors, permitting newly enfranchised voters to do what Madison would have abhorred: to vote for president, even if indirectly. New norms of egalitarianism and the decay of social hierarchy,

[56] John, *Spreading the News.*   [57] Fang, *A History of Mass Communication.*
[58] Harold W. Stanley and Richard G. Niemi, *Vital Statistics on American Politics, 1997–1998* (Washington, D.C.: Congressional Quarterly, 1998).

as well as expanding education and literacy, formed a cultural foundation for political participation.[59]

At the center of this democratization were the newly nationalizing parties. Unlike the Federalists and Democratic Republicans, the Whigs and Democrats institutionalized themselves as professional political organizations, driving the development of political identity and loyalty, and organizing the political behavior of the electorate. The energy of the parties and their central position in American politics from the time of Jackson on, as well as the coherent and organized political behavior of the public itself, depended on the new information and communication capacity. The new parties could use the postal–press system to do something the protoparties of the 1790s and 1800s could not: communicate with citizens on a national scale. To be sure, the Federalists and Republicans had been deeply involved in the newspaper business. One of the basic functions of party organizing before the 1820s had been the founding and operation of newspapers. In many cases, newspapers had not been viable financially without party sponsorship.[60] As a result, the media and the protoparties of the early postcolonial period were more tightly linked than they would ever again be. However, the newspapers operated by the protoparties were aimed at elite audiences who might control or influence votes, rather than at the citizenry at large. Ironically, the parties benefited most from newspapers only after they yielded economic control in the 1820s and '30s. The rise of the paper as a business fueled mass politics and therefore the creation of nation-wide audiences. Loss of the economic connection between papers and parties ultimately led to deeper institutionalization of both into the fabric of American politics. By 1831, when the first national party convention was held by the Anti-Masonics, and in 1832 when the Democrats followed with their own, communication with citizens through newspapers was becoming a central instrument of party power in a new way.

Many of the institutional changes for which the 1830s and 1840s are so widely known, such as the expanded franchise or the nominating convention in place of the caucus, in fact committed parties to mass campaigns of information and persuasion if they were to succeed, and were premised on the capacity of citizens to receive politically relevant information.

---

[59] See Formisano, "Federalists and Republicans: Parties, Yes – System, No"; McCormick, *The Second American Party System;* Goodman, "The First American Party System"; Schudson, *The Good Citizen;* Arthur M. Schlesinger, Jr., *The Age of Jackson* (Boston: Little, Brown, 1946).

[60] Cook, *Governing with the News.*

These structural developments, which would have been impossible in 1800, proceeded because of the new communication capacity and in turn deepened the dependence of the political system on the new communication. In other words, broad, citizen-level politics both depended on and fostered broad, citizen-level exchange of political information.

The question of slavery was in many ways the first political proving ground for the new forms of collective action made possible by the information revolution of the 1820s and '30s. The scores of antislavery societies formed during and following this period depended on the new communication system to reach members and sympathizers. By the 1830s, citizen groups mobilized through mail and newspapers were flooding Congress with letters about slavery in what was arguably the first sustained "grassroots" policy campaign in the United States.[61] In 1835, a group called the American Anti-Slavery Society undertook a remarkably modern effort, acquiring the names of 20,000 prominent southerners and mailing them well over 100,000 abolitionist pamphlets.[62] At the same time, the American Temperance Society and other groups were experimenting with mass mail for distribution of antialcohol tracts and educational information.[63] The long-term success of the parties themselves depended even more on the new communication capacity, both because citizens could themselves engage in issues of the day and because party elites could reach out to citizens in strategic ways.

The terrain of American politics was therefore fundamentally different by midcentury than it had been at the start, for reasons that are rooted as much in communication as in processes that political scientists traditionally label institution building. The newspapers were a key vehicle for generating and directing political interest in the newly active electorate. Party officials used the local papers to call meetings, to list delegates to conventions and caucuses, and to publicize the political rallies and events that eventually became such an important feature of nineteenth-century politics. At the same time, the papers also published notices of meetings and events involving the broader array of civic organizations, from religious clubs to boards of directors of local banks and businesses.[64] The

[61] James L. Sundquist, *Dynamics of the Party System: Alignment and Realignment of Political Parties in the United States*, rev. ed. (Washington, D.C.: Brookings Institution, 1983).

[62] John, *Spreading the News*.

[63] Jack S. Blocker, Jr., *American Temperance Movements: Cycles of Reform* (Boston: Twayne Publishers, 1989).

[64] Glenn C. Altschuler and Stuart M. Blumin, *Rude Republic: Americans and Their Politics in the Nineteenth Century* (Princeton: Princeton University Press, 2000).

story of the Jacksonian democratization is not just one of new party labels and larger voter rolls, but also one of new ways of organizing politics made possible by a new information infrastructure.

The effects of newly vibrant communication went deep in the political psyche, as Michael Schudsen has argued, affecting how the public understood itself and its role in democracy with respect to elites.[65] A large part of what happened in these decades was the decay of the strong tradition of political deference by the public to elites that had characterized the postfounding period. A new individualism in politics and the increasing legitimization of private political discourse by the public flowed out of the new information environment. Along with these came increasing legitimacy attached to the idea of political competition among organized bodies, a concept anathema to Madison and the founders. These were the values and connections between the public and political elites necessary to the effective exercise of democratic power.

The American political party in the early and mid-nineteenth century can be understood as a novel organizational form, adapted to take specific advantage of new communication capacities and opportunities. The parties' tasks were to integrate and mobilize on a national scale a set of political interests with two chief characteristics, simplicity and spatiality. In modern terms, the policy agenda was less than lean. With highly circumscribed national policy jurisdiction and a simple economic system to oversee, the government apparatus contested by the parties dealt with just a few big issues at a time: banking, tariffs, the westward expansion, and, of course, abolition. No party would need to offer a well-developed policy platform across an array of issue areas for decades. Spatial location was important to the organization of interests, not simply between North and South, but between the Atlantic seaboard and the near-interior as well as the "far" West.

Within this "state of courts and parties," the flows of information and communication associated with policy-making apparatus were simple.[66] The legislature was elementary in structure and work load. In 1829, Congress had just twenty-five staff members, roughly one for every ten legislators.[67] The Thirty-second Congress, which met from 1851 to 1853, passed just 137 public laws in two years, not many more than the First

---

[65] Schudson, *The Good Citizen.*
[66] Stephen Skowronek, *Building a New American State: The Expansion of National Administrative Capacities 1877–1920* (Cambridge, Eng.: Cambridge University Press, 1982).
[67] Young, *The Washington Community.*

Congress had passed between 1789 and 1791.[68] The executive branch was even less well developed, since no "bureaucracy" in the modern sense of the word existed until late in the century. Apart from the Navy and War departments, the only cabinet departments until midcentury were State and Treasury. Interior was added in 1849, but no others until Reconstruction. Prior to the Civil War, government agencies were thinly distributed, comprising the Coast Survey, the Steamboat Inspection Service (the sole regulatory agency), and land and customs offices. It was what Stephen Skowronek calls "a serviceable but unassuming government . . . [that] provided promotional and support services for the state governments and left the substantive tasks of governing to these regional units."[69]

Prior to the Civil War, there were comparatively few organized political voices in the polity apart from parties and abolitionist groups to add to the complexity or heterogeneity of political communication. The age of major corporations and the union had not yet arrived, explicitly political interest groups had yet to engage government or the public on a large scale, and "lobbying" was yet to develop as a normal practice.

All this meant that the numbers of governmental and organized public actors involved in the communication of political information, as well as the number of issues to which they addressed themselves, were small – far smaller than they would be half a century later. This set of conditions, including the press–postal medium, made dominance over political communication by the parties straightforward, especially given the absence of institutional competitors in the realm of information, such as national religious institutions, or an organized aristocracy. These characteristics of political communication that emerged from the developments of the 1820s and '30s constituted an *information regime*, one that would prove dominant and stable for about five decades. Its chief features were the simple, spatially organized structure of political information itself, opportunities for national-scale communication dependent on and restricted mainly to newspapers, and a particular form of political organization, the party, exploiting and dominating those opportunities.

During the existence of this regime, other technological developments eventually extended the new communications capacity. These included the steamboat, which had first been used commercially in 1807 on the Hudson, but which did not expand into commercial importance until midcentury, and then the railroad, which became commercially

---

[68] Roger Davidson and Walter Oleszek, *Congress and Its Members*, 7th ed. (Washington, D.C.: CQ Press, 2000).
[69] Skowronek, *Building a New American State*, p. 23.

important after midcentury. These added to the possibilities for the movement of information in the United States, but they did not alter in any fundamental way the features of the regime. The railroad meant that information could move faster, but it did not alter the simple, spatial characteristics of communication nor dislodge the newspaper as the central medium.

Even the telegraph – the true antecedent to the Internet technically, politically, and economically – only consolidated the first information regime.[70] Interestingly, the very earliest telegraphed messages in the United States were political, one of them transmitted by Morse in 1842 between congressional committee rooms in a bid to win funding for the telegraph itself.[71] The first geographically significant telegraph line linked Washington, D.C., and Baltimore. In 1844, developments at the Whig convention occurring in Baltimore were telegraphed to Washington an hour before reporters could present the news in person.[72] By 1848, there were 2,000 miles of telegraph cable in the United States, and by 1850, some 12,000 miles. By at least one estimate, at the midcentury mark the telegraph was as important as the postal service to the American economy.[73] This explosive growth of the telegraph in the 1840s was a product almost exclusively of commercial enterprise. The federal government provided essentially no subsidy except for an initial grant to Morse of $30,000, declined to purchase patent rights offered to it, and imposed no regulations.

Built and developed by private firms, the telegraph had vitally important effects on at least two areas of American society: business and the press. Replacing slower ground transportation for the movement of information, the telegraph increased the pace of business substantially. In the late 1840s, the best travel time for information from the Atlantic states to reach St. Louis by physical means had been six days, and another eight to ten days to reach California. The telegraph put out of business many enterprises that had been engaged in land transportation

---

[70] Technically, the telegraph was an electrical medium using a primitive form of binary signal, not entirely unlike the more sophisticated binary logic of electronic computing. Politically, the telegraph was advanced early on by its military applications, as was radio in World War I. While the Internet was not a battlefield tool, its early development was funded and organized by the U.S. military establishment. Economically, both the telegraph and the Internet were commercialized and distributed rapidly by market forces in the near absence of government regulation, unlike radio and television.

[71] Tom Standage, *The Victorian Internet: The Remarkable Story of the Telegraph and the Nineteenth Century's On-Line Pioneers* (New York: Walker and Company, 1998).

[72] Fang, *A History of Mass Communication.*

[73] These data on the telegraph come from Standage, *The Victorian Internet.*

of information, and it reduced the importance of the postal service by permitting businesses of all kinds to operate faster. Businesses that could transmit information nearly instantly across the country could operate in new ways, handling more transactions and placing less emphasis on physical proximity and more on price and availability of goods. Pricing of goods therefore become more uniform and more responsive to national rather than local market forces. In this way, telegraph-based information flows contributed to the beginnings of national economic markets in the United States.

In the world of newspapers, the telegraph exerted similar influences. The new wires permitted newspaper businesses to acquire and exchange information much more rapidly. Some major papers took advantage of the increased flow of information to produce multiple daily editions, while smaller, rural papers were able to present national news more readily and promptly than using the old exchange-paper methods. Early on, some smaller papers incorporated the telegraph into their exchange system. One local paper might receive wire news, then use an exchange with other local papers to distribute information regionally.[74]

The newspaper business thus changed, as new national news networks and pools formed around the telegraph-based flow of information. Newspapers like the *Baltimore Sun,* which had promoted the original Washington–Baltimore line, contributed enthusiastically to the development of the telegraph, giving it publicity as well as funding. In particular, the penny papers exploited and promoted the telegraph, eventually integrating it into the media business.[75] By the 1850s and 1860s, telegraph-based news agencies were fueling the continued expansion and growth of the newspaper business. By this time, the postal service was no longer such a vital link in the news chain. It would never again be so important for moving information between news businesses and getting newspapers into the hands of citizens outside the major urban areas.

While the telegraph sped the flow of political information dramatically, it was not a medium to *supplant* the newspaper as television one day would, nor did it alter the basic content and characteristics of political information. It left undiminished the relevance and command of parties. While it constituted new infrastructure of great importance, to be sure, it was not an alternative channel for communication between elites and citizens nor a force for reorganizing political information itself.

---

[74] Fang, *A History of Mass Communication.*   [75] Schudson, *Discovering the News.*

THE SECOND INFORMATION REVOLUTION AND THE
ROOTS OF PLURALISM

The first information regime would finally be altered in a substantial way toward the end of the nineteenth century. During the Gilded Age, the structure of political information as well as opportunities and constraints on communication began to change, in conjunction with the industrial revolution.[76] Industrialization would bring more than mechanization, mass production, urbanization, and demographic shifts; it also entailed a new scale of organization, radically altered communication patterns, and vastly more complex information of all kinds permeating human activities. As sociologist James Beniger has argued, industrialization and Progressivism entailed as much a revolution in information as in industry.[77]

This point can be seen most obviously in the economy, where industrialization brought increased complexity and differentiation of function. That in turn left mechanisms of communication and coordination from the preindustrial economy inadequate for businesses and individuals. In businesses, one result was new industrial control technologies, bureaucracy and rationalized administration, new systems for the distribution of goods, new methods for advertising and communicating with mass markets, and the use of techniques such as polling for obtaining feedback from the public.[78]

For their part, consumers were faced with new goods, unfamiliar retailers, and a growing culture of advertising. The trust once placed in familiar local shopkeepers and sellers was inadequate in the face of large-scale retailing activities. Walter Lippmann captured vividly the new complexity:

> For the scale on which the world is organized to-day discrimination has become impossible for the ordinary purchaser. He hasn't time

---

[76] Scholars assign various beginning and ending dates to this period of general transformation in U.S. society, economics, and politics, but most agree within a margin of five or six years that the two decades before and two after 1900 capture industrialization and its immediate consequences.

[77] Beniger, *The Control Revolution*.

[78] For an argument that the origins of the information revolution lie in the industrial revolution, see Beniger, *The Control Revolution*, who argues that solving these information problems was requisite to the maturation of the industrial revolution. Without new informational techniques adequate to an industrial economy, the capacity to make mass-produced goods could hardly be fully realized. This argument expands the ancestors of the Internet beyond simply the telegraph and stagecoach, to encompass regularized freight and delivery schedules for goods, standardized wire sizes and railroad gauges, vertical integration of firms, uniform standard time, and other informational innovations of the nineteenth century.

to candle every egg he buys, test the milk, inquire into the origins of the meat, analyze the canned food, distinguish the shoddy, find out whether the newspapers are lying, avoid meretricious plays, and choose only railroads equipped with safety devices. . . . In our intricate civilization the purchaser can't pit himself against the producer, for he lacks knowledge and power to make the bargain a fair one.[79]

As the Gilded Age passed into the Progressive Era, the nature of work changed, placing more people in organizations or positions involving direct contact with other citizens. In 1880, the 13 million people in the American work force were divided roughly evenly between agricultural workers, who were comparatively isolated economically, and nonagricultural workers. By the end of the 1920s, nonfarmworkers outnumbered farmworkers by more than three to one. Manual work and service jobs that brought people into contact with one another accounted for the bulk of this change, while the fastest rate of growth occurred in professional and so-called white collar jobs where information and communication were often central.[80]

Another feature of the industrializing economy was the growth in the number of small businesses, a phenomenon sometimes overshadowed by the rise of major corporations in the railroad, steel, telegraph, oil, and food industries. The number of small- and medium-sized firms exploded around the turn of the century and contributed as much or more to the complexity of the nation's economy as the industrial giants. According to Census Bureau data, the American economy in 1870 comprised about 427,000 businesses, about one for every 90 citizens. By 1929, this figure had quintupled, to around 2,200,000, or one for every 56 citizens. After the adjustments of the Depression, the total number of business enterprises in the United States would remain roughly stable for nearly half a century, settling at 2,400,000 until the mid-1970s.[81] The turn of the century was a high-water mark for the multiplication of small businesses in the United States as well as the founding era for the large industrial firm.

[79] Walter Lippmann, *Drift and Mastery* (New York: Mitchell Mennerly, 1914) pp. 68–69.
[80] Bureau of the Census, *Historical Statistics of the United States: Colonial Times to 1970*, part 1, Series D 1–10, D 11–25, D 182–232 (Washington, D.C.: Government Printing Office, 1975), pp. 126–127, 139.
[81] Bureau of the Census, *Historical Statistics of the United States: Colonial Times to 1970*, part 2, Series V 20–30, p. 912; Bureau of the Census, *Statistical Abstract of the United States*, 114th ed., table no. 846 (Washington, D.C.: Government Printing Office, 1994), p. 547.

In society, as in the economy, industrialization created new problems of information and communication. Maintaining social bonds with others became more difficult. As Durkheim observed in *Division of Labor in Society*, industrialization and urbanization stressed and overburdened old processes of communication and information exchange that were the basis of social integration and cohesion. Patterns of simple, neighborly communication and social intercourse that had bound communities together in the preindustrial era grew increasingly inadequate by the early years of the twentieth century.

The rise of the city was a central part of this process. In 1880, the small town was the center of social gravity in the United States, with its small scale, personal relationships and inward-focused, parochial concerns. By 1920, some 51 percent of Americans lived in urban areas, with all that urban life entailed: a large scale of social and political activity, new rules and norms, and a larger number of impersonal relationships.[82] The demographic changes also led in the direction of complexity. Not only was the population growing in size, from 39 million in 1880 to 123 million in 1930; it was growing much more diverse. From 1901 to 1930, the United States admitted just under 19 million immigrants – more than half the Civil War–era population of the entire country.[83]

Political scientists recognize in this history the interdependent ingredients of the twentieth-century interest-group pluralism that would eventually flourish in the United States. Traditional explanations of the linkages between industrialization and the rise of the modern state, however, typically do not attend sufficiently to information and complexity. Rather, the traditional account adopts roughly the following causal story. Changes in economy and society lead to stresses and dislocations that result in demands for new public policies and state action; those demands in turn lead to the creation of new state capacities and powers, with the result being a larger and more powerful state apparatus.[84] This model makes appearances in various forms in the work of many scholars, from Tocqueville and Marx through Weber and Durkheim: Capitalism leads to

[82] Samuel P. Hays, *The Response to Industrialism 1885–1914*, 2nd ed. (Chicago: University of Chicago Press, 1995); Robert H. Wiebe, *The Search for Order, 1877–1920* (New York: Hill and Wang, 1967).

[83] Bureau of the Census, *Statistical Abstract of the United States*, table no. 1, p. 8; table no. 5, p. 10.

[84] E.g., see: Skowronek, *Building a New American State*; and David Truman, *The Governmental Process: Political Interests and Public Opinion* (New York: Alfred E. Knopf, 1965), p. 55.

industrialization, industrialization to social stresses and the subsequent failure of markets to meet human needs adequately, and market failures to state building or state change of one kind or another.

This familiar account provides a great deal of insight into changes in democracy at the turn of the century. But it leaves out the role of the changing information regime. No less important than new demands for state action was the fact that the complexity, scale, and intensification of relationships overloaded old communication and information channels in the economy, in civil society, and in the political system. Whereas information had before been simply and spatially organized, it was now highly specific, associated with narrower and more diverse groups of actors and issues, and organized in particularistic, cross-cutting ways. As human relationships grew far more complex, they required new, more complex patterns of communication to sustain them. These new patterns had to accommodate social reality: a multiplication of relationships, interdependence, and heterogeneity.

A number of scholars writing about these changes have commented on matters of information, communication, and complexity, although few have made these matters the central focus of their analysis.[85] Robert Wiebe describes the effect of these changes on individuals as the decay of the "personal society" of the early and mid-nineteenth century. A society once comprehensible to its members in terms of individuals had become a society comprehensible only in much larger, more complex terms, and it "lacked those national centers of authority and information which might have given order to such swift changes."[86] For Samuel Hays, the changes of 1880 to 1920 entailed a "massive reorganization in the scale and scope of human activities."[87] For Durkheim, it was a society whose complexity made it susceptible to *anomie*.

The fact that Americans were increasingly taking their problems to government for redress created a mushrooming public agenda unlike anything that had gone before. New issues that piled up before the federal government included labor matters, punctuated by strikes and riots; battles over regulation of industries, from railroads to utilities; child labor in factories and mines; community services, such as water and sewage; public health, including food and drug safety; education; and management of the public domain. It was not simply that the public as a whole

---

[85] The important exception is Beniger's *The Control Revolution*, although this volume does not address political development.

[86] Wiebe, *The Search for Order*, p. 12.   [87] Hays, *The Response to Industrialism*, p. 69.

demanded new state capacity; its demands also affected who could communicate best and who could dominate the flow of political information.

One indicator of the changing demands on policy communication is the output of laws from Congress. Between Reconstruction and the turn of the century, the number of bills introduced in Congress grew about seven-fold, from 3,000 in the Fortieth Congress (1867–69) to over 20,000 in the Fifty-sixth (1899–1900). By 1917, the Sixty-fourth Congress introduced 29,000 bills, a record that survived the New Deal and policy activism of the 1960s and 1970s, and that still remains. The number of measures enacted into law grew nearly as rapidly, from 765 in the Fortieth Congress to 1,942 in the Fifty-sixth.[88] For legislators as well as others in public life, this legislative energy created huge new demands, both for information about policy problems and possible responses and for communication with constituents and other private interests. To be a competent public official by 1920 required new levels of expertise in communication, whether one served in Congress or in the agencies that were taking on new responsibilities. By the same token, to influence government and successfully advocate for policy, citizens and groups were required to engage in intensified communication and coordination under circumstances of greatly heightened competition for legislative and bureaucratic attention.

A second element of complexity and changing communication arrangements flows directly from this expanding policy agenda: institutional development and specialization. In Congress, committees and subcommittees were formed during a period of growth that has never been matched. The Senate doubled its complement of committees and subcommittees between 1880 and 1920, a feat not repeated even after World War II. In 1900, the House had 391 members, up from 243 at the outset of the Civil War, and by 1910 had reached its modern plateau of 435. Developments in the executive branch surpassed those of Congress. New cabinet departments were added, including Agriculture, Commerce, and Labor (which was soon split in two), as were dozens of new agencies: the Interstate Commerce Commission, the Food and Drug Administration, the Federal Reserve, the National Park Service, the Forest Service, and more. The total number of independent agencies alone grew four-fold between 1880 and 1920.[89] In 1871, the federal government had about 51,000 employees, a majority of whom worked for the post office. By

[88] Davidson and Oleszek, *Congress and Its Members*, table 2-2.
[89] Superintendent of Documents, *Congressional Directory* (Washington, D.C.: Government Printing Office, various years 1873–1921).

1920, the total was 650,000, with the post office no longer dominating the ranks.[90]

The complexity of political communication was affected also by the evolving electoral arena. The primaries, which spread steadily following the 1904 debut in Wisconsin, doubled the number of occasions in which citizens were called to the polls. At roughly the same time, the spread across states of mechanisms for tying Senate appointments to the outcome of popular votes increased electoral options. By the time the ratification of the Seventeenth Amendment in 1913 finalized the process, citizens had to choose three rather than two national officials, as well as contend with the primary and general election. The rise of ballot propositions in the same period added to the intricacy of elections, beginning with the initiative in South Dakota in 1898 and the referendum in Oregon in 1902. Even the adoption of the Australian ballot added incrementally to political complexity, since it eliminated the automatic straight-ticket vote and provided citizens more degrees of freedom at the ballot box. The electoral process had become substantially more information-intensive than it had been during the previous information regime.

A final contributor to complexity was the multiplication of private and public actors with an interest in politics. In civil society, a comparatively homogeneous nation, characterized mainly by regional divisions on a few major issues, had mutated into a complex, heterogeneous society of groups with specialized interests that did not overlay neatly on old regional patterns. At the heart of this new body of political interests were private associations. The period 1880 to 1920 was characterized by a massive, nationwide frenzy of association formation – what Elizabeth Clemens calls a "mania" for the creation of new organized groups.[91]

The variety and vibrancy of new associations would likely have astonished even Tocqueville. New women's groups formed, some for Jewish women, some for all business and professional women, others for female artists, one for women in universities. Some groups focused on historical connections, such as the Daughters of the American Revolution and the Daughters of the Confederacy. Social improvement and health-related associations included the Boy Scouts, the Girl Scouts, the

---

[90] Hays, *The Response to Industrialism*; Stanley and Niemi, *Vital Statistics on American Politics*.

[91] Elizabeth Stephanie Clemens, *The People's Lobby: Organizational Innovation and the Rise of Interest Group Politics in the United States* (Chicago: University of Chicago Press, 1997). Also see: Schudson, *The Good Citizen*; Wiebe, *The Search for Order*; Truman, *The Governmental Process*.

YWCA, Planned Parenthood, Big Brothers/Big Sisters, the National Easter Seal Society, the American Lung Association, and the Mental Health Association, along with service organizations such as Rotary International and Lions Clubs.

New religious associations also sprang up between 1880 and 1920 (especially for Catholics and Jews), as did educational organizations and sports and hobby groups tailored to bowling, chess, gardening, golf, cat and dog ownership, skiing, soccer, power boating, and stamp and coin collecting. New national identity associations were also founded during this period for the Danes, Irish, Italians, Norwegians, and Poles.

The transforming economy sparked a wealth of new business groups. In the retail sector, new groups included the National Automobile Dealers Association, the American Association of Booksellers, the Direct Marketing Association, the National Association of Grocers, the National Association of Retail Merchants, and the National Restaurant Association. Other business groups formed in this forty-year window for contractors, advertisers, motor vehicle manufacturers, food supply industries, and oil companies, as well as the U.S. Chamber of Commerce. Agricultural associations formed around the interests of the fading agricultural sectors of the economy, such as the National Dairy Council and the American Farm Bureau Federation.

The association category with the greatest growth was the professional group. Distinct national-level associations developed for these and other professionals: engineers (electrical, chemical, agricultural, mechanical, safety, and naval), foresters, geographers, geologists, economists, entomologists, historians, illustrators, journalists, physicians, accountants, mathematicians, actors, anthropologists, archeologists, astronomers, zoologists, school principals, legal secretaries, sociologists, surgeons, English teachers, nurses, photographers, and psychologists.[92] Capping off this ferment in association-building was the establishment in 1920 of the American Society of Association Executives.

Before the Civil War, there had been were less than ten major civic associations in the United States, and only two with memberships totaling 1 percent of eligible citizens: the International Order of Odd Fellows and the Order of the Sons of Temperance. By the 1920s, twenty-six groups enrolled over 1 percent of the eligible citizens, from the Farm Bureau to

---

[92] For a list of groups founded in the United States between 1880 and 1920, see *World Almanac and Book of Facts* (Mahwah, N.J.: Funk and Wagnalls, 1994).

the American Automobile Association.[93] About half of all such groups ever created in United States were founded between 1870 and 1920.[94] By 1920, the United States had been transformed from a society of individuals to a society of groups and individuals.[95] In all of these ways, the complexity of the democratic system was increasing rapidly through a greatly expanded policy agenda, a much larger and more specialized set of political institutions, a more elaborate electoral apparatus, and a dramatically expanded body of private organizations, in addition to individuals, as constituents. By the end of this period, the number of sources and destinations for the flow of political information, as well as its content, had expanded geometrically.

The key implication for the information regime was that neither the parties nor the newspapers could continue to satisfy on their own the bulk of demands by political actors for political information and communication under these new conditions. The newspaper business did grow more specialized, with salutary business consequences, but it could not maintain its central position in the flow of information. The mass papers of the Gilded and Progressive Ages focused to a greater extent on issues, emphasizing the currency of news. To a degree not reached by newspapers of the early and mid-nineteenth century, turn-of-the-century newspapers prioritized the delivery of information.[96] Like other economic enterprises, the newspapers themselves became large, specialized, complex institutions operating in an environment where the management and control of information was an increasingly central theme. Papers were filled with the sensationalism and "yellow journalism" of the turn of century, even as they experimented with the more serious kind of informational reporting that was becoming the norm at newspapers such as the *New York Times*. And without a doubt the media were capable of great and grave political influence, as Hearst demonstrated. So certainly the press was helped on the whole financially rather that hurt by the changes.

Yet for those engaged in politics, neither Hearst, Pulitzer, Ochs, nor their lesser known contemporaries could provide the necessary

[93] Theda Skocpol, "How Americans Became Civic," in Theda Skocpol and Morris P. Fiorina, eds., *Civic Engagement in American Democracy* (Washington, D.C.: Brookings Institution and Russell Sage Foundation, 1999), pp. 27–80.

[94] Ibid.; Robert D. Putnam, *Bowling Alone: The Collapse and Revival of American Community* (New York: Simon and Schuster, 2000).

[95] Wiebe, *The Search for Order.*   [96] Cook, *Governing with the News.*

information regarding the actions of the new agencies, the movement of bills in Congress, the positions and intentions of politicians, the interests of the new associations and groups, or the deals that would have to be made for politics and policy to proceed. Complexity in government far outstripped the capacity of newspapers to inform, especially where the demands of political professionals and elites were concerned.

The parties confronted a parallel problem. Newly realigned as they were, and destined for political stability (except for 1912) until the Great Depression, they increasingly lost their centrality to the flow of policy information. As organizations adapted to brokering compromises among blocs of citizens and to building large electoral coalitions, parties were poorly suited to master or dominate the new information environment. That environment called for specialization and expertise in policy information, and they could not communicate in the right ways to remain dominant over the information moving among business, government officials, and constituent groups.

In the business arena, executives wanted rapid, detailed information about government and policy making. Had parties been able to provide it, they might have retained some of their nineteenth-century power. Instead, businesses turned to new channels for information. As Wiebe writes, "the corporate leader needed a continuous flow of political information, so he paid strategically placed men to supply it."[97] Indeed, one of the major challenges facing businesses at the turn of the century was obtaining information about government and finding ways to communicate effectively their interests to government officials. A great many of the business associations made explicit efforts to provide a systematic flow of politically relevant information among firms and between firms and government. Those associations that initially formed without explicitly political agendas found themselves by 1900 to be engaged fully in the game of political information and communication. In fact, for most associations formed after 1900, political communication was typically a central function from the outset. The National Association of Manufacturers is a good example. It formed in 1896, and was active in policy on labor issues by 1903.[98]

For government officials, the situation was similar. They wanted information about constituent demands that parties could not ably provide. Instead, officials found it more satisfactory to respond directly to the clearly articulated demands and information provided by groups than to

[97] Ibid., pp. 183–184.   [98] Truman, *The Governmental Process*.

the diffuse interests and communications of parties, particularly in the policy arena. Wiebe describes the problem as follows:

> Now it was the politician who required information. . . . Varieties of competing organizations, often with diversified programs, left the legislative leader without the basis for decisions. Nor could he depend upon partisan loyalties to mellow their spirits. Only if the lobbyists translated the wishes of their clients, negotiated with other agents, and offered reasonable assurance of how their constituents would react to particular measures could the politician broker calculated risks and fashion the compromises.[99]

This orientation of managing and distributing information as a response to complexity led to new government practices for informing the public as well. Government agencies increasingly made it a practice to publish proceedings and press bulletins and to engage in "public education."[100] Following the Civil War, Presidents made tentative ventures into regularized communication with the press. McKinley eventually began a practice of daily White House briefings with reporters, with Roosevelt and Wilson later institutionalizing this practice. The naming of Wilson's World War I propaganda organization the "Committee on Public Information" symbolizes the new information vogue.

On top of the institutional changes of the period that weakened their power, and the Progressive climate of antiparty sentiment, this information revolution of the 1880s to 1910s left the parties increasingly on the sidelines of communication, especially about public policy. As business and government developed new arrangements for information and communication that bypassed parties, so did citizens themselves. The new associations discovered that they were well suited to press their cases directly with government; that is, they were able to assume a good part of the mantle of political intermediation from parties. The American Medical Association (AMA), for instance, created in the middle of the nineteenth century, grew into a modern professional organization with an interest in civic affairs by the 1910s.[101] It evolved from an arcane association to which very few doctors belonged prior to the 1890s into a powerful organization involved in public information and education as well as in policy making. It set up Bureaus of Organization and Public Instruction to disseminate information to communities and argued before

[99] Ibid., p. 184.   [100] Cook, *Governing with the News.*
[101] Wiebe, *The Search for Order,* p. 115.

government about policies dealing with food, drugs, occupational safety, and so on. As its membership grew from 8,400 in 1900 to 83,000 in 1920, the AMA became one of the central distributors of public information about health in the United States.[102] The National Education Association followed a pattern not unlike that of the AMA. It emerged from an old, quiet organization into a modernized, politicized group situated for engagement in policy and the marshaling of information about public policy.

It is interesting to note that the new forms of communication led to changes in understandings of what was legitimate in politics, not unlike some of the changes of the first information revolution. Perhaps the most important involved formal "lobbying." As late as 1874, the Supreme Court had ruled on nonconstitutional grounds in *Trist* v. *Child* that contracts for attorneys or other agents to represent clients before Congress were void. The Court's rejection of "lobby" services reflected what had long been a widespread perception of the unacceptability of a professional relationship intervening between citizens and government, other than that offered by political parties. The implicit premise of *Trist* was that the flow of information and communication in the process of representation should not be professionally mediated. As contracts with a "base purpose," the Court held that lobbying contracts were not binding.[103]

This view of lobbying changed rapidly as the Gilded Age passed into the Progressive Era. Businesses wanted lobbyists to do what parties could not, and so, increasingly, did members of Congress. By the turn of the century, many private nonbusiness associations would take the same view. Following *Trist*, members of Congress in both chambers took up bills to recognize lobbyists. Such a nonbinding resolution passed the House two years after the *Trist* decision, and while no other formal recognition was forthcoming, by the 1890s and 1900s, lobbying had become an accepted professional practice and was not impeded again by the Court. What would later be called "grassroots lobbying" also increased during this period. Businesses first experimented with it in the 1870s, and other groups later incorporated it as part of their efforts to manage political information. In 1919, for example, the Anti-Saloon League developed a

---

[102] James G. Burrows, *AMA: Voice of American Medicine* (Baltimore: Johns Hopkins University Press, 1963); Morris Fishbein, *A History of the American Medical Association, 1847–1947* (New York: Kraus Reprint, 1969).

[103] See Margaret Susan Thompson, *The "Spider Web": Congress and Lobbying in the Age of Grant* (Ithaca: Cornell University Press, 1985).

mailing list of half a million citizens, which it used to good effect in the successful pursuit of prohibition.[104]

The new practices of lobbying constituted more than just a political strategy; it was an orientation toward the public sphere. As groups created press offices of their own, engaged in public education campaigns and publicity drives, and provided information directly to government officials, they institutionalized the idea that to be in politics was to engage with information and communication on one's own terms.[105] As Aileen Kraditor writes about women's groups, "the women had meetings, published manifestoes, testified at legislative hearings, edited newspapers, and distributed leaflets" in the effort to persuade men to provide them the vote.[106] By the turn of the century, the General Federation of Women's Clubs had opened in addition to a "Press Bureau" its own "Bureau of Information" – a symbol of the new decentralized, specialized information environment in politics.[107] Democracy had become a game of information, not merely one of party loyalty.

Lobbying by groups and associations like this proved reliably successful in a comparatively short time. The new civic and professional associations proved perfectly adapted to take up the flow of political information under conditions of complexity, which in turn facilitated their incursions into the parties' old domain of communication. They could provide targeted information about specific policy problems and link constituencies with the appropriate decision makers. In a 1911 address to Congress, President Taft recognized the role of groups as information intermediaries in at least one domain of activity: "In the dissemination of useful information and in the coordination of effort certain unofficial associations have done good work toward the promotion of foreign commerce."[108] Taft's blessing symbolizes how the informational terms of

[104] Kenneth M. Goldstein, *Interest Groups, Lobbying, and Participation in America* (Cambridge, Eng.: Cambridge University Press, 1999).
[105] Pendleton Herring, *Group Representation before Congress* (Baltimore: Johns Hopkins University Press, 1929).
[106] Aileen S. Kraditor, *The Ideas of the Woman Suffrage Movement, 1890–1920* (New York: Columbia University Press, 1965), p. 226.
[107] Clemens, *The People's Lobby*, p. 216. Certainly, not all associations were aggressive about the strategic use of information like this. In civil rights, the NAACP eschewed public information and political persuasion in favor of legal action, while labor groups such as the Knights of Labor, the American Federation of Labor, and the International Workers of the World focused on economic actions.
[108] President Taft, Dec. 7, 1911, message to Congress, cited in Truman, *The Governmental Process*, p. 85.

politics had changed. Democracy had come to involve "new contexts of control," in the phrase of Samuel Hays. In these, the expanded scope of enterprises "increased many fold the factors which one had to take into account if he wished to influence the course of events . . . . The vast world of complex circumstances intruded into decision-making and required new perceptions of the scope and complexity of the political arena and new devices for gathering information upon which decisions could be based."[109] When Walter Lippmann writes that the complexity of society and politics had advanced sufficiently that "men have had to organize associations of all kinds in order to create some order in the world," the order to which he refers is an informational phenomenon as well as an organizational one, and it was indeed a central issue of the day.[110] A new information regime had emerged, featuring complex structures of information; opportunities and demands for particularistic, direct communication; and a newly dominant form of organization at the center, the specialized group.

One of the most important consequences of these developments is the connection they entailed between information and financial resources. In the regime that emerged from the 1920s, information did not come cheaply. Monitoring government actions required paid staff. Identifying interested citizens or businesses and soliciting them to join a group required time and effort and money, as did producing studies and reports. Mass mailings of any scale were costly. Virtually all of the information and communication functions performed by groups required substantial resources. As the twentieth century progressed, technological developments bolstered the capacities of groups and at the same time added to resource requirements. The evolution of the telephone system, fax technology, computerized mailing lists, polling, and the like contributed to the maturing and consolidation of this information regime and the importance of money in it. Even more so than in the first regime, where the newspaper business and postal system had in effect subsidized political communication, bearing the cost of information and communication became an increasingly central part of politics.

Scholars typically date the beginning of the American interest group system to the New Deal and they often associate it with modern technologies of computing and telecommunication. In his remark in *The Governmental Process* that "a precondition of the development of a vast

---

[109] Samuel P. Hays, "Political Parties and the Community-Society Continuum," in Chambers and Burnham, eds., *The American Party Systems*, p. 166.
[110] Lippmann, *Drift and Mastery*, p. 162.

multiplicity of groups, itself an instance of technological change of the most dramatic sort, is the revolution in means of communication," David Truman had in mind the utility of telephones, direct mail, and other pluralistic communication technologies that eventually came on the American political scene.[111] But these technologies did more to consolidate pluralism than to give birth to it. A truer "precondition" for the power of interest groups was a political environment throughout most of the twentieth century featuring decentralized, complex structures of information and communication.

THE THIRD INFORMATION REVOLUTION AND THE MASS AUDIENCE

The course of the information regime born out of the industrial revolution was different from its predecessor's, because technologies of communication evolved differently in the twentieth century than they had in the nineteenth. Whereas the major technological milestones of the 1840s to 1870s tended to reinforce the party-dominated press–postal system until its abrupt displacement at the end of the century, the technologies of the 1920s to 1940s soon laid the groundwork for change in the second information regime. By the 1950s and '60s these technologies had blossomed into a full-scale information revolution, but this revolution did not so much displace the interest group–based second regime as hybridize it, adding a new kind of dynamic centered on the mass audience. By at least the 1980s, this new revolution led to an information regime featuring both group-based and mass communication.

The central impetus in these developments was the emergence of broadcast media: the rise of radio, which was put to political purposes from the very start, and several decades later, television. Characterizing the emergence of these technologies as revolutionary for culture and politics is well-traveled ground, and I will not recapitulate or summarize existing scholarship dealing with the profound impacts of mass media on candidate selection and campaigning, leadership styles and strategies, political identification, socialization, and media effects such as framing, agenda setting, and priming.

Of greater concern here are the consequences of broadcast telecommunications for political intermediaries – especially, parties and interest groups, the forms of organization to emerge in prior information

---

[111] Truman, *The Governmental Process*, p. 55.

revolutions. The standard claim in the literature on this topic concerns the contribution of television to the changing nature of electoral campaigns. The history of campaigning in the twentieth century is typically told in terms of the evolution of candidate-centered politics: a "change in focus," as Martin Wattenberg writes, "from parties to candidates."[112] Television is a central figure in this story, although not the only important actor. The familiar account is roughly as follows. Along with the destruction of patronage systems and structural changes such as adoption of the primary system and the Australian ballot, the technologies of television as well as polling led to the demise of the party-based campaign and the rise of the candidate-centered campaign in its place. At the same time that changes in political process were weakening the grip of parties on voters' behavior and necessitating competition between candidates of the same party, the new technologies provided candidates with capabilities for communicating and mobilizing that substituted for some of the traditional services of parties. This process of party decline in electoral politics began in the Progressive Era, at the same time as the decline in the party's role in policy communication, and extended well past the midcentury mark. By the 1950s, at least, changes had evolved far enough that congressional candidates no longer needed party organizations to win them office.[113] The situation was similar for presidential campaigns not long thereafter.

This story of the shift from parties to candidates is very much a story of organizational change, of a decline in the influence of one form of organization and ascendance in place of another. As political intermediaries, interest groups had exploited and benefited from the second information revolution, just as parties did from the first. As broadcasting and associated technologies developed, the candidate campaign organization emerged as a newly important organizational form better adapted to the new communication and information environment than the old party form. The candidate campaign organization belonged to a new class that would grow more important: the ad hoc, event-centered organization, created for the duration of one event or political episode and very much unlike the more institutionalized party or interest group. It was a temporary political team – not unlike the teams in a pick-up

---

[112] Martin P. Wattenberg, *The Rise of Candidate-Centered Politics: Presidential Elections in the 1980s* (Cambridge, Mass.: Harvard University Press, 1991), p. 1.

[113] Paul S. Herrnson, "Hired Guns and House Races: The Impact of Campaign Professionals on Fundraising, Strategy, Communications, and Electoral Success," paper for the Role of Political Consultants in Elections Conference, School of Public Affairs, American University, June 19, 1998, Washington, D.C.

game of neighborhood basketball – built of various specialists brought in to serve a particular function at a particular time: pollsters, media advisers, policy experts, campaign consultants, and the like. Indeed, the story of the modest resurgence in influence by parties that occurred in the 1990s is again a story of organizational change in the face of new modes of communication and information management. The resurgent modern party did not succeed by returning to the days of centralized, hierarchical party-based communication, but by reorganizing as a kind of organized political consultant who could offer a menu of political services and assistance to networks of candidate organizations.[114] This "service organization" model of parties highlights their adaptation to a new organizational environment for communication and campaign functions. It is in this organizational sense that the pattern of political change from the first and second information revolutions carries over into the broadcast era.

From the very beginnings of broadcasting, in the pretelevision period, the potential for new communication channels eventually to displace the party in campaign communication was clear. Although it would take years for the process to mature, the most important political lesson of radio prior to the midcentury mark was a kind of proof-of-concept: Use of broadcast telecommunications could build a direct relationship between politicians and citizens that did not involve party organizations. One of the first radio broadcasts in the United States occurred on November 2, 1920, to an audience numbering perhaps a few thousand in Pittsburgh.[115] In a repetition of the political nature of the first telegraph

---

[114] John J. Coleman, "Resurgent or Just Busy? Party Organizations in Contemporary America," in John C. Green and Daniel M. Shea, eds., *The State of the Parties: The Changing Role of Contemporary American Parties* (Lanham, Md.: Rowman and Littlefield, 1997), pp. 367–384.

[115] Identification of the first radio broadcast in the United States is a subject of debate. Many authors cite the Cox-Harding broadcast as the first. Others cite an experimental broadcast by Woodrow Wilson in 1919, and others an earlier broadcast in San Jose and an amateur broadcast in Detroit. Part of the dispute stems from problems of classification as to what constitutes an official or commercial "broadcast" as opposed to private uses of radio. See: Douglas B. Craig, *Fireside Politics: Radio and Political Culture in the United States, 1920–1940* (Baltimore: Johns Hopkins University Press, 2000); George H. Douglas, *The Early Days of Radio Broadcasting* (Jefferson, N.C.: McFarland, 1987); Irving Settel, *A Pictorial History of Radio* (New York: Citadel Press, 1960); Christopher H. Sterling and John H. Kitross, *Stay Tuned: A Concise History of American Broadcasting*, 2nd ed. (Belmont, Calif.: Wadsworth Publishing, 1990); Sydney W. Head, with Christopher H. Sterling, *Broadcasting in America: A Survey of Television, Radio and New Technologies*, 4th ed. (Boston: Houghton Mifflin, 1982).

message announcing the outcome of the Whig convention in 1844, the broadcast covered the outcome of the presidential race between Harding and Cox. The next year, New York City Mayoral candidate John F. Hylan made what is generally accepted as the first radio campaign speech.[116] As President, Harding made occasional addresses carried by radio, beginning with his inaugural speech on March 4, 1921.[117] Coolidge was the first President to use radio regularly and effectively. His radio delivery likely contributed to his successful election in 1924 against Davis and LaFollette, making Coolidge arguably the first President whose political success can be attributed at least in part to broadcast media.[118]

Hoover relied on radio regularly on the campaign trail, and in a move symbolic of what was to come, the Republican Party rescheduled a Hoover campaign speech from a Saturday evening to Monday, when officials estimated that the radio audience would be larger, the first recorded instance of a presidential campaign event being structured around the dynamics of the broadcast audience.[119] Both the Democratic and Republican conventions had been broadcast in 1924, and by the 1928 race between Hoover and Smith, radio had become a regular part of presidential campaigning. If there is to be a single election that stands as a marker for the beginning of the long displacement of the party organization by broadcast technologies, it was the Hoover–Smith race of 1928.

Between 1924 and the elections of 1928 and 1932, the modern advertising-based model of campaign communication emerged. In the 1924 race, the Republican Party spent about $120,000 and the Democratic Party about $40,000 on the purchase of commercial radio time.[120] For the most part, however, these funds went toward the broadcasting of speeches. Commercial advertising of products by businesses was developing at the same time, and strong norms existed moderating the aggressiveness and directness of radio salesmanship. Many advertisers in the early to mid-1920s avoided announcing prices or making direct pitches

---

[116] Craig, *Fireside Politics.*

[117] William Banning, *Commercial Broadcasting Pioneer: The WEAF Experiment 1922–1926* (Cambridge, Mass.: Harvard University Press, 1946); Craig, *Fireside Politics*; Lawrence Wilson Lichty and Malachi C. Topping, *American Broadcasting: A Source Book on the History of Radio and Television* (New York: Hastings House Publishers, 1975); Settel, *A Pictorial History of Radio.*

[118] Several scholars of radio credit Coolidge's radio skills as contributing to the magnitude of his win against Davis and LaFollette. See Head, *Broadcasting in America,* and Settel, *A Pictorial History of Radio.*

[119] Orrin Elmer Dunlap, *Advertising by Radio* (New York: Ronald Press, 1929).

[120] Edwin Diamond and Stephen Bates, *The Spot: The Rise of Political Advertising on Television* (Cambridge, Mass.: MIT Press 1984).

for their wares. These norms, which faded by the 1930s, likely contributed to the brief, initial hesitancy of candidates to produce commercial-like advertising. But by 1928 and 1932 the political spot ad had emerged as a technique alongside the broadcasting of speeches. An early radio advertising handbook published in 1929 and providing instruction on the new medium to businesses listed among categories of advertising clients "political speakers" sponsored by the Democratic and Republican parties – evidence that paid political advertising was recognized early on as a source of revenue to media businesses.[121] A list of NBC customers for 1930–31 includes the national Republican Committee, the campaign of San Francisco Mayor James Rolph for Governor of California, and the Tammany Hall organization.[122] By one estimate, the total spent on radio-based campaign advertising in 1932 was $5 million, a sum equivalent to nearly $70 million today.[123]

At the presidential level, Hoover made regular use of radio in office, and along with Coolidge was known by contemporaries as a radio President. By the time of Roosevelt's famous fireside chats, radio had already become the most effective means for Presidents to communicate with a national audience, and the fact that citizens could build strong political preferences based on perceptions of individual officeholders built through broadcasting was proven. Those twenty-eight fireside addresses did not so much inaugurate radio as a political tool as consolidate what had already become a standard channel for political communication. By 1938, Congress was beginning to board the new bandwagon as well. Both chambers of Congress had functional radio galleries with facilities for commentators, although live broadcasts from Congress would not come until the 1970s. The 1930s were also the time of the "press–radio" war, when print journalists sought to block or constrain the emergence of broadcast news, which initially had amounted to little more than the reading of newspaper articles by radio announcers. By the late 1930s, radio had prevailed in the war after a series of moves and countermoves by the industries, establishing itself as a permanent and important new medium for news.

Even before World War II, then, it was possible in principle for a candidate with an independent source of funds to communicate effectively with citizens outside the channels created by party organizations.

[121] Dunlap, *Advertising by Radio*, p. 178.
[122] Frank A. Arnold, *Broadcast Advertising, the Fourth Dimension* (New York: J. Wiley and Sons, 1931).
[123] Sterling and Kitross, *Stay Tuned*.

In practice, such bypassing of the parties occurred chiefly at the local and state levels. For example, John Brinkley, a quack radio doctor with a huge audience, ran a write-in campaign for Governor of Kansas in 1930 on the basis of his radio constituency, nearly winning with 30 percent of the vote in the multicandidate race.[124] Charles Coughlin, who never actually ran for office, built a weekly political audience in the 1930s ranging from 15 million to 45 million people – a potentially potent mass audience outside the party channels.[125] In 1935, Coughlin appealed to listeners to contact the White House opposing the proposal for a World Court supported by Roosevelt. His effort succeeded in producing 200,000 telegrams, a striking feat for an independent political figure operating without the backing of an established political organization.[126]

Political communication through television occurred far earlier than is generally recognized, and its very early political history is nearly coincident with that of radio. Al Smith's acceptance speech at the 1928 convention was broadcast by General Electric in Schenectady, New York, on the highly experimental new technology of television, although the viewing audience was negligible, since no commercial production of television sets yet existed.[127] The 1940 Republican convention was broadcast, also to a tiny audience, and when the wartime freeze on television production finally ended, the audience for the new medium soared in the late 1940s and '50s. Truman has been called the first "television President" for his broadcast address to Congress in 1947 and his televised programs from the Oval Office.[128]

The year 1952 was in many ways the tipping point for the new medium, as 1928 was for radio. Commercially, television was by that year seriously threatening radio station revenues, and political candidates were paying increasing attention to television over radio. The 1952 presidential race featured the first televised coverage of primaries and the famous "Checkers" speech by Richard Nixon, and it was the first in which television-based political communication was available to a majority of

---

[124] Kansas State Historical Society, "A Kansas Portrait: John R. Brinkley," 2001, http://www.kshs.org/people/brinkley.htm.

[125] Rodger Streitmatter, *Mightier Than the Sword: How the News Media Have Shaped American History* (Boulder, Colo.: Westview Press, 1997).

[126] Ibid.

[127] J. Leonard Reinsch, *Getting Elected: From Radio and Roosevelt to Television and Reagan* (New York: Hippocrene Books, 1988).

[128] Ibid., p. 46.

the population.[129] The televised spot ad also developed as a mass technique in Eisenhower's 1952 campaign.[130] By the time an audience estimated at 75 million watched Eisenhower's first inaugural address in 1953, television had arrived as the new force in political broadcast communication.[131] And by the 1956 presidential rematch, nearly one-third of the expenditures for national campaign committees went to broadcasting, with television the dominant medium.[132]

One of the crucial political developments in the years that followed was the discovery by political figures that individual, candidate-based organizations could exploit and use this new medium as well or better than the party committees. Availability of the new medium meant that campaign communication could easily be managed by specialized organizations focused candidate by candidate and campaign by campaign. It was not just that citizens would respond to candidates on the basis of individual characteristics rather than party identification, but that the parties as organizations had no particular selective advantage at dominating the new modes of communication and information. The structure of one important form of information and communication had been changed by the technology. The mass audience, defined by the media market, provided a new structure and new opportunities for information management and communication, and that brought organizational change and adaptation.

Parallel to this story of organizational change involving parties and campaigning is the relationship between the broadcast revolution and interest groups. Research on the use of broadcast media by political organizations other than parties prior to the 1970s is sketchy. It is clear, though, that a broad range of groups experimented to advantage with radio and then television from the earliest. In the 1920s, for instance, women's organizations such as the National League of Women Voters and the

---

[129] Sterling and Kitross, *Stay Tuned*; Reinsch, *Getting Elected*; Head, *Broadcasting in America.*

[130] Diamond and Bates, *The Spot;* Head, *Broadcasting in America.*

[131] Reinsch, *Getting Elected.*

[132] There are several markers of television's ascendance over radio, even though sales of radio receivers were booming and audiences growing. By 1956, average radio station advertising revenues from all sources were half of what they had been in 1946, as commercial and political advertisers shifted to television. By the early 1960s, polls first showed that television had become the most widely used and the most trusted medium for news. See: V. O. Key, Jr., *Politics, Parties, and Pressure Groups*, 5th ed. (New York: Thomas Y. Crowell, 1964); Head, *Broadcasting in America.*

National Woman's Party used radio to broadcast messages in support of women's rights.[133] Labor unions also used radio early on, sponsoring radio programs and purchasing advertising well before 1930.[134] The CIO in particular used radio aggressively as an organizing tool in the 1930s, despite eventual denial of access by NBC and CBS, even using radio to organize strikes and other labor actions.[135] The Anti-Saloon League distributed messages using radio as well as film in the 1920s, and farmers' organizations did the same.[136] The National Grange, for example, broadcast an hour-long program on its annual conventions from 1922 to 1942.[137] The same 1930–31 list of NBC clients including Tammany Hall and the Republican Party also includes what would now be called interest groups: the Citizens Anti-Charter League and the Tax Payers Committee.[138] During a Federal Trade Commission investigation in the late 1920s and early 1930s into whether a trust existed in the power utility industry, utility firms and groups used radio extensively in an effort to build public support. Among the most important users of radio were the Edison Company of Boston and the National Industrial Conservation Board, a utility company advocacy group.[139] The NAACP took a wary stance toward radio because of its typically denigrating portrayals of African-Americans, but did run a few membership recruitment ads as early as 1948.[140]

One of the most interesting cases of interest group broadcasting involves the American Medical Association. The AMA used radio extensively in the 1930s in the form of public health broadcasting on subjects such as cancer, tuberculosis, and children's growth. By the late 1930s and '40s, its broadcasts became explicitly political as the group opposed proposals for national health insurance. In 1946, for example, it hired a public relations firm to mount a "National Education Campaign" timed to influence the congressional elections. It spent over $1 million in that

---

[133] Susan D. Becker, *The Origins of the Equal Rights Amendment: American Feminism between the Wars* (Westport, Conn.: Greenwood Press, 1981).

[134] Ross Evans Paulson, *Liberty, Equality and Justice: Civil Rights, Women's Rights, and the Regulation of Business, 1865–1932* (Durham, N.C.: Duke University Press, 1997); Nathan Godfried, "The Origins of Labor Radio: WCFL, the 'Voice of Labor,' 1925–1928," *Historical Journal of Film, Radio and Television* 7, no. 2 (1987): 143–59.

[135] Godfried, "The Origins of Labor Radio."

[136] K. Austin Kerr, *Organized for Prohibition: A New History of the Anti-Saloon League* (New Haven and London: Yale University Press, 1985).

[137] Bruce E. Field, *Harvest of Dissent* (Lawrence: University of Kansas Press, 1998).

[138] Arnold, *Broadcast Advertising*.

[139] Carl D. Thompson, *Confessions of the Power Trust* (New York: E. P. Dutton, 1932).

[140] Leonard Archer, *Black Images in the American Theatre* (Brooklyn: Pageant-Poseidon, 1973).

campaign – equivalent to about $10 million now – to "arouse public op-position to compulsory health insurance," with the expenditures divided among radio, newspaper, and magazine advertisements.

The AMA also purchased campaign ads through subsidiary commit-tees that endorsed congressional candidates directly.[141] By the 1960s, the AMA's embrace of television was complete. Howard Wolinsky and Tom Brune describe the AMA's efforts against national health insurance as bat-tling President Kennedy "on his own turf, and in his favorite medium, television."[142] When the Medicare Act passed in 1965, the AMA had be-come one of the nation's largest nonparty political advertisers, using both radio and television. Its efforts foreshadowed the "Harry and Louise" tele-vision campaign run so successfully by the Health Insurance Association of America in 1993 and 1994 against President Clinton's health insurance proposal.

In the 1960s and '70s other industries and groups employed television selectively. In the 1960 campaign, the group Seniors for Kennedy, which later became National Council for Senior Citizens, ran spot ads on tele-vision and radio.[143] Two years later and at the other end of the political spectrum, the Ku Klux Klan used television to promote a Republican can-didate for Congress in Tennessee.[144] By the 1970s, various public service announcements with politically relevant messages were common, and by the 1980s some groups ran occasional advertisements for their issues.

Not all interest organizations made an aggressive shift from radio to television, and certainly no groups came to rely *mainly* on television for external communication, as did campaign organizations. This fact is im-portant to understanding the differences between radio and television. Radio with its thousands of stations spread around the country provided opportunities for comparatively focused, targeted political communi-cation. Television offered something quite different: a mass audience dominated by three major broadcast firms, at least prior to the 1980s. From the perspective of many groups, this made radio and television very different for reasons beyond cost. Television offered something valuable

---

[141] Donald C. Blaisdell et al., "Unofficial Government: Pressure Groups and Lobbies." *Annals of the American Academy of Political and Social Science* 319 (Sept. 1958); David R. Hyde et al., *The American Medical Association: Power, Purpose, and Politics in Organized Medicine* (Washington, D.C.: Committee for the Nation's Health, 1955).

[142] Howard Wolinsky and Tom Brune, *The Serpent on the Staff: The Unhealthy Politics of the American Medical Association* (New York: G. P. Putnam's Sons, 1994), p. 27.

[143] Henry J. Pratt, *The Gray Lobby* (Chicago: University of Chicago Press, 1977).

[144] David M. Chalmers, *Hooded Americanism: The History of the Ku Klux Klan* (Durham, N.C.: Duke University Press, 1987).

to well-funded groups seeking to influence public opinion on a national scale. Radio offered the opportunity to reach targeted audiences at far lower cost. For purposes of identifying potential members or recruiting members into action, television was in many instances too much a mass medium for the interest groups.

Some groups selectively adopted television techniques without abandoning radio, and some avoided television all together. Religious organizations, for example, had used radio reliably in the 1950s and '60s for evangelical purposes – the first Christian broadcast took place in 1921 from Calvary Episcopal Church in Pittsburgh – and by the 1970s and '80s some religious broadcasters had turned explicitly political.[145] As they did, these broadcasters focused on both radio and television: television for its great reach and radio for its greater capacity to target audiences. By 1987, there were over 1,000 full-time Christian radio stations and 200 television stations in the United States, many of which had a mixture of religious and political aims. The rise in the 1980s of television broadcasters such as Jerry Falwell and Pat Robertson represented the exploitation of these established audiences for political purposes in a television-intensive era.[146] The National Association of Manufacturers (NAM), on the other hand, never made that transition. It was an aggressive user of radio as early as the 1930 debates over the Wagner Act. By the early 1940s, it was running a weekly radio program carried by over 500 radio stations.[147] But, like labor organizations, NAM did not take up television aggressively in the 1960s and '70s or after.

Television became part of the arsenal of groups, used chiefly on occasions where organizations sought to influence public opinion widely, as in national health care debates in the 1960s and 1990s. But those functions were less important to the interest groups than to candidates running for office. In his early-1990s sample of fifty interest groups, Ken Kollman found that only 2 percent engaged in general-audience television advertising, compared with 4 percent using general-audience radio,

[145] George Hill, *Airwaves to the Soul: The Influence and Growth of Religious Broadcasting in America* (Saratoga, Calif.: R&E Publishers, 1983); William Fore, *Television and Religion: The Shaping of Faith, Values, and Culture* (Minneapolis: Augsburg Publishing, 1987); Hal Erikson, *Religious Radio and Television in the United States, 1921–1991* (Jefferson, N.C.: McFarland, 1992).
[146] Sara Diamond, *Spiritual Warfare: The Politics of the Christian Right* (Boston: South End Press, 1989).
[147] Nathan Godfried, *WCFL: Chicago's Voice of Labor 1926–78* (Urbana and Chicago: University of Illinois Press, 1997).

8 percent using cable or other targeted television, and 26 percent using local newspapers.[148]

The most important development in the use of mass media by interest groups was the surge in independent campaign advertising in the early 1990s. Groups across the political spectrum embraced this form of broadcast communication, including business and labor organizations, environmental groups, education groups, and others. Data compiled by the Federal Election Commission do not include figures on independent expenditures because they are unregulated, but estimates are available. Erika Falk at the University of Pennsylvania found about eighty interest groups in the 2000 election cycle airing a total of about 400 issue ads at a cost of at least $250 million. Of these, seven groups spent at least $10 million each (Business Roundtable, Federation for American Immigration Reform, National Rifle Association, AFL-CIO, U.S. Term Limits, Citizens for Better Medicare, and the Coalition to Protect America's Health), and another two dozen at least $1 million.[149] Their encroachment into campaigning notwithstanding, the interest groups remained information specialists, operating for the most part as they had throughout the second information regime. The broadcast revolution layered on top of the interest group system a new set of informational and organizational dynamics.

A distinction is traditionally drawn between two phases of mass media, one of channel scarcity and one of channel abundance. This division is important to the outcome of the third information revolution and the features of the regime that briefly followed. The channel scarcity phase of mass media begins with film and radio and continues through television until roughly the late 1980s. This was the age of conventional broadcast television, with its long oligopoly of the three major broadcast networks. Its hallmark was the mass audience consuming a comparatively homogeneous diet of news and political communication.

The phase of channel abundance resulted from the multiplication and diversification of mass media outlets and content. This phase is characterized by the availability of dozens or even hundreds of channels

[148] Ken Kollman, *Outside Lobbying: Public Opinion and Interest Group Strategies* (Princeton: Princeton University Press, 1998).
[149] Erika Falk, "Issue Advocacy Advertising through the Presidential Primary 1999–2000 Election Cycle," *Issue Ads @ APPC*, the Annenberg Public Policy Center of the University of Pennsylvania, Sept. 20, 2000, http://www.appcpenn.org/issueads/2000issuead.htm.

through cable and satellite television, and also includes the multiplication of special-interest magazines and the flourishing market in recorded video.[150] The 1980s are traditionally considered the transition period between these two phases. By the early 1990s, a majority of households subscribed to cable television, and by the mid-1990s, over half of those with cable subscribed to more than fifty channels.[151] By 1999, cable service was available to 97 percent of households, virtually every household with a television set. The key feature of this phase of mass media is the fragmentation of the audience and the divergence in the content of political communication and news.

The politics of these two phases are in some ways in opposition to one another. The rise of the mass audience after midcentury and the increasingly central role played by broadcast television constituted an important break from the second information regime. The mass dynamics of scarce-channel television after 1960 exerted countereffects to the specialization and fragmentation of that earlier regime, namely, a tendency to homogenize communication and elevate the importance of mass opinion in politics. Channel abundance in the 1990s, on the other hand, eroded the mass audience for the traditional networks and re-created opportunities for more specialized, individualized, fragmented communication reminiscent of a century before.

The broadcast information regime that emerged from the 1970s therefore did not last long. It never displaced the second regime but complemented it, and by the 1990s it was in tension with the effects of channel multiplication as well. The mass audience was to remain alive and

---

[150] Several periodization schemes for communication are available, none of which are particularly suitable for understanding the coevolution of political communication and political structure in the United States from a long-term perspective. For instance, Mark Poster divides the modern period into two media "ages": the era of film, radio, and television constitutes the first media age, while that of the Internet and post-broadcast technologies constitutes the second. Jay Blumler and Dennis Kavanaugh divide roughly the same period into three "ages": the first running until the mid-1960s and characterized by high levels of consensus organized by institutional structures, especially parties; the second associated with limited-channel broadcast from the mid-1960s to the end of the century; and the third emergent now as a function of media abundance. The importance of the shift from channel scarcity to channel abundance is one of the central points of agreement among various periodization schemes such as these. See Mark Poster, *The Second Media Age* (Cambridge, Mass.: Polity Press, 1995); and Jay G. Blumler and Dennis Kavanaugh, "The Third Age of Political Communication: Influences and Features," *Political Communication* 16 (1999): 209–230.

[151] W. Russell Neuman, *The Future of the Mass Audience* (Cambridge, Eng.: Cambridge University Press, 1990); Owen, *The Internet Challenge to Television*.

well into the twenty-first century, but was to be layered with the newer possibilities for audience selection and fragmentation. This tension between audience dynamics and the information regimes they represent became a central characteristic of telecommunications at the outset of the new century.[152]

Structurally, the tension between mass audience dynamics and more fragmented, individuated communication contributes to the larger tension in modern politics between majoritarian and pluralistic political processes in the United States. As one of the defining features of American democracy since the third information revolution, the coexistence of mass politics and group politics is central to many political outcomes. One of the most interesting questions about contemporary American democracy involves the circumstances under which pluralistic forms of political action do or do not prevail over majoritarian forms. Any attempt at explaining the structure of contemporary political power in the United States must accommodate the fact that policy making is sometimes pluralistic in orientation, and sometimes majoritarian. Conceptualizing politics in informational terms provides the best approach to that problem.

A few scholars have recognized this point, including Susan Lohmann and Douglas Arnold.[153] They each observe that organized groups are typically better able to bear the costs of monitoring and communicating legislators' actions than are diffuse, unorganized majorities. As information specialists with robust financial resources, groups are typically better informed about government intentions and better able to communicate what they know than are parties or the public at large. Public officials direct policy toward those best able to monitor government actions and thereby pose credible threats of retaliation or reward for policies at the voting booth. The result is that groups typically prevail over majorities, not simply because they are more intensely interested in politics, as classical pluralist theory would have it, but also because they are typically better situated in terms of information and communication. But it is not always so, and when on occasion the asymmetry in information between the mass public and groups disappears, public officials tend to respond accordingly. One important mechanism for the leveling of the informational playing field is the mass media. When issues are framed

---

[152] On this issue, see Neuman, *The Future of the Mass Audience*.

[153] R. Douglas Arnold, *The Logic of Congressional Action* (New Haven: Yale University Press, 1990); Susan Lohmann, "An Information Rationale for the Power of Special Interests," *American Political Science Review* 92, no. 4 (1998): 811.

in such a way that a credible possibility of mass attention to them arises, government officials tend to favor the interests of broad publics, even at the expense of interested groups. In either case, *policy and political influence tend to flow to the best informed.* The general principle is that variation in the extent of pluralistic and majoritarian power in the United States is explained by an information dynamic, and this dynamic rests on what is essentially the tension between the politics of the second and third information regimes.

3

The Fourth Information Revolution
and Postbureaucratic Pluralism

THE QUESTION OF INFORMATION ABUNDANCE

The capacities of competing political actors and organizations are most often measured by yardsticks involving money, staff, experience, and organization, but rarely information. The idea that democratic power tends to flow to the most well-endowed political actors, financially and organizationally, exerts a far-reaching influence on conceptions of politics and democracy. Much research on pluralism and interest group politics in the United States is based on the premise that financial and organizational requirements pose a barrier to national-scale collective action, and that in policy competition, those with more financial and organizational resources tend to prevail in the long run over those with fewer resources. The conclusion from the last chapter that policy and political influence tend to flow to the best informed provides an explanation for this resources–power relationship: Resources confer command over information and communication, and command over these enhances political influence.

This approach to explaining political power leads to an interesting question. Throughout the series of information revolutions and regimes thus far in American history, developments at each step have strengthened the link between resources and command of information, making organizational and financial infrastructure of one kind or another ever more important for facility with information and political communication. Information and communication have been comparatively scarce, costly, and unevenly available to political actors, and on this foundation historical developments in the complexity and organization of information have proceeded, facilitating in turn the evolution of parties, interest groups, and candidate organizations. If technological or other developments somehow altered this foundation, so that information and communication became abundant and readily accessible, what might be the result organizationally and politically?

This is precisely the question raised by developments in contemporary information technology since the early 1990s. As the Internet became commercialized and moved out of the exclusive domain of universities, government agencies, and selected corporations, societies have grown more information-intensive in nearly every area. The many functions and characteristics of the Internet and associated new media are widely discussed and need not be itemized. Five main aspects of information intensiveness in the political realm are important, however. First, the new information environment involves a multiplication of low-cost channels for the distribution of information by political elites and organizations. Candidates for office have new means for communication with voters that are in some cases less costly than old ones. Electronic mail and web-based communication provide a means of communication affordable in principle to every candidate, not only those able to bear the expense of direct mail, broadcast advertising, telephone banks, press offices, or precinct walking. Not only are the new channels for communication comparatively inexpensive, but they provide for a richer array of content and the possibility of greater control by candidates over the flow of information. By the mid-1990s, candidates were offering issue papers, biographies, video clips, and other carefully constructed information to any interested citizen, group, rival candidate, or journalist anywhere in the country, around the clock. In theoretical terms at least, this constitutes a substantial change in the cost and structure of political communication. While it hardly makes old modes of communication obsolete, the new media of the 1990s dramatically expand the possibilities for candidates to distribute information. Technological developments of the 1990s brought similar opportunities to interest groups and other political organizations. Virtually every major interest group and advocacy organization in the United States was operating some form of Internet-based political communication system by the late 1990s. These new systems permitted groups to offer to the public a wide array of policy statements, reports, news items, video, endorsements, and the like.

A second feature of information-intensiveness is the capacity that new technology provides to elites and organizations to *acquire* highly detailed information at low cost. One of the most interesting technological developments is the spread of data-driven web sites, in which the candidate or organization sponsoring the site solicits citizens to provide contact information as well as details about political interests or preferences.

This information in turn permits groups and candidate organizations to tailor their messages and appeals to citizens on a largely unprecedented level. New capacities to capture large amounts of political information inexpensively constitute an enormous departure from previous media, especially those of broadcasting and print news. Another feature of information-intensiveness is the capacities of new technology to provide for citizens to communicate directly with one another. Forums for publicly displaying messages and for meeting and conversing "on line" among people who share political concerns constitute perhaps the largest break functionally from previous media.

Changes in the media business add additional elements to the information-intensiveness of contemporary politics. The fact that any news organization, including small newspapers and radio stations, can readily distribute information globally constitutes an enormous acceleration in historical efforts to link news organizations together and to expand their reach. The nineteenth-century practice of exchanging papers among news businesses is evolving in the early twenty-first century toward a situation in which any citizen can read any newspaper at any time, and perhaps, one day, watch any television show from any nation at any time. Already the *Bangor Daily News* is available in Boise and Birmingham, to those who would read it. The practice of some citizens (and government officials) following events during the U.S. war in Afghanistan by tuning into Qatar's Al Jazeera television station through the Internet is one of the most dramatic examples of the media losing their spatial boundaries.

A final feature of contemporary developments in information is a more subtle one. It involves the archiving of news and other information. In previous information regimes, the recording and preservation of political information was rudimentary and fragmented at best, symbolized well by the term "news." For the most part, information in news was available to the public at large only contemporaneously; a week-old newspaper was not readily accessible and a week-old television broadcast gone forever. The archiving of news, political broadcasting, campaign information, interest group records, and even citizen discussions in network-based "bulletin boards" reorganizes political information in a way that makes the past more accessible to the present.

The evolution of the Internet and associated technologies are popularly labeled an "information revolution," especially for their effects on business and commerce. And, indeed, these five features of the new information environment for politics since the 1990s fit the historical pattern of information revolutions in American democracy. They constitute a potentially important change in the structure of political information and the opportunities and constraints on communication afforded political actors. New means for elites to distribute and acquire information, new possibilities for citizens to identify and communicate with one another, changes in the ways that citizens interact with the news system, and the historical preservation of information, among other developments, contribute toward a state of *information abundance* in the political system.

The lesson of the sequence of historical information revolutions is that information abundance should have important effects on political organizations as intermediaries. It is possible to develop specific expectations about what those effects likely are by examining theories of association and organization. These can illuminate the possible responses of the political system to information abundance as it has developed so far.

THE BUREAUCRATIC CONCEPTION OF PLURALISM

Alexis de Tocqueville is the first theorist of information and political association following the Federalists and Antifederalists. His observations about American democracy in the 1830s, at the time of the first information revolution, are useful for understanding what information abundance might mean for political association and organization. Tocqueville's claim that Americans were obsessed with the formation of civic and political associations remains entrenched in scholarship on American civil society and political pluralism. However, more often forgotten is Tocqueville's theory of the relationship between information and group formation. Tocqueville believed that while Americans possessed a natural habit of association and an inclination toward cooperation, their efforts at collective action also confronted natural problems of information.

Forming associations requires information and communication, Tocqueville wrote in *Democracy in America*. First, citizens must recognize mutual interests in one another. Doing so requires the flow of information, and so the richer the information environment in which citizens live, the more likely they are to recognize others with compatible or complementary concerns and position themselves to act mutually. Second, citizens must establish some form of communication with those sharing their interests. Without adequate information, these steps from common interest to common action are precarious. "It frequently happens that a great number of men who wish or who want to combine cannot accomplish it because as they are very insignificant and lost amid the crowd, they cannot see and do not know where to find one another."[1] Tocqueville also observed that information and communication problems persist once citizens with common interests identify one another, because the success of an association or group depends on coordination and a continued exchange of information among people who may not be physically proximate. Once located, "means must then be found to converse every day without seeing one another, and to take steps in common without having met."[2] Therefore, associations depend on the flow of information and communication both to form and to survive.

How can these information and communication requirements be met? Tocqueville believed it would be through the newspaper. He observed that Americans surpassed Europeans in both the vibrancy of their newspapers and their many civic associations, and that this was not coincidental. He believed that newspapers provided the vital flow of information that stimulates the formation of individual interests in the first place, which helps citizens identify others of like mind and eventually permits the coordination of activities and operations within associations. In his words, "The effect of a newspaper is not only to suggest the same purpose to a great number of persons, but to furnish means for executing in common the designs which they may have singly conceived."[3] He summarizes: "Consequently, there is a necessary connection between public associations and newspapers: newspapers make associations, and associations make newspapers."[4]

Informational obstacles occupy a position in Tocqueville's theory of collective action similar to that of free riding in the work of Mancur Olson and other contemporary scholars of groups. Tocqueville's theory of collective action also contrasts with much of modern collective action theory, in that he believed it is easier to entice people to join large organizations than small. He argued that potential group members more readily see the impact and value of a large group, and so are more inclined to participate. Although he failed to recognize the problem of free riding and the possibility of its differential effects on large and small groups, Tocqueville's acknowledgment of the role of media and information flow

---

[1] Alexis de Tocqueville, *Democracy in America*, vol. 2 (1840; rpt., New York: Vintage, 1945), p. 120.

[2] Ibid., p. 121. For a larger discussion of Tocqueville and information technology, see Hans K. Klein, "Tocqueville in Cyberspace: Using the Internet for Citizen Associations," *The Information Society* 15, no. 4 (1999): 213–220.

[3] Alexis de Tocqueville, *Democracy in America*, p. 119.   [4] Ibid., p. 120.

in group formation was far ahead of its time. His analysis suggests that richer flows of information in society should lead to more numerous and intense associations among citizens. Tocqueville's hypothesis for the contemporary period is that information abundance should be associated with associational richness.

The work of Max Weber and of other theorists of organization provides insights into the form that those associations might take. Like Tocqueville, Weber recognized the importance of the flow of information in society to the functioning of organizations. The administration of businesses, he argued in *Wirtschaft und Gesellshaft*, rests in large measure on the speed of operations, and speed in turn is "determined by the peculiar nature of the modern means of communication, including, among other things, the news service of the press."[5] In his day, Weber observed a rapid increase in the speed by which "public announcements, as well as economic and political facts," flow throughout society, and he believed that this increased speed demanded faster and better administrative reaction that could be optimized by only bureaucratic forms of organization.[6]

What Weber observed was a set of changes in the information environment, as information moved more rapidly and presented new challenges to organizations. He believed that the success of administrative organizations was in part a function of how they adapted to the current state of information and communication. He understood the relationship to encompass both the external communication environment and the ways that organizations handled information internally. Weber wrote that "the degree to which the means of communication have been developed is a condition of decisive importance for the possibility of bureaucratic administration, although it is not the only decisive condition."[7] So it is, he observed, in Egypt, in Persia, and in Asia, where administrative states at the end of the nineteenth century depended on river communication, the telegraph, the mail, and railroads for their external communication. That is, effective administration requires that an organization have effective means for the communication of information throughout the social or economic system. In this, Weber echoes Tocqueville.

At the same time, effective administration for Weber requires that an organization adapt its internal structure and procedures to manage information adequately. Within the organization, the flow of information

---

[5] H. H. Gerth and C. Wright Mills, *From Max Weber: Essays in Sociology* (New York: Oxford University Press, 1958), p. 215.
[6] Ibid., p. 215.   [7] Ibid., p. 213.

between bureaucrats and managers must be organized in a hierarchical system that emphasizes knowledge and skill over personality or identity. The classical Weberian conception of bureaucracy is a body of arrangements for organizing information and communication into a system for rational decision making and administration. He believed that the successful pursuit of efficiency and expert administration leads naturally to bureaucracy: well-delineated and fixed jurisdictions and functions, with layers of clerk-like workers having specific knowledge of the all-important files, the bureaucracy's system for preserving information.

There is an important premise implicit in this familiar conception, namely, that the information necessary for efficient administration is not easy to come by. Weber's argument assumes that information is scarce and costly to assimilate and manage over time. Locating the right information, storing it, and making it available within an organization at the right time and place to people with the skill or expertise to use it is a difficult task. Coordinating the activities of workers and decision makers and communicating the results of their activities outside the organization is also challenging. What Weber calls "the rational specialization of functions and the rule of expert knowledge" is a system for organizing information and bringing it to bear on decision making and the exercise of private or public authority.[8] The challenges associated with costly, scarce information and effective communication are important reasons why the pursuit of efficiency in administration leads to bureaucracy.

For Weber, then, bureaucracy is associated with the opposite of information abundance: scarcity and costliness. Weber did not consider what forms organizations might take if information were no longer scarce and costly, because he and his contemporaries could observe no such examples. Contemporary scholars, on the other hand, have addressed that question more directly. Sociologist Manuel Castells is one. In *The Information Age*, an interpretation of economics, society, and culture in informational terms, Castells argues that a new sociocultural system called "informationalism" is replacing "industrialism.[9] He interprets social fabrics and cultures as regularized, "crystallized" patterns of communication and information exchange. In this view, flows of information and communication among human actors and institutions represent a kind of historical variable with patterns and features that are distinctive to specific places and times. These may be a function of available technologies,

---

[8] Ibid., p. 237.
[9] Manuel Castells, *The Rise of the Network Society* (Malden, Mass.: Blackwell, 1996).

economic activity, geophysical circumstance, or historical contingency. Whatever their particular sources in a given place and time, characteristics of information and communication contribute powerfully to the creation and definition of culture, identity, and social structure. In this view, the Weberian bureaucracy represents the congealing of a characteristic pattern of communication under conditions of information scarcity.

Social theorist Pierre Levy's term for this relationship between informational and structural or cultural features of society is "communications ecology."[10] An "ecology" is comprised of the dominant modes of information flow and the forms of organization and social structure that adapt themselves accordingly. For Levy, like Castells, features of communication take on characteristic patterns in particular eras of history as a function of various factors such as technology. These characteristic patterns in turn exert influences on the nature of public and private institutions, economic practices, social arrangements, and cultures.

In the ecology that prevailed in the United States throughout most of the nineteenth and twentieth centuries, the salient characteristics of information and communication were the high cost and asymmetric distribution that resulted from resource requirements and scarcity. The information and communication necessary for group formation, business transactions, and the maintenance of social ties were expensive, lending themselves to particular kinds of organizational arrangements that were typically variants on the hierarchical, Weberian administrative form. In this way, costly information led to decision-making arrangements and organizations of all kinds that employed bureaucracy for their internal structures, and that also constructed rigid and impermeable boundaries to separate them from other organizations with which they communicated, cooperated, or competed. Such arrangements characterized corporations, private citizens' associations, universities, and even armies. As characteristics of information change as a result of technological developments, so should these structures.

Economic theories of the firm provide the most well-developed characterization of that process. These theories, which originated prior to the Second World War, held that costs of information and communication are typically higher in market-like transactions between organizations than within single hierarchical organizations of the sort that Weber described. Transaction costs drive producers toward hierarchy and vertical

---

[10] Pierre Levy, *Collective Intelligence: Mankind's Emerging World in Cyberspace* (Cambridge, Mass.: Perseus, 1997).

integration, rather than market-based forms of organization and coordination. Therefore, production, marketing, finance, and other functions tend to be integrated into classical bureaucratic forms inside businesses. On the other hand, low transaction costs, if and where they occurred, would tend to favor non-Weberian organizational forms. Ronald Coase's 1937 argument that high transaction costs lead to bureaucratic organization while low transaction costs lead to nonbureaucratic structures is the classic statement, and it implies that the evolution of societies toward information abundance should reduce the occurrence of bureaucratically structured organizations.[11]

This implication was born out by developments in the world of business organizations by roughly the 1980s. Technological change did in fact prove to decrease the cost of many kinds of information and transactions in business, with the result that market-like mechanisms for organizing firms' functions replaced some traditional hierarchical forms.[12] Scholars of business and organization observing these changes added new models of market- and network-based economic structure to the neoclassical theory of the firm. In these models, firms exhibit reduced levels of vertical integration, reconfigured external boundaries and so-called outsourcing of functions to other businesses, and flexible new ways of organizing expertise and tasks. The organizations in these models go by many names: "organic," "network," "interactive," and so on, all of which highlight their "postbureaucratic" characteristics.[13] The models do not reject the classical view that high information costs lead to hierarchical organization but, rather, add the idea that low information costs can lead to nonhierarchical structures.

Postbureaucratic models of organization therefore constitute the contemporary complement to Weber's observations about the role of information in administration. Applied to politics, this body of theory

[11] R. H. Coase, "The Nature of the Firm," *Economica* 6, no. 4 (1937): 423–435; O. E. Williamson, *Markets and Hierarchies* (New York: Free Press, 1975). Also see Frederick W. Taylor, *The Principles of Scientific Management* (1911; rpt., New York: W. W. Norton, 1967).

[12] Thomas W. Malone, Joanne Yates, and Robert I. Benjamin, "Electronic Markets and Electronic Hierarchies," *Communications of the ACM* 30, no. 6 (1987): 484–497.

[13] Charles Heckscher and Anne Donnellon, eds., *The Post Bureaucratic Organization: New Perspectives on Organizational Change* (Thousand Oaks, Calif.: Sage Publications, 1994); Michael Best, *The New Competition: Institutions of Industrial Restructuring* (Cambridge, Mass.: Harvard University Press, 1990); Walter W. Powell, "Neither Market nor Hierarchy: Network Forms of Organization," *Research in Organizational Behavior* 12 (1990): 295–336; Francis Fukuyama, *The Great Disruption: Human Nature and the Reconstitution of Social Order* (New York: Free Press, 1999).

suggests that certain political organizations might also evolve in the direction of nonbureaucratic structure as a result of information abundance. The class of political organization most like the firm is collective action organizations: the kinds of associations that concerned Tocqueville, as well as the modern interest group that emerged from the second information revolution and developments following it. Like firms, collective action organizations are competitive and private. Both are regulated only to a point and, unlike political parties, are not connected by law to the state in any substantial way. Like firms, but not parties and especially not like government institutions, collective action organizations are largely free to reorganize and adapt themselves independently to changing conditions in their environment without the necessity of agreement by other institutions, public support, or legislative or constitutional action.

And collective action organizations are above all else, truly *organizations*, not merely groups or movements. As Mancur Olson writes in *The Logic of Collective Action*, "most (though by no means all) of the action taken by or on behalf of groups of individuals is taken through organizations."[14] For Olson, a group is not simply a number of individuals who share a common interest, and the collective action problem is not simply the failure to overcome free-riding inertia; it is also a problem of organization building. Free riding results in the failure "to organize a lobby to obtain a collective benefit," that is, to build organization.[15] Olson's attack on "analytical pluralists" such as David Truman is addressed largely to "their lack of concern for organization."[16] Truman's mistake, Olson argues, was to believe that a "latent group" is the theoretical equivalent of the organized group. Since Olson, most scholars have implicitly or explicitly accepted the premise that groups who are active in politics are organizations; this implies that the pluralistic structure of American politics throughout most of the twentieth century was a marketplace of political organizations, not simply a realm of interested groups. As Jeffrey Berry writes, "an interest group is an organized body of individuals. . . . 'Farmers' do not constitute an interest group, yet the National Association of Wheat Growers, the American Farm Bureau Federation, and the National Milk Producers Federation are all bona fide interest groups. The central distinction between farmers and any one of these is *organization*" (emphasis in the original).[17] Interest groups

[14] Mancur Olson, *The Logic of Collective Action: Public Goods and the Theory of Groups* (Cambridge, Mass.: Harvard University Press, 1971), p. 5.
[15] Ibid., p. 132.   [16] Ibid., p. 129.
[17] Jeffrey M. Berry, *The Interest Group Society* (Boston: Little, Brown, 1984), p. 5.

and related collective action groups, the defining structural feature of American pluralism in the twentieth century, are therefore likely to be among the organizations most susceptible to changes in the nature of political information and communication.

Collective action organizations are typically not conceived of as bureaucracies, but in fact most constitute one variant or another on roughly the Weberian administrative form. They rely on offices administered by a central headquarters, they employ staff at fixed functions according to their expertise, and they raise and spend funds in pursuit of priorities established by leaders at the top through regularized planning processes.[18] As the size of the group increases, so does the degree of functional specialization into areas such as research, lobbying, press relations, and management.[19] Most rely somehow on memberships, unlike the firm, but even these are formalized with membership terms, dues, and a strategic and centrally determined body of selective incentives. The typical interest organization is, in short, vertically integrated and well bounded, much like the classical firm.

POSTBUREAUCRATIC POLITICAL ORGANIZATION

If the evolution of information abundance implies intensified social and political association, as Tocqueville suggests, and also less bureaucratized structures for collective action, as organization theory suggests, what might the result look like? One feature of postbureaucratic political organization[20] involves the resources required to organize collective action. As "outside" lobbying and "grassroots" campaigns have become more important in American politics, their costs have risen.[21] Many local groups, minor parties, and other poorly endowed political actors have been unable for the most part to participate in the game of large-scale political mobilization. Often, even local-scale collective action is beyond the means of political actors without access to substantial material resources. This means that major efforts at collective action are largely the luxury of well-endowed organizations. Costs for organizing collective action by

---

[18] As Berry notes, this fact is typically independent of the nature of group membership or the extent of democratic process the group publicly avows.

[19] See Berry on this point.

[20] For this terminology and some of the theoretical constructs, I am especially indebted to Charles Heckscher for his chapter "Defining the Post-Bureaucratic Type" in Heckscher and Donnellon, eds., *The Post-Bureaucratic Organization*, pp. 14–62.

[21] Steven E. Schier, *By Invitation Only: The Rise of Exclusive Politics in the United States* (Pittsburgh: University of Pittsburgh Press, 2000).

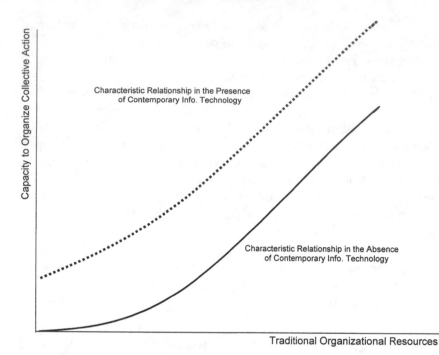

Figure 3.1. Hypothetical effects of contemporary information technology on the capacity to organize collective action.

direct mail, for example, average 30 cents to one dollar per letter sent, depending on how elaborate the message.[22] These costs require larger, resource-rich groups to choose carefully how to expend their resources, and they cause more modest groups to often forgo efforts at organizing collective action altogether.

The relationship between capacity to organize collective action and marginal resource requirements is illustrated schematically in Figure 3.1 by the solid line. In this theoretical curve, the relationship between resources and organizational capacity has a key feature: a threshold near the origin. The small slope near the origin reflects the fact that groups with very few resources are typically unable to mount effective collective action on any substantial scale. In many cases, only after resources reach a critical threshold, which should vary by group and issue area, are groups able to begin to mobilize citizens in an appreciable way. Research by

---

[22] Direct mail campaigns to 100,000 citizens cost from $30,000 for a simple letter in a printed envelope using an internal mailing list, to $100,000 for a letter, brochure, and reply-card envelope, along with the purchase of a mailing list. Source: Direct Marketing Association, 2000.

Paul Johnson provides empirical support for this curve, showing that in a sample of fifty groups, the extent of direct mail activity was a function of size, and that among small groups, such activity dropped off altogether. About 56 percent of groups with fewer than 5,000 members undertake no collective action at all, compared with only 14 percent of those groups with 100,000 members or more.[23]

The evolution toward information abundance should affect this curve by reducing the threshold effect and, in some cases, reducing the overall resources required for a particular level of collective effort. One estimate provided to the author by a political consultant is that an organizing effort targeted at 100,000 citizens and costing $25,000 to $75,000 using direct mail could be undertaken for $4,000 to $5,000 using electronic mail instead. So, as information grows more abundant and communication costs fall, collective action can more readily be initiated by actors with more modest access to material resources. In principle, collective efforts might even be self-organizing under conditions of information abundance. This implies increased opportunities for collective action by organization-poor or even organization-less groups.

In the area of political campaigning, information abundance suggests that candidates with fewer traditional resources might better be able to undertake some of the costly, information-intensive aspects of campaign-oriented collective action, such as identifying volunteers and donors. On the other hand, broadcast campaign advertising should be affected little by information abundance, since advertising is an information-poor activity. In general, the more dominant television is in a campaign, the less significant should be the effects of information abundance. Since the significance of broadcast media in campaigns is roughly proportional to the level of office involved, information abundance should be expected to affect some campaigns more than others. Television costs consume more of a presidential campaign's funds than a Senate campaign's, and television is more important in Senate races than House races. In the

---

[23] It is also interesting to note that the most resource-poor group in Schlozman and Tierney's sample of 175 organizations was the National Low Income Housing Coalition, which managed in 1981 on a budget of $61,000 and the volunteer time of two exceptionally skilled individuals to coordinate a coalition of 1,500 supporting groups using poorly mimeographed flyers. See Schlozman and Tierney, *Organized Interests and American Democracy*. Also see Paul E. Johnson, "Interest Group Recruiting: Finding Members and Keeping Them," in Allan J. Cigler and Burdett A. Loomis, eds., *Interest Group Politics*, 5th ed. (Washington, D.C.: CQ Press, 1998), pp. 35–62; and Ken Kollman, *Outside Lobbying: Public Opinion and Interest Group Strategies* (Princeton: Princeton University Press, 1998).

1988 and 1992 presidential races, for instance, television accounted for roughly 60 percent of major candidates' campaign budgets.[24] In the 1990 Senate races, by comparison, incumbents spent an average of 33 percent and challengers 40 percent of their budgets on broadcast advertising, while House incumbents spent 20 percent and challengers 27 percent.[25]

In both interest groups and some campaign organizations, therefore, information abundance might diminish the importance of traditional material resources. This is hardly to suggest, however, that simply because information is abundant and inexpensive, money should no longer be a key resource in predicting outcomes, or that poorly endowed organizations could perform equally well compared with well-endowed organizations. It is only to suggest a weakened relationship and diminished threshold effect. This expectation is illustrated schematically in the dotted line in Figure 3.1.

Another implication of information abundance is a possibility for change in the nature of organizational form and boundaries. In general terms, the changing communication ecology implies that political organizations should become less rigidly structured, more malleable, and more responsive to changes in their environments. As the flow of information inside political organizations grows increasingly independent of people's official functions or roles, one of the foundations of Weberian bureaucracy is weakened: the formal distinction among roles and the segregation of information and communication as a function of those roles. Under such conditions, informal, flexible structures can take on substantially increased importance. Heckscher and Applegate call this "the opening of formerly closed organizational boundaries."[26] As information becomes less costly, contract-style relationships, temporary alliances, and ad hoc collaborations and partnerships become more viable as alternatives to traditional hierarchical organizational structure.

A third implication of information abundance involves the nature of membership. Membership in traditional political organizations has several characteristics: a defined span, the transfer of money, and selective benefits. People join organizations typically by paying dues, which entitle them to a specified duration of membership, typically a year. In

[24] Darrell M. West, *Air Wars: Television Advertising in Election Campaigns*, 3rd ed. (Washington, D.C.: CQ Press, 2001).

[25] Sara Fritz and Dwight Morris, *Handbook of Campaign Spending: Money in the 1990 Congressional Races* (Washington, D.C.: CQ Press, 1992).

[26] Charles Heckscher and Lynda M. Applegate, "Introduction" to Heckscher and Donnellon, eds., *The Post-Bureaucratic Organization*, p. 2.

return, they receive selective benefits of some kind, often a magazine or other literature. Under conditions of information abundance, where the exchange of detailed information is easy and the cost of communication low, all three of these features of membership are subject to change. When organizations can identify interested people and communicate with them at very low marginal cost, some of the impetus for collecting dues is diminished. Similarly, as the effort and cost required to communicate with a group and to engage in collective action falls for citizens, the need for selective benefits to motivate engagement and participation is also weakened. Information abundance implies the possibility of less bureaucratized forms of political membership.

As a result, the focus of collective action can in principle change. Citizen involvement in public affairs has traditionally involved a tension between two factors. The first is the impetus for localism, or the tendency for people to understand and approach political issues through their local perspectives. The second is the national scale and general orientation of most media, especially up through the broadcast era historically, which tend to direct citizens toward national issues. Because of the cost and structure of political information, interest organizations have in the past generally been forced to operate at either one scale or the other, but not both. Information abundance makes possible flexible, scalable, network-style organizational structures that are not fixed around either national or local issues. An organization rich in information and communication capacity might readily adapt from one scale of issue to the next and back again.

In the past, most membership-based groups have traditionally experienced high annual turnover and have dedicated substantial resources to retaining members and attracting new recruits to make up for that attrition.[27] Abundant information has the potential to reorient this process so that "membership" turnover could approach 100 percent *per event*, as citizens "join" an organization solely for the purpose of participating in a particular activity. This means that the motivation to protect the environment, promote civil rights, or save the lives of the unborn may be less important to citizens' affiliations with political groups than the motivation to speak out about a specific environmental decision, register a view about a civil rights law being considered in Congress, or attend an abortion-clinic protest. This constitutes event-based rather than interest-based political affiliation.

---

[27] Johnson, "Interest Group Recruiting."

Together these possibilities imply an acceleration of the speed of politics, as organizations grow more nimble and their capacity to mobilize citizens selectively is enhanced. This represents the ultimate solution to Tocqueville's information problem: As the marginal cost of information and communication tends toward zero, political associations can form and disband at will. To the extent that they do, events should in theory increasingly drive political structure and organization. To be sure, government and other political processes have in the past been driven by events as well as by interests and more stable internal agendas of political organizations. Votes, decisions, elections, economic developments, social affairs, and media practices have influenced greatly who participates in politics and what the issues of the day are. But the pace of events has been overlaid on a structure of comparatively stable, distinct organizations operating from established agendas and strategies. The resulting political action has been shaped by a balanced interplay between events and organizational interests. Conditions of growing information abundance imply a shift in that balance toward greater event-based political structures.

These features of political organization under conditions of information abundance are summarized in Table 3.1 They constitute possibilities for a form of postbureaucratic pluralism. In it, group-based politics remain vitally important and in tension with the majoritarian politics of the mass media. But in postbureaucratic pluralism, the structure of collective action is less tightly coupled than in the past to a marketplace of formal political organizations. Interest organizations exist, to be sure, but the patterns and structures of collective action are less reflective and representative of traditional organizational boundaries and forms.

Theoretically, several important limitations on postbureaucratic pluralism are clear. First, it is important to note that postbureaucratic pluralism is not the product solely of technological developments after 1990. Some postbureaucratic features of politics extend back into the third information revolution, particularly in the phase of channel abundance, while others extend further back into trends in civil society and interest group politics of the 1960s and '70s. And as Samuel Kernell and others have noted, changes in communication patterns over the last few decades of the twentieth century undermined "institutionalized pluralism" and contributed to a more "individualized pluralism."[28]

---

[28] Samuel Kernell, *Going Public: New Strategies of Presidential Leadership*, 3rd ed. (Washington, D.C.: CQ Press, 1997), p. 30. For related arguments regarding Congress,

Table 3.1. Organizational Types in Politics

Bureaucratic political organization	Postbureaucratic political organization
1. Collective action requires substantial material resources on the part of organizers.	1. Collective action does not necessarily require substantial staff, money, or organization on the part of organizers.
2. Organizational boundaries are sharply defined.	2. Organizational boundaries are often permeable and not sharply defined.
3. Membership is formally defined and structured.	3. Informal association and affiliation are important and sometimes replace formal membership.
4. Collective action is typically broad-based and oriented toward entire memberships, with the organization seeking to act as a whole on the basis of centrally determined priorities.	4. Collective action is often narrowly focused on subsets of members or affiliates, with the organization reconfiguring itself between issues in opportunistic responses to the flow of political events.

Technological trends of the 1990s and 2000s have accelerated and consolidated some of those older trends in information and communication, expanding the possibilities for organizational adaptation and change.

The spread of postbureaucratic pluralism in response to information abundance will necessarily be constrained by the psychology and market dynamics of the traditional mass media. This is especially likely in the area of campaigning, since the function of attracting the attention of citizens to a campaign is comparatively low in information-intensiveness. Campaigning is more a game of citizen attention than citizen information and learning, and traditional mass media, especially broadcasting, should remain superior at this task. In the 2000 elections, the cost of political advertising approached $1 billion.[29] For parties and candidates, as well

see Thomas E. Mann and Norman J. Ornstein, eds., *The New Congress* (Washington, D.C.: American Enterprise Institute, 1981).

[29] Source: Alliance for Better Campaigns, http://www.bettercampaigns.org/documents/rele30601.htm.

as interest groups and issue groups who on occasion undertake mass media campaigns, new information abundance does little to reduce such costs.

On the other hand, information abundance weakens the gate-keeping function of the traditional mass media. Mass media institutions are less able to exert editorial and strategic control over the stories to which the public attends in the new information environment. Bruce Williams and Michael Delli Carpini identify several mechanisms by which traditional gate-keeping functions are being eroded to the point of elimination, including multiplication and expansion of media outlets, which creates competition for gate keeping; growth of the twenty-four-hour news cycle, which provides fewer opportunities for editors to control which stories are covered and which are not; and the interactivity and multiplication of noninstitutionalized means for citizens to share information. The result is a multiplication in the number of gates, and the consequent collapse of control over gate keeping.[30] By similar mechanisms, other chief political functions of media – agenda setting and priming – may also erode. The endpoint of this transition is hardly a utopia of alternative media. The traditional dynamics of the mass audience and political attention will remain in place, but the extent to which a few businesses can dominate political communication is clearly changing.

Issue-based politics and political fragmentation as a consequence of information abundance hardly precludes the focusing of mass attention on particular events. Clearly, mass media – especially broadcast media – possess an enormous capacity to direct the attention of large numbers of citizens to individual events, from O. J. Simpson to the vote count in Florida to the "war" against terrorism. The dynamics of mass attention and the politics of majoritarianism remain a potentially powerful counterbalance to group politics.

Another powerful constraint on postbureaucratic pluralism is the structure of the state apparatus itself. Formal political institutions do not reconfigure themselves in response to changes in information and trans-action costs. One reason is that their structures are rooted in the politics of legislation and the Constitution. Another is that, unlike collective action organizations, many formal institutions perform functions that are distributive or redistributive rather than informational in nature, Hamilton and Madison's characterization of the state as a center of information

---

[30] Bruce A. Williams and Michael X. Delli Carpini, "Unchained Reaction: The Collapse of Media Gatekeeping and the Lewinsky-Clinton Scandal," *Journalism: Theory, Practice and Criticism* 1, no. 1 (2001): 61–85.

notwithstanding. The need for collective action organizations to orient themselves to the structures and processes of largely unchanging institutions of the state creates limits on the advantages of postbureaucratic forms.

A related constraint stems from the need for personal relationships between state officials and representatives of civil society. The kinds of interpersonal actions and relationships that connect public officials to lobbyists, industry leaders, academics, and others are not driven by information costs, and their importance is hardly diminished by technological advances that produce information abundance. While some forms of interpersonal interaction may be facilitated by such abundance, a vast array of political relationships based on familiarity and trust lie at the center of politics. Familiarity and trust are only marginally matters of information.

A fourth constraint on postbureaucratic organization involves the need for sustained performance across events and issues. The event-driven orientation of postbureaucratic pluralism makes it less well suited to repeated collective action and sustained performance throughout the policy process than more traditional bureaucratic pluralism. Many of the features that make postbureaucratic organization highly adaptive to event-driven politics are disadvantages to the group faced with working through a lengthy legislative or rule-making process.

Perhaps the most important and pervasive limitation on postbureaucratic forms involves cheap-talk effects and the tendency for any item of information or communication to mean less as the overall volume of information and communication rises. Information abundance can lead to information fatigue as well as the reasonable calculation by political actors that a message sent cheaply means less than one sent expensively. One useful feature of an information economy with great variation in the price of communication is that senders can more easily signal the importance of a message. Information abundance tends to flatten the price of communication and weaken this signaling function. It is for this reason, as is sometimes said, that employers post job advertisements on the Internet but send the offer letter by Federal Express. In an environment of abundant political information and communication, it remains important to find comparable strategies for differentiating important messages from the routine.

A small body of research dealing with cheap-talk effects already exists in connection with congressional politics. This research has shown that citizen communication with Congress can be effective in influencing congressional policy.[31] Government officials pay attention when constituents write, occasionally even when the number of communicating constituents is not high. Most important, they are most likely to attend to constituent communications when messages show signs of substantial effort: when they are lengthy, personalized, handwritten, or otherwise indicative of thoughtfulness and real concern. These kinds of constituent communications signal to government officials the salience of an issue and also the likelihood that constituents' electoral behavior in the future might be conditioned upon an official's response to the current issue.

Research shows that the effectiveness of citizen communication with Congress is partly a function of the effort to which constituents have gone to convey their concerns. Members of Congress tend to discount constituent communications that appear to be centrally orchestrated through databases and mailing lists or subsidized by organizations through preprinted postcards or letters. Ken Kollman finds that the growing incidence of such "astroturf" campaigns in the 1980s and '90s diminished the marginal value of constituent communications. The problem with centrally orchestrated, "cheap" communication is not that none of the citizens participating are serious about the issue at hand, but that such efforts *conceal* the extent to which various citizens are interested and serious. Elected officials have little incentive to ignore serious and interested constituents and much greater incentive to ignore the background noise of the nonserious. Research on communication with Congress shows that over time, as members of Congress learned to recognize and discount centrally orchestrated communication, interest groups in turn adopted more sophisticated techniques aimed at either masking the cost of the message or actually elevating it; these included replacing the prewritten message with efforts to coach constituents by telephone on how to write their own personal letters.

In more general ways, information abundance plagues political communication of all kinds: between citizens and government, interest groups and citizens, and even among citizens themselves. These problems tend to limit the adoption of inexpensive means of communication throughout the political system. Together with the dynamics of mass media and public attention, the need to respond to stable institutions of government, the need for personal relationships based on trust and

---

[31] John Kingdon, *Congressmen's Voting Decisions*, 3rd ed. (Ann Arbor: University of Michigan Press, 1989); Kollman, *Outside Lobbying*; Stephen Frantzich, *Write Your Congressman: Citizen Communications and Representation* (New York: Praeger, 1986).

Table 3.2. Constraints on Postbureaucratic Political Organization

1. The dynamics of mass media and public attention.
2. The need to interact with unchanging formal institutions of government.
3. The importance of personal relationships based on familiarity and trust.
4. The requirement of sustained performance across events and throughout the policy process.
5. The discounted value of inexpensive information and communication.

familiarity, and the need for sustained performance across events and processes, this problem of the discounted value of inexpensive information constrains the exploitation of postbureaucratic forms by organizations. These five factors are summarized in Table 3.2.

Moreover, no single organizational structure is superior for all situations in any case, regardless of era or informational context. Not all industrial-era organizations resembled classical Weberian bureaucracies, but the Weberian model still provided powerful insights into organization and administration. Similarly, not all information-era organizations are likely to exhibit postbureaucratic features such as these. Large organizations may differ from small ones; organizations aimed at one political strategy or function should differ from those pursuing others; organizations whose leaders have autocratic styles should differ from those whose leaders tend toward collaboration, consultation, and delegation; organizations facing instability in their environments should be organized differently from those operating under conditions of certainty and stability. Even within individual organizations, substructures vary. For all these reasons, the connection between information abundance and postbureaucratic pluralism indicates a theoretical direction for changes in politics rather than a universal condition.

This connection raises the empirical question of evidence: In practice, do postbureaucratic organizations exist in politics, and if so, what do they look like? To what extent does contemporary politics conform to the bureaucratic conception of political organization, and to what extent to the postbureaucratic conception? These questions are the subject of the next chapter.

4

Political Organizations in the Fourth Information Revolution

INTRODUCTION

Between 1995 and 1998, Mike McCurry grew to become one of the most familiar figures occupying the borderland between American political institutions and mass media. As Press Secretary for the Clinton White House, McCurry delivered the White House message and managed press relations during part of Clinton's second term. He had moved to the White House from his position as spokesman for the State Department following the election of 1994. His mission was to shore up the White House press operation after the midterm setback that had returned Republicans to power, and he brought to the job a long resume in media–state relations. He had previously worked as Communications Director of the Democratic National Committee; political strategist for Senator John Glenn, Senator Bob Kerrey, and Governor Bruce Babbitt; and press secretary to the Senate Labor Committee and Senator Daniel Patrick Moynihan. In May of 1998, in the middle of the Lewinsky scandal, McCurry resigned. To cover hard feelings with the President, he offered the traditional euphemism of wanting to spend time with his family, but he had in mind a more strategic goal: shifting position in the government–press borderland by becoming a principal in the Washington lobbying and communications firm Public Strategies, Inc.[1]

Two and a half years later and one week following the indecisive election day of 2000, McCurry announced another career move. He had accepted the position of CEO of a political Internet business, Grassroots.com. Headquartered not in Washington but in San Francisco, the firm's aim was to provide "Internet-based communications and

---

[1] James Bennett, "Clinton's Spokesman Will Leave in the Fall," *New York Times*, July 24, 1998, p. A18, http://archives.nytimes.com.

mobilization products for the American political market."[2] This move to the world of Internet-related politics by a figure so deeply rooted in the traditional press was symbolic of changes in the world of political organization and media. In the firm's press release, McCurry offered a characteristic spin on the venture: "There is an 'Old Politics' based on the conventional way of doing business in Washington, DC, and there is an emerging 'New Politics' that is based on savvy use of the Internet."[3] McCurry had in mind something akin to postbureaucratic politics.

The sources of McCurry's enthusiasm for change were twofold. Like many others, he saw a viable means for political professionals to profit from the Internet revolution, and he was not reluctant to speak about the financial rewards of involvement in the new politics. This and the desire for a new kind of challenge explain much of McCurry's motivation. But he also offered a familiar critique of the traditional mass media for attending too closely to the agendas and interests of political institutions and being more interested in scandal than the policy concerns of citizens.[4] McCurry's firm would work against that trend, he argued, attempting to organize citizens through the Internet and to bypass some of the traditional institutionalized interests in politics. In addition, it would offer related Internet-based services, such as electronic filing of campaign finance information for campaigns, political action committees, and ballot measure organizations.

McCurry's move from the world of old media to new reflected the efforts of many professionals to promote and profit from new political processes and opportunities associated with changes in the information environment of American politics. An official of Burson-Marsteller, one of the world's largest public relations firms, observed in an interview for this project that a central task facing his company is "to help customers understand that communication is different now in the web age; what we are trying to do is help our clients develop and send information." He says that "we are trying to change how the Internet is used. . . . We don't want the Internet to be another tool, we want it to be the first tool."[5] In

---

[2] "Mike McCurry Appointed CEO of Grassroots.com," press release (San Francisco, Calif.: Grassroots.com, Nov. 15, 2000).

[3] Ibid., p. 2.

[4] Mike McCurry, "Keynote Address," at Measuring Success: 2000 Politics Online Conference of the George Washington University Graduate School of Political Management, George Washington University, Washington D.C., Dec. 4, 2000.

[5] Anonymous staff member, Burson-Marsteller, telephone interview by Eric Patterson for the author, Aug. 1, 2000.

this new age, information functions would stand visibly on the stage of politics.

By 1999, it was clear that increasing information abundance was influencing the market for lobbying and political mobilization. Like the market for retail goods, this one featured competition between established lobbying organizations and new start-ups, a strong reliance on venture capitalists, and rapid churn as some business models failed and others thrived and as businesses recombined in mergers and consolidations. At the time of McCurry's change of venue, the market for new political advocacy services already had highly visible players: PoliticsOnline, Mindshare, the Juno Advocacy Network (a subscriber-based general Internet services provider with a political organizing capacity), and a firm called e-advocates. Old-media consultants including Capitol Advantage and Issue Dynamics were also offering products in the new arena.

Until the late 1990s, instances of political organizations or groups employing new information infrastructure to accomplish political tasks – let alone hiring consultants to do it for them – remained novel enough to warrant mention whenever they occurred. Some of the earliest examples reported in the academic literature date to the early 1990s, when political activists and organizers began using new means of communication to organize collective action. One of the first was an Internet-based protest in 1990 by about 30,000 people, which was directed at a private firm, Lotus Development Corporation. A small organization, Computer Professionals for Social Responsibility (CPSR), initiated the effort out of concerns that a forthcoming product, Lotus Market Place, would facilitate violations of consumers' privacy. CPSR's call to protest against Lotus took a theoretically important course. As participants communicated with one another on line, they rapidly generated sympathizers outside the group's own membership. Without any noteworthy expenditures of resources or a centrally coordinated media campaign, a small, insular group had been transformed into a large, self-organized, and potentially threatening group with prominent postbureaucratic features. Flooded with messages, Lotus withdrew its product.[6]

A similar effort in 1993 involved a successful protest directed at the Clinton administration over the proposed "Clipper Chip" policy, which would have created a ready technological means for law enforcement officials to intercept computer-based messages. A coalition of small

---

[6] Laura Gurak, *Persuasion and Privacy in Cyberspace: The Online Protests over Lotus Marketplace and the Clipper Chip* (New Haven: Yale University Press, 1997).

organizations, including CPSR, initiated an effort to mobilize computer professionals and users into political action against this challenge to privacy without relying heavily on traditional media techniques, mailing lists, or large memberships. Instead, the groups asked citizens through electronic mail to protest the policy directly to the White House. The result was another vociferous, ad hoc, self-organized network, which was large and loud enough to command national political attention and thereby generate a debate over the pending policy, which the White House eventually withdrew.[7]

Some of these early instances of new forms of collective action were dismissed by observers in the mid-1990s as too idiosyncratic to have theoretical significance. They involved political actions by people within the computer industry, using computer technology, in order to affect private and public policies aimed at computer use. They seemed to have little bearing on broader politics, because the percentage of adults who had access to the Internet was in the single digits and the web had not yet emerged as a commercial force. More important, few mainstream political groups and organizations were involved in these Internet-dependent political strategies, so episodes like Lotus Notes and the Clipper Chip seemed peripheral. It appeared entirely speculative to think that the organizational features of these political events were indicative of any larger phenomenon that might affect collective action more broadly.

By the late 1990s, that no longer seemed true. Reports of lobbying and advertising that employed new means of communication increasingly involved groups outside the computer industry. From the Christian Coalition to the Democratic Socialists of America, groups were using the Internet to inform and organize citizens, and the result looked less and less like traditional, bureaucratically organized advocacy. The "Move On" protest, for instance, involved the important political question of impeachment. Move On was initiated by two Colorado residents who used electronic mail and the web to create a nationwide mail and petition drive aimed first at persuading the House not to impeach President Clinton, and later at convincing the Senate to acquit. Like the privacy protests earlier in the 1990s, the Move On protest exhibited a rapidly accelerating, self-organizing character. As the number of participants swelled, it caught the attention of the major media, who in reporting on Move On contributed even further to its size. Between September 1998 and January 1999, the Move On effort generated about 500,000 messages from constituents

---

[7] Ibid.

to Congress. The two Coloradans who started the effort report having spent about $100, making Move On arguably the least expensive mass petition effort in American history.[8] While the cost of the underlying technological infrastructure that made it possible was enormous, the directly attributable marginal cost to the protest organizers was on the order of one-fiftieth of a cent per person. It is unlikely that Move On materially affected the impeachment proceedings, given the overwhelming media attention dedicated to them; however, here was another instance of collective action in the absence of traditional organization.

Mainstream interest groups were also exploring new approaches to collective action. In 1998 and 1999, the National Association of Manufacturers (NAM) relied heavily on the Internet to obtain legislation it sought from Congress. NAM is the largest and most powerful organization representing business interests, claiming to have 14,000 member corporations along with 350 member associations. As a product of late nineteenth-century industrialization, the association has its roots in the second information revolution and a long history of forming coalitions and cooperating with other groups outside its already formidable membership base.[9] In the late 1990s, the association and its member businesses were concerned with the possibility of widespread lawsuits against businesses whose computer systems might fail temporarily at the outset of 2001, due to ambiguity in the two-digit date records used by computers and other electronic devices. In 1997 and 1998, as awareness spread of the potential for computer failures at the beginning of the new millennium, NAM created a coalition that was unusual for its size and speed.

The coalition included about 100 business groups, including organizations in the banking, insurance, retail, and finance sectors. NAM officials claimed the coalition represented 80 percent of the American economy; while that figure is more symbolic than literal, this was clearly a business coalition of enormous proportions. It used electronic mail

---

[8] Jeri Clausing, "Anti-Impeachment Web Site Tallies Millions in Pledges," *New York Times*, Jan. 8, 1999, http://www.nytimes.com/library/tech/99/01/cyber/articles/08move.html; Benny Evangelista, "A Way to Petition Congress on Clinton: Web Site Lets You Tell Your Lawmaker to Censure, Move On," *San Francisco Chronicle*, Oct. 15, 1998, p. B3; Kevin Merida, "Moving Down Off the Fence; An Undecided Democrat Makes Up His Mind," *Washington Post*, Oct. 9, 1998, p. D1; Melissa Healy, "Grass-Roots Organizing Effort Gets a Big Boost From Internet," *Los Angeles Times*, Jan. 13, 1999, http://www.latimes.com/home/news/reports/scandal/stories/lat_public990113.htm; Chris Carr, "On-Line Call against Impeachment Is on Fire," *Washington Post*, Feb. 1, 1999, p. A10.

[9] National Association of Manufacturers, March 2001, http://www.nam.org.

networks and a password-secured web site to coordinate a very rapid and intense exchange of information among groups, including working drafts of legislation that would be requested of Congress. According to a senior counsel of the American Banking Association, this system permitted creation of consensus positions on policy among groups in record time, as well as permitting outward flow of requests for contacts with members of Congress to the many coalition partners and the tens of thousands of businesses represented by them. He says, "The Internet has brought more people into the loop . . . it just picks up the pace on everything . . . [and] gives everyone more time to communicate."[10] The impetus for such a large-scale cooperative effort was inherent in the breadth of the policy question at hand, but organizers at NAM insist that the new modes of communication dramatically enhanced the capacity of the groups to interact and coordinate very rapidly across the various business sectors. Virtually all information moved among organizations through the Internet, and the group claimed it could produce lobbyists in members' offices from many groups at once within half an hour of distributing a call for action. According to Jan Amundsen, Vice President and General Counsel of NAM, the group came under extraordinary pressure from members of Congress to break apart, because legislators wanted to create individual deals for each industry. The capacity to move information rapidly among the groups using new technology twice helped hold the diverse coalition together all the way through the legislative process.[11] By August of 1998, the group had won passage of its first bill, the Information Readiness and Disclosure Act of 1998, and by June of 1999, a second bill, the Y2K Liability Act. Amundsen believes that this coalition's connections through high-speed, information-rich communication channels was a prototype for the future formation of business coalitions spanning traditional groups.

Stories similar to NAM's appeared throughout the political system in the late 1990s. For example, in 1999, Congress completed a last-minute reauthorization of the 1994 Violence Against Women Act. The reauthorization funded legal and health services for women and also provided rape and abuse prevention education, law enforcement grants, and other measures. It was in jeopardy of stalling in early 1999 despite years of lobbying by a large and disparate coalition of women's groups, in large

---

[10] Gordon Glaza, Senior Counsel, American Banking Association, telephone interview by Diane Johnson for the author, May 29, 2000.

[11] Jan Amundsen, Vice President and General Counsel, National Association of Manufacturers, telephone interview by Diane Johnson for the author, May 11, 2000.

part because of perceptions by Republicans that it was a "Democratic bill."[12] As the deadline on the original bill's five-year authorization approached and the outcome of the reauthorization remained uncertain, the groups intensified their efforts at grassroots mobilization as well as "inside" lobbying. Participants found that the Internet could play two major roles in those processes: providing a means for highly responsive, rapid coordination among groups, and facilitating the large-scale mobilization of citizens. The Public Policy Director of the National Coalition Against Domestic Violence, one of several umbrella groups advocating for the bill, claims that the Internet was "critical" to coordination among the groups as well as to communication within the organizations.[13] The sponsors of the largest web site dedicated to passage of the bill brokered over 150,000 e-mail messages from citizens to members of Congress during the final twelve weeks of the campaign, as well as facilitating a great deal of traditional mail, faxes, and telephone calls.[14]

This case again exhibited some of the features of postbureaucratic politics: flexible, event-based organization in which the boundaries of groups were sometimes vague, and mobilization occurring outside formal membership rolls. So too with the Gay and Lesbian Alliance Against Defamation (GLAAD), which began using new communication techniques as early as 1996. In 1998, when the U.S. Navy moved to discharge gay sailor Tim McVeigh, an advocacy network sprang up in his defense using the Internet for coordination.[15] McVeigh had revealed his sexual orientation in an America Online (AOL) venue, and through that act came to the attention of his naval superiors. As the Navy prepared to discharge him for being gay, McVeigh distributed electronic messages to every AOL member with the word "gay" in their personal profile – accomplishing the first steps in Tocqueville's model of information and association formation. Many of these AOL members passed the messages on to others, and a rapidly expanding group of advocates emerged. With help from John Aravosis, a political consultant in Washington, D.C., and Rex Wockner, a gay activist in San Francisco, the group attracted the attention of the mass media. Despite its initial disinterest in McVeigh's

---

[12] Bonnie Robin-Vergeer, former staff aide to Senator Joseph Biden, telephone interview by Diane Johnson for the author, May 7, 2001.

[13] Juley Fulcher, Public Policy Director, National Coalition Against Domestic Violence, telephone interview by Diane Johnson for the author, May 4, 2001.

[14] Erica D. Rowell, "Spurring an Online Movement," ABCNews.com, Oct. 18, 2000, http://more.abcnews.go.com/sections/tech/dailynews/onlineactivism001018.html.

[15] This person is not related to Oklahoma City bomber Timothy McVeigh.

situation by itself, the story of a network of gay rights supporters backing a sailor being drummed out of the Navy became newsworthy. Eventually, the *New York Times* and ABC's *World News Tonight* covered the story. According to Aravosis, the Internet permitted a few activists to bypass the originally uninterested media outlets, creating public interest without them. Once a threshold of interest was crossed, the media took on the story. He says, "What's new here is the ability to get the message out without going through the [traditional] media. We were able to get [McVeigh's story] to thousands of people without ever calling one print reporter."[16] With only a little hyperbole, Wockner observes, "In the old days, Activist A had to call Reporter B at Paper C and hope that the editor was interested. That strategy used to take two weeks to get anything out and only reached the readers of gay newspapers. The Net has changed all that. Now it takes 10 minutes to reach millions."[17] The effort failed to save McVeigh's job at the Navy, but it demonstrated how a group with few resources and essentially no organizational structure could place an issue on the national policy agenda, even if only briefly.

The same year, the protests and violence at the 1999 Seattle meeting of the World Trade Organization (WTO) illustrated similar organizational dynamics. The far-flung collection of activist, labor, and student groups that comprised the late 1990s antisweatshop movement operated through a decentralized network of electronic mail, chat rooms, and eventually a web site dedicated solely to organizing for the protest. They used these tools to recruit participants for Seattle, share information, and coordinate activities. According to one participant during the organizing phase, "Right now, every time we do an action, we send out an e-mail and a hundred people show up. It's like magic. We couldn't do it without e-mail."[18] By one account, the genesis of the protests can be traced to an electronic mail campaign initiated eleven months before the WTO meetings, with a single message distributed by Public Citizens' Global Trade Watch. From that event through the street protests in Seattle, events had a self-organizing character independent of central planning and finance. Protesters drew together from several nations a disparate

---

[16] Quoted in Steve Friess, "Cyberactivism," *The Advocate*, no. 780 (March 2, 1999), p. 37.

[17] Quoted in Steve Silberman, "Wiring the Gay World," *Wired*, on-line edition, Aug. 5, 1998, http://www.wired.com/news/culture/0,1284,14229,00.html.

[18] Cited in B. J. Bullert, "Strategic Public Relations, Sweatshops, and the Making of a Global Movement," unpublished paper, Seattle University, May 18, 2000, p. 3.

coalition of labor and civil rights organizations, women's groups, and environmentalists, who had in most cases no history of cooperation or even interaction.[19]

Even the American Association of Political Consultants (AAPC), the bastion of mass media–based politics, recognized by the late 1990s that important new possibilities for communication were at hand. As the main membership organization for traditional political campaign and advertising professionals, AAPC distributes awards after each election cycle for a variety of campaign accomplishments. These include awards for best television advertisements, best radio advertisements, and best print and direct mail campaigns. By 1998, AAPC acknowledged that its members were increasingly involved in communication using new media, and after the elections that year it gave new awards for best candidate web site, best organization web site, and best initiative web site. By the 2000 cycle, one in five of its awards went for Internet-based communication strategies, in the categories of best presidential, statewide, congressional, legislative, local initiative, and independent expenditure web sites; best use of the web for fund raising, persuasion, and negative advertising; best banner ads on web sites; and best overall Internet campaign. According to Richard Schlackman, president of a direct mail firm in San Francisco and member of the board of directors of AAPC, the association created the new awards because "new technology has shown that it is beginning to work."[20]

By the turn of the century, then, political groups across the spectrum were exploring new means of communicating and managing political information. Virtually all established advocacy groups, such as NAM, were using some form of Internet-based tools. Groups without a presence in the traditional political landscape were forming and often disappearing after a political event had run its course, as in the case of Move On and others. These had a new name emphasizing their speed and unpredictability: "flash campaigns."[21] On the surface, many of these cases exhibited intriguing organizational structures bearing at least some of the markings of postbureaucracy. Yet, certainly, for each one of these cases there

[19] Greg Miller, "Internet Fueled Global Interest in Disruptions," *Los Angeles Times*, Dec. 2, 1999, p. A24.

[20] Richard Schlackman, Campaign Performance Group; telephone interview with the author, Dec. 5, 2000.

[21] Rebecca Fairley Raney, "Flash Campaigns: Online Activism at Warp Speed," *New York Times*, Cybertimes Edition, June 3, 1999, http://www.politicsonline.com/archives/usnews/usnews1999.html.

were far more examples of traditional interest groups with bureaucratic organizational forms going about their business in traditional ways. The Internet-based political efforts represented something largely new, to be sure, but just how deeply changes in the information and communication environment might be connected to changes in organizational forms is still not clear. How can the extent of postbureaucratic organization be assessed more systematically and compared with traditional organizational structure? For a quantitatively oriented social scientist, the natural inclination when confronted with such a question is to seek population samples and test for trends or differences. In a world of ideal evidence, one would sample groups and organizations active in politics at points prior to the contemporary information revolution and again at points after. Coding these organizations as to their conformity with elements of bureaucratic and postbureaucratic organizational forms would then permit the appropriate inferences to be made about changes over time.

Unfortunately, that approach is unworkable, since opportunities for assembling anything approaching a probability sample of political organizations are scarce. Selecting groups and organizations requires a priori judgment about which are likely to be of interest. It is also clear that the boundaries of whatever information regime might eventually solidify out of the fourth information revolution will take time to become clear. History provides chastening lessons in this regard. As Charles Hecksher warns, a study of market economics conducted in 1650 and examining a wide or random cross-section could have documented much about how markets work theoretically, but empirically would have had to conclude that markets function effectively only in cloth-producing areas. The wise observer would have focused attention on the cloth sector and extrapolated from there rather than sampling many sectors. By the same token, a study of new economic organizations conducted in 1870 and bound by the methodology of random sampling might have concluded that bureaucratic management is only appropriate for railroads.[22] Such cases warn against attempting to make final claims about the extent of change in organizational structures at the beginning of periods of dramatic change. They also warn against concluding prematurely that limited developments cannot one day become profound.

---

[22] Charles Hecksher, "Defining the Post-Bureaucratic Type," in Charles Hecksher and Anne Donnellon, eds., *The Post-Bureaucratic Organization: New Perspectives on Organizational Change* (Thousand Oaks, Calif.: Sage Publications, 1994), pp. 14–62.

In an effort to explore the ramifications of these brief stories above, I examined a selective set of cases in greater depth and focused on the possibility of relationships among properties of information and communication and properties of organization. For this analysis, I chose to study organizations and groups whose main purpose is national policy advocacy, or "lobbying," because of their importance to the structure of contemporary American politics. Such organizations are also one of the main features of the second information regime, and it is important to ask how those organizations are faring in the midst of the contemporary revolution.

In choosing lobbying organizations, I sought a set of cases sufficiently diverse to allay concern that the results would be specific to a particular policy domain or type of organization. I sought cases also with a high level of visibility on the political agenda. These provide a better indicator of structural change than organizations involved in minor policy-making episodes, because prominent cases typically involve a greater investment of resources in traditional political processes and techniques by established interests. Toward this end, members of my research team and I conducted a wide-ranging search across national policy areas.[23] I began by drawing up a list of major policy areas to survey, with the main criteria being salience and heterogeneity. These were: abortion and "family" issues, civil rights, the economy, education, the environment, gun control, health care, and taxation.[24] With this list in hand, we reviewed and discussed scholarly literature and news accounts pertinent to each area over the last decade. For the news accounts we relied on the *New York Times*, the *Los Angeles Times*, several news magazines, and political news clipping services dealing with politics. We worked from the premise that throughout the 1990s, most organizations were adopting new information technology in various ways. We therefore looked for prominent cases covered in the media that appeared to illustrate a range of consequences. Where we found cases of postbureaucratic forms, we pursued them. Where we found cases of bureaucratic forms persisting,

---

[23] I chose explicitly to exclude state-level cases and minor national policy-making episodes. My research team for the case studies included three doctoral students in the Department of Political Science at the University of California, Santa Barbara (UCSB): Joe Gardner, Diane Johnson, and Eric Patterson. Notes indicate the cases to which each researcher contributed most.

[24] Compare with Thomas Dye's categories in his classic textbook on American public policy, *Understanding Public Policy*, 7th ed. (Englewood Cliffs: Prentice Hall, 1997). Dye's categories are civil rights, criminal justice, health and welfare, education, environment, defense, economics, and taxes.

we noted these and asked why. This process produced a list of thirty-nine interest groups and other nongovernmental organizations involved in prominent episodes of national policy making and apparently reliant in some important way on information technology.[25]

Next, members of my research team contacted the thirty-nine organizations in writing and by telephone, making preliminary inquiries about their political activities. Our aim was to select about five cases for closer inquiry. My criteria for reducing the list from thirty-nine were three-fold. First, I wanted cases where policy advocates got what they wanted from government in the form of a new policy or the withdrawal of a policy under consideration, as well as cases where they failed. I wanted a set of cases with mixed outcomes precisely because these typify real advocacy and policy making. Descriptions of interest groups reliant exclusively on successful cases of lobbying can lead to errors of inference about what works in politics and what does not, because often the same strategies and efforts that succeed in one case fail in another. In the case studies, I did not seek to explain why decision makers acted as they did, nor attempt to attribute causation for policy outcomes. Instead, I took as the phenomenon of primary interest to be the existence and form of the group's or organization's engagement with the policy process, regardless of how successful any one group was in any particular case.

Second, I sought to maintain policy heterogeneity among the cases, and third, I sought a spectrum of organization types. Specifically, I

[25] The list of organizations is as follows (some were involved in the same episodes of policy making): AFL-CIO, American Banking Association, American Federation of Teachers, American Gulf War Veterans Association, American Insurance Association, American Legion, American Library Association, American Association of University Women, B'nai B'rith, Brotherhood of Locomotive Engineers, California National Guard Public Affairs, Children Now, Children's Defense Fund, Christian Coalition, Communication Organization On-Line Conference on Community Organizing and Development, Concerned Women for America, Conservative Enterprise Institute, Covering Kids, Edison Electric Institute, Families USA, Human Rights Campaign, Information Technology Industry Council, International Brotherhood of Boilermakers, International Womens Network, Information Technology Association of America, Juno Advocacy Network, Lambda Legal Defense Fund, Million Mom March, National Organization of Women, National Association of Manufacturers, National Association of School Boards, National Association of Teachers, National Coalition on Health Care, National Gay and Lesbian Task Force, National School Principals Association, OMB Watch, OneNation, Orange County Citizens Against Handgun Violence, Pacific Center for the Study of Gun Violence, Quaker House, Securities Industry Council, US Chamber of Commerce, Veterans of Foreign Wars, Victory Fund, Vietnam Veterans Association, Y2K Coalition.

sought at least one large, well-endowed, traditional political organization, at least one modest organization with a history in American politics but not a great deal of political influence, and at least one new organization with no political history whatever. The result was the following list: the Libertarian Party; the Environmental Defense Fund and other environmental groups; a coalition of education groups including the National Education Association and others; and the Million Mom March.

To develop case studies of these groups, members of my research team and I read further into the secondary literature relevant to the organizations, obtained public records and documents where available, and conducted almost a hundred telephone and face-to-face interviews. Our informants were organization officials, participants in advocacy efforts, congressional staff, and federal agency officials and staff. The aim of the interviews was to explore how the new information environment in politics affected the efforts of these organizations to pursue their political goals as well as their organizational arrangements. My goal for interviewing in each case involved a four-step strategy to which I was able to adhere with varying but reasonable success. First, we began by interviewing mid-ranking staff with close, day-to-day involvement in the use of information technology for political communication and other functions. The goal of this step was to develop an understanding of the insider's view of the organizational dynamics of technology. At this level we continued interviewing inside the group using a "snowball-sampling" technique until we felt we had a complete insider's view. The second step involved moving upward in the organization's hierarchy to reach the highest-ranking staff person with direct responsibility for political communication and information technology. The aim of this step was to develop a broader understanding of how the technology-intensive operations fit within the larger organizational context. We inquired specifically about strategic matters involving information technology rather than the tactical and day-to-day issues we discussed at the first step.

The third step involved attempting to interview at least one even higher-ranking official with responsibility for overall operations and who could give the broadest possible perspective on the organization. These interviews provided a check on some of the enthusiastic claims of those directly involved with the technology on a daily basis. Not surprisingly, we found in some cases that those with daily involvement overstated the importance of technology within the organization as measured against the views of those at the top – but not always. The final step in the interviewing strategy was to interview officials outside the organization who were either located in the government offices that the organization sought to influence or who were located in similar organizations and were in a position to comment on the issues and events under investigation.[26]

Because I selected cases in which there was reason to suspect that information technology had made a difference organizationally, one of the major goals of the interviews was to assess the reasons for that relationship between technology and organizational form. I also sought to learn about the persistence of organizational change over time, and toward this end I employed the technique of reinterviewing selected informants for each case six to twelve months after the initial set of interviews. In the reinterviews, we inquired about the stability of organizational innovations associated with new technology and examined constraints and limitations on the kinds of innovations that initially attracted us to the case.

These cases emphasize interest groups because they have been so important in defining the structure of American pluralism. I was also interested in comparing policy organizations with campaign organizations, which theory suggests should exhibit less organizational change. Without redirecting the main focus of the case studies from interest groups, I created a fifth case dealing with the most recent national election, the 2000 cycle.[27] I had two selection criteria: to include both the primary and general presidential elections and to include all significant candidates with either a chance of winning or a chance of influencing the outcome. In the general election, this led to four candidates: Al Gore, George Bush, Ralph Nader, and Pat Buchanan. For the primaries, these criteria included Bill Bradley and John McCain. To construct the case, members

---

[26] In practice, success at adhering to this interviewing strategy varied somewhat across cases, as a function of the type of organization involved and the particulars of the case. For instance, in one case, where the goal of policy advocacy was to influence a specific agency decision, it was possible at the fourth step to interview as many as half a dozen agency officials directly involved in the decision making and who could comment quite specifically on what informants in the advocacy organization claimed to be true. In another case, where the goal of the organization was to influence a congressional decision, we were able to interview congressional staff but were unable, as one would expect, to draw conclusions about influence with the same level of confidence. In another case, step three proved especially difficult. The conclusions in the case narratives reflect this varying level of reliability and confidence in the evidence. In the case involving gun control, the temporary nature of the organization, including the absence of an office or staff following the event, meant that it was impossible to reach any key staff at steps one through three; this case is unlike the rest in that it is built chiefly from documentary sources and newspaper reporting.

[27] In a separate project to be reported subsequently, I am examining information technology and campaign dynamics exclusively.

of my research team and I interviewed officials of each campaign in person. Where possible, we again used the interview/reinterview technique, speaking with officials during the heat of the campaign season and then after the election was over.[28]

For yet another perspective on interest groups as well as election campaigns, we also interviewed officials at a set of public relations and political advertising firms. My goal was to get behind the symbolic AAPC adoption of Internet awards and understand how the efforts of professional lobbyists to advocate on behalf of interest groups, corporations, and candidates might be sensitive to the changing information environment. My criterion in selecting these lobbyists was simply to include officials from firms in three categories: leading traditional firms offering political communications consulting or public relations involving "grassroots advocacy" and "outside" lobbying; leading traditional firms focused on "inside" lobbying and advocacy; and new political consulting firms focused on Internet-based strategies. We compiled a list of such firms and contacted the most prominent in each category. Our final selection produced four traditional public relations firms, one inside lobbying firm, and two new Internet specialists, for a total of seven firms. The results of these interviews are not organized as a separate case study, but are presented below in the narrative where appropriate and are cited individually.

I chose not to include distinct cases involving mass media organizations, despite their importance to contemporary politics and the apparently great implications of information technology for them. My chief reasons for not including mass media as parallel cases are their theoretical differences from interest groups and campaign organizations, and the scope of analysis needed to deal with them thoroughly. I exclude them not because they are unimportant but rather because they are sufficiently important to require their own study. However, interaction between new media and old media proves to be an important subtopic in the cases below.

I also excluded civic organizations and other nongovernmental organizations, also mainly for reasons of scope. Clearly, such groups are important contributors to the pluralistic structure of American politics, and without a doubt the possibility of postbureaucratic organization applies to them. I interpret part of the debate over social

---

[28] The exception is the Buchanan campaign, whose officials were not amenable to talking with us the second time.

capital in the United States as a dispute over the classification of associations. Robert Putnam's observation of the decline in traditional civic organizations, such as the PTA and the Boy Scouts, is largely an assessment of the state of *bureaucratic* civic associations.[29] Critics of this argument who claim that social capital is now borne instead by informal parents groups, "soccer mom" networks, singles groups, fitness clubs, and the like invoke organizations with many postbureaucratic features.[30] The so-called on-line communities of the Internet may be the best example of postbureaucratic civic association. It will take more time to see whether and how contemporary associations such as these build social capital or in other ways produce meaningful consequences. In any event, I do not pursue matters of purely civic association here.

The case studies are organized below by group and policy area, not technology. In the study of information technology and politics, considerable attention is typically paid to web sites as a unit of analysis, in large part because they are one of the most readily observable of all political phenomena. Though web sites themselves are indeed important and can serve as a useful focus of analysis, it should be clear that in this study, my focus and unit of analysis is much broader than the web site as a particular form of technology. In the case studies, I sought to examine how collective action occurs in an information-rich environment where a variety of technologies contribute toward information abundance of one kind or another. The case narratives below give a description of each group, and their strategies and the structure of advocacy resulting from use of information technology. Following the narratives is a summary that analyzes the cases together for what they illustrate about postbureaucratic political organization.

CONSUMER PROTECTION AND PRIVACY

The short story of the Libertarians and the Federal Deposit Insurance Corporation (FDIC) at the beginning of Chapter 1 is in several ways an archetypal case of information infrastructure substituting for traditional

---

[29] Robert D. Putnam, *Bowling Alone: The Collapse and Revival of American Community* (New York: Simon and Schuster, 2000).

[30] Nicholas Lemann, "Kicking in Groups," *The Atlantic Monthly* 277, no. 4 (April 1996), http://xroads.virginia.edu/~HYPER/DETOC/assoc/kicking.html; Michael Schudson, "What If Civic Life Didn't Die?" *The American Prospect* 25 (March–April 1996), http://www.prospect.org/archives/25/25-cnt1.html; Theda Skocpol, "Unravelling from Above," *The American Prospect* 25 (March–April 1996), http://www.prospect.org/archives/ 25/25-cnt2.html.

political infrastructure, and it bears a closer examination as the first of the full case studies.[31] The "Know Your Customer" regulations proposed by the FDIC and other federal agencies in 1998 constituted the latest move in a long series of efforts to identify money laundering through the nations' banks.[32] The Bank Secrecy Act of 1970 requires private banks to file currency transaction reports for banking transactions involving more than $10,000 in cash and also to report any "suspicious" activities, such as customer refusals to show identification.

In the 1980s and early 1990s, Congress tightened efforts to control money laundering through half a dozen new laws.[33] For instance, the Money Laundering Control Act of 1986 made it a federal crime knowingly to help launder money from a criminal activity, engage in a transaction of more than $10,000 involving property from a criminal activity, or structure transactions so as to avoid the Bank Secrecy Act. The Federal Deposit Insurance Corporation Improvement Act of 1991 allowed banking authorities in the United States to share with foreign governments financial information gained through their own monitoring or investigations of banking transactions in the United States. The Housing and Community Development Act of 1992, also known as the Annunzio-Wylie Anti-Money Laundering Act, authorized the federal government to seize banks found guilty of money laundering.[34] To comply with the various

---

[31] This case is based on an examination of public records and sixteen interviews. Interviewees include five staff members of the Federal Deposit Insurance Corporation; one staff member of the Office of Thrift Supervision; one official of the Federal Reserve; one of the Office of the Comptroller of the Currency; one staff member of the House Committee on Banking and the Senate Committee on Banking, Housing and Urban Affairs; two staff members of the Senate Committee on Banking, Housing and Urban Affairs; one staff member of the office of Representative Robert Barr; and two officials of the Libertarian Party. Names and affiliations are provided in citations below in cases where informants granted permission. Most of the research and an initial written description of the case was prepared by Diane Johnson, doctoral student in the Department of Political Science at UCSB.

[32] "Money laundering" refers to efforts at concealing the illegal nature of a source of money, such as drug trafficking, though a series of financial transactions. Moving money through bank accounts, for example, can obscure its original origins in a criminal activity.

[33] These are: the Money Laundering Control Act of 1986; the Anti-Drug Abuse Act of 1988; the Crime Control Act of 1990; the Federal Deposit Insurance Corporation Improvement Act of 1991; the Housing and Community Development Act of 1992, also known as the Annunzio-Wylie Anti-Money Laundering Act; and the Money Laundering Suppression Act of 1994.

[34] Department of the Treasury, Office of the Comptroller of the Currency, "Money Laundering: A Banker's Guide to Avoiding Problems," Washington, D.C., 2001, http://www.occ.treas.gov/launder/origa.htm.

disclosure and reporting requirements of the network of laws and regulations organized around the original Bank Secrecy Act, U.S. banks in 1998 filed about 100,000 reports of suspicious activities and 13 million reports of currency transactions.[35]

As a matter of private banking policy, most banks operating in the United States in the 1980s and 1990s also employed some form of voluntary practice referred to in the industry as "knowing your customer." These practices were based on the principle that by learning individual customers' banking habits and patterns, banks can more readily distinguish legitimate and illegitimate financial dealings. Regular, large cash transactions could be routine for one customer, who might be involved in a retail business in a fully legal way, while a single large cash transaction by another customer might signal illegal activity. A report by the American Bankers Association in 1994 showed that 86 percent of member associations operated a "know your customer" policy of some kind to aid in identifying crimes.[36]

In the early and mid-1990s, some banks, as well as federal banking authorities, developed interest in standardizing and formalizing these policies.[37] Standardization would provide banks with clearer guidelines as to what constitutes "suspicious" activity, thereby helping them comply with their reporting obligations, and it would streamline the workload at the Treasury department where suspicious activity reports were managed. In 1992, the Treasury department began discussing the possibility of drafting federal regulations. In 1994, the American Bankers Association released a position paper stating that "the banking industry is poised to cooperate with the Treasury's efforts to formalize what, to a large degree, already exists in the commercial banking industry." Many bankers sought new rules to help them define their own requirements and avoid potential competition between banks that were profiling their customers and those that were not. By 1997, agency officials were prepared to advance regulations, and throughout that year and the next, Federal Reserve Board staff and officials of the FDIC, the Office of the Comptroller of the Currency, and the Office of Thrift Supervision prepared and revised

---

[35] Robert O'Harrow, Jr., "Disputed Bank Plan Dropped: Regulators Bow to Privacy Fears," *Washington Post*, March 24, 1999, pp. E1–E2.

[36] American Bankers Association, "ABA Money Laundering Task Force Position on Establishing a Know Your Customer Policy," position paper (Washington, D.C.: American Bankers Association, 1994).

[37] Scott Barancik, "Know Your Customer Debate Cases a Widening Shadow," *American Banker*, Feb. 10, 1999, p. 4.

preliminary regulations that would be called "Know Your Customer." According to officials of the agencies, members of the banking industry were very active in crafting the regulations with agency staff. Although the four agencies possessed the authority to act without additional authorization from Congress, in 1998, a bill passed the House without fanfare that required the Treasury Secretary to promulgate "Know Your Customer" rules within 120 days.[38]

By the end of the year, the House bill had not been taken up in the Senate, but the four agencies proceeded with the rule-making process anyway. On December 7, they published Notices of Proposed Rulemaking for nearly identical versions of a "Know Your Customer" policy that was structured as further implementation of the Bank Secrecy Act.[39] The proposed regulations "would require each banking organization to develop a program designed to determine the identity of its customers; determine its customers' sources of funds; determine, understand and monitor the normal and expected transactions of its customers; and report appropriately any transactions of its customers that are determined to be suspicious."[40]

In their regulations, the agencies revealed more of the nature of industry support than perhaps they should have. They wrote that the rules were an aid to banks who were already required to report "suspicious" activity and in particular to those already profiling their customers who might have found it "difficult to convince customers of the need to provide certain information." Because customer profiling and reporting would "now be required by regulation, financial institutions will not be prejudiced or criticized for needlessly inquiring into the affairs of their customers" as compared with banks not using Know Your Customer rules.[41] The regulations therefore constituted support for major, mainstream banks over institutions not engaged in typical ABA practices and provided them with an excuse for actions that might be offensive to customers. From the perspective of December 7, when the Federal Register published the proposed regulations, "Know Your Customer" had all the earmarks of favored regulation provided by the

[38] The Money Laundering Deterrence Act of 1998. See http://www.house.gov/banking/hr4005rp.pdf.

[39] *Federal Register* vol. 63, no. 234, part 2 (Washington, D.C.: Government Printing Office), Dec. 7, 1998 (Federal Reserve System, 12 CFR Parts 208, 211, 225; U.S. Department of the Treasury, Office of the Comptroller of the Currency, 12 CFR Part 21; Federal Deposit Insurance Corporation 12 CFR Part 326; Department of the Treasury, Office of Thrift Supervision, 12 CFR Part 563).

[40] *Federal Register*, p. 67516.   [41] Ibid., p. 67517.

federal government in close consultation with the major players in a valued industry.

The banking industry is not associated with a network of watchdog groups, customer organizations, or other lobbies that monitor the industry and its relationship with government officials. Up until December 7, no groups who might potentially oppose the regulations had been active, and there appeared to be virtually no prospects for organized opposition. In the October hearing on the House bill that would have mandated the rules, all witnesses had spoken in favor of the bill, and on the floor the bill had proven entirely uncontroversial, passing under suspension of the rules and a voice vote.[42]

After the Notice of Proposed Rulemaking was published, spotty opposition began to emerge. Representative Ron Paul of Texas, the Libertarian Party's presidential nominee in 1988, along with other members of the House Banking Committee, sent a letter to the FDIC criticizing the proposed rules.[43] The first organized group to become active was the Libertarian Party. According to their national director, Libertarian Party officials had been previously unaware of the development of the rules, which came to their attention only after the publication of the notice and an article in an Internet-based news journal, WorldNetDaily.[44] In early January, the party officials decided to take on the issue by adopting two strategies: a traditional set of press releases and interviews with journalists, and an electronic mail distribution. Their January press releases proved to be among the party's most popular ever. Their press secretary reports that they received a stream of demands for interviews in January, which let the party know that the topic had a great deal of potential public resonance.[45] On February 3, Ron Paul held a press conference to

---

[42] House Committee on Banking and Financial Services, *Full Committee Hearing/ Markup of H.R. 4005, the "Money Laundering Deterrence Act of 1998" and H.R. 1756, the "Money Laundering and Financial Crimes Strategy Act of 1997,"* 105th Cong., 2nd sess., June 11, 1998, http://www.house.gov/banking/61198toc.htm. The bill was considered directly by the full committee without subcommittee hearings or markup. The only recorded dissention was a single view published in the Banking Committee report by privacy advocate Rep. Ron Paul, who objected to the bill on the grounds that "constitutionally there are only three federal crimes . . . treason, piracy on the high seas, and counterfeiting." See the House Committee Report.

[43] Scott Barancik, "Texan Plans to Push Bills to Kill Bank Secrecy Act, Know Your Customer," *American Banker,* Jan. 19, 1999, p. 2.

[44] Steve Dasbach, National Director, Libertarian Party, personal interview by Diane Johnson for the author, May 23, 2000.

[45] George Getz, Press Secretary, Libertarian Party, personal interview by Diane Johnson for the author, May 23, 2000.

announce sunset legislation aimed at killing Know Your Customer, as did Republican Representative Bob Barr.[46] This action in the House signaled that public efforts to oppose Know Your Customer might have found at least limited support inside Congress.

From the perspective of the Libertarian Party, however, directly generating much public attention to the issue was beyond its traditional reach. The party lacked both the funds for a major mass media advertising campaign and a sufficiently large membership to provide much of a direct political threat. Dues-paying members numbered fewer than 40,000, making the Libertarian Party about the size of a modest interest group. However, the party did possess a list of 10,000 electronic mail addresses it had collected through its web site, and it was to these interested citizens that it sent a notice in January. This mailing produced a modest response – strong enough to signal to the party that the issue might be a good one, but too small to influence public officials.

By early February, party officials felt potential public sentiment against Know Your Customer to be large enough possibly to derail the rules, if a sufficiently large number of citizens could be mobilized. On the Hill, opposition was strengthening among Republicans on the House and Senate banking committees, and at the same time the American Civil Liberties Union was preparing opposition.[47] Libertarian officials felt that the electronic mail campaign they had initiated during the prior month held the greatest promise for leveraging citizen involvement beyond the party's own membership if it could be repeated on a larger scale. Libertarians were aware of the Move On effort and explicitly interested in repeating it.[48] The new electronic campaign would be far less expensive than direct mail or broadcast advertising, but would still require paying for web site design and an information system for managing larger volumes of electronic mail.

On February 17, the party launched a web site called DefendYourPrivacy.com that permitted citizens to file their official comments on the proposed rules. It also permitted citizens to send electronic mail to members

---

[46] Paul's bill was H.R. 516 and Barr's H.R. 530.

[47] See House Committee on Banking and Financial Services, "Leach Urges Revision to Proposed Know Your Customer Rules," Press Release, Feb. 4, 1999; House Committee on Banking and Financial Services, Subcommittee on Commercial and Administrative Law, *The "Know Your Customer" Rules: Privacy in the Hands of Federal Regulators: Hearing before the Subcommittee on Commercial and Administrative Law*, 106th Cong., 1st sess., March 4, 1999; U.S. Senate, letter from Senators Phil Gramm and Robert F. Bennett to Alan Greenspan, Feb. 10, 1999.

[48] Dasbach interview.

of Congress after using a zip-code lookup mechanism to identify their representative's name and contact information. Their strategy also involved reducing the visibility of the Libertarian connection, framing the matter as a simple privacy concern of interest to all citizens. The party then sent another message to its 10,000 electronic mail addresses, asking recipients to do two things: visit the web site and pass the message on other citizens. The party explained its strategy as follows: "We're hoping to create a chain letter–type phenomenon . . . we hope to generate tens of thousands of hits on this new web site – and tens of thousands of complaints to the FDIC." The party chose the FDIC from among the four agencies because it would accept public comments electronically.[49]

Almost as much to the party's own surprise as anyone else's, a "chain letter–type phenomenon" is precisely what occurred. Party members filed their comments, then solicited others who repeated the process. In the three weeks between the launching of the web campaign and the closing of the public comment period, the party directly brokered 171,000 messages from citizens to the FDIC, more than four times the size of its own membership and far more than agency officials had ever received.[50] It was a stunning amplification of the strength of the Libertarian Party. Other involved agencies also received loud public messages, but on a far smaller scale. The Office of Thrift Supervision and the Office of the Comptroller of the Currency were not targets of the Libertarian-initiated effort, and they each received but a few thousand comments, according to agency officials.[51] The Federal Reserve, by far the most prominent of the four Know Your Customer agencies, received about 75,000 written comments.[52]

The remarkable public response to the previously obscure banking rules helped Republicans on the two banking committees succeed. By March, there was enough political momentum to kill the rules. At a March 4 hearing of the House Judiciary Subcommittee on Commercial

---

[49] Libertarian Party, "LP Launches New Website to Defeat FDIC's Know Your Customer Proposal: Party's Campaign Picks Up Speed as March 8 Public Comment Deadline Looms," *Libertarian Party News*, online edition, March 1999, http://www.lp.org/lpn/9903-KYC.html.

[50] Source: Libertarian Party records, from personal interviews with Steve Dasbach and George Getz.

[51] Anonymous officials, U.S. Office of Thrift Supervision, personal interviews with Diane Johnson for the author, May 22, 2000; anonymous officials, Office of the Comptroller of the Currency, personal interviews with Diane Johnson for the author, May 26, 2000.

[52] Anonymous official, Federal Reserve, telephone interview with Diane Johnson for the author, May 9, 2000.

and Administrative Law, the American Bankers Association, the ACLU, the Federal Trade Commission, and the Comptroller of the Currency all spoke against the rules, while the FDIC and Office of Thrift Supervision wavered, neither defending the rules nor backing off. The same day, the House Banking Committee passed an amendment with language killing Know Your Customer, and the next day Senator Phil Gramm successfully attached language to an education bill terminating the policy. On March 23, the four banking agencies withdrew Know Your Customer.

Libertarian Party officials claim much credit for the outcome, and their enthusiasm is largely on the mark. It is clear that they played a key role in generating public comments and directing them at FDIC, although the efforts of Republicans in Congress are an important part of the reason why the policy was dropped. In the years since, the party has made smaller efforts of a similar kind, including an effort to oppose the 2000 census and a protest over American military involvement in Kosovo that produced approximately 20,000 comments from citizens to Congress. According to the party's national director, cost has limited repetition of the Know Your Customer campaign.[53] Although far less costly than other techniques, the technology required for such large-scale Internet efforts is still expensive, and the party claims it is building the technological infrastructure needed to engage in such efforts regularly. Party officials also claim to be learning what kinds of issues are most promising for "chain letter" style political efforts. They believe that noncontroversial issues are best, in that citizens who do not necessarily support the solicitation might nonetheless pass it on to others. They also believe that issues with a clear deadline for action are more suitable because citizens are more likely to respond to approaching events, such as votes or public comment periods, than to issues without a time-based imperative. The party is also sensitive to the problem of overloading citizens with calls for action, and so believes that it must approach them sparingly with requests for participation.

The Libertarians' experience with Know Your Customer amounts to a preliminary exploration of new means for organizing collective action. The party has not yet consolidated or regularized the procedures it used, although it is attempting to learn how. The effects of reduced costs were concentrated on the organization's external relationships rather than its internal structure. The new environment for information and communication provided a means to reach beyond its own limited membership and to mobilize citizens who do not and would not identify with

[53] Dasbach interview.

Libertarianism or the party's candidates. The size of the organization's membership and its endowment of material resources mattered less to the outcome than the organization's capacity to choose an issue wisely, target political action appropriately, and time its efforts accurately.

ENVIRONMENTAL ADVOCACY

The environmental lobby in the United States comprises about a dozen interest groups with memberships of 100,000 or more,[54] for a combined total of around 8 million, along with several dozen smaller groups.[55] Their organizational structures vary, although most represent some variation on the classic bureaucratic form. For instance, the Sierra Club, which is the oldest of the groups, operates on a chapter structure, with its main office in San Francisco managing top-priority national issues and a set of chapters spread around the country disseminating information up and down the organization as well as concentrating on local issues. It focuses both on "grassroots" lobbying strategies and "inside" lobbying and legal action. Defenders of Wildlife, on the other hand, is a smaller unitary organization without chapters that has traditionally focused exclusively on inside lobbying and legal action directed at issues chosen by its top leadership. The World Wildlife Fund is similar. Like Defenders, it accepts members, but operates as a unitary organization pursuing traditional lobbying and legal action on national and international issues.

---

[54] Groups with 2001 memberships of at least 100,000: the Center for Marine Conservation, Defenders of Wildlife, Environmental Defense, the Fund for Animals, Greenpeace USA, National Audubon Society, National Parks Conservation Association, National Wildlife Federation, National Resources Defense Council, the Nature Conservancy, Sierra Club, the Wilderness Society, the World Wildlife Fund (USA). Groups with memberships between 10,000 and 100,000: American Rivers; Center for Health, Environment and Justice; Earth Island Institute; Friends of the Earth; League of Conservation Voters; Rainforest Action Network. Source: Foundation for Public Affairs and Congressional Quarterly, Inc., *Public Interest Profiles 2001–2002* (Washington, D.C.: Foundation for Public Affairs, 2001).

[55] This case study is based chiefly on three dozen in-person and telephone interviews, supplemented with an examination of documents and electronic materials. The interviewees include three officials of the World Wildlife Fund, six officials of Environmental Defense, one official of the Sierra Club, one official of the National Resources Defense Council, one official of the Save Our Environment Coalition, two officials of Defenders of Wildlife, and one official of the Turner Foundation, along with fifteen congressional staff. Names and affiliations are revealed in notes below in those cases where informants gave permission. In some cases, informants were interviewed more than once. Most of the research and an initial analysis of the case was prepared by Joe Gardner, doctoral student in the Department of Political Science at UCSB.

Groups like these exhibit as a whole five main organizational characteristics: a tension within groups over devoting attention to national as opposed to subnational policy processes; a tension between groups as to ideological positioning; increasing institutionalization and bureaucratization over time; a history of coordination among organizations; and a strong orientation toward treating information as a political resource. The tension between national versus subnational policy involves organizations' changing calculations about how many resources to devote to policy at the national level as opposed to the state and local levels. This tension is the product of at least two general forces: changing receptivity on the part of national and subnational institutions to environmental groups' agendas and the sometimes internally conflicting logic of membership. During the late 1960s and 1970s, when environmentalism came to the fore in American politics, government institutions at the national level, such as the Environmental Protection Agency (EPA) after its creation during the Nixon administration, were widely judged to be more receptive to new policy. The states, on the other hand, were perceived by most environmental groups to be poor at policy innovation and too beholden to economic interests to respond to demands for environmental protection.[56] Throughout this period, most groups organized themselves as national interest groups oriented toward the federal government, aligning themselves with key members of Congress and committees, as well as the suite of federal agencies involved in environmental issues: the EPA, Interior agencies, the Forest Service, and the Energy and Transportation departments, among others. It also meant that they attracted and mobilized citizen members on the basis of national issues within the jurisdictions of the various federal institutions. Whether or not their assessment of conditions in the states was correct, the wealth of national legislation and regulations produced in the 1960s and 1970s confirmed their judgment that the national arena was productive for them.

Beginning during the Reagan administration, environmental organizations changed their assessments of where new policy could best be made.[57] The hostility of the Reagan White House was coupled with what groups perceived as a decreasing capacity of the national government to innovate. That lack of innovation persisted throughout the 1990s, even

[56] Barry G. Rabe, "Power to the States: The Promise and Pitfalls of Decentralization," in Norman J. Vig and Michael E. Kraft, eds., *Environmental Policy in the 1990s*, 3rd ed. (Washington, D.C.: CQ Press, 1997), pp. 31–52.

[57] See Barry Rabe, "Power to the States," on the "decentralization" of environmental policy.

with more congenial occupants in the White House. Many organizations felt frustrated by the national policy process because their capacity to oppose antienvironmental policy was not matched by an equal capacity to obtain new proenvironment policy.[58] At the same time, some groups found that new state-level institutions – some adapted from the federal level – were increasingly responsive and well situated to make environmental policy. The result was what Barry Rabe calls a "decentralization mantra" among some organizations during the 1990s to reorganize and attend to policy at the state, rather than national, level.

The other contributor to evolving tension within environmental groups over whether to align themselves nationally or subnationally has been a membership issue. The groups originally most successful in attracting large memberships were organizations with a national focus and wide name recognition. Yet by the 1990s, many of these organizations found that citizens were animated and motivated most by local or regional environmental issues with which they could identify closely. Also, with national institutions in the hands of Democrats by the mid-1990s and the threats of the Reagan years gone, many groups found it hard to sustain national membership growth. The rapid membership expansions of the 1970s and 1980s for most national groups leveled off by the 1990s.[59] Some groups stagnated, while some actually lost substantial numbers of members between 1990 and 1995, including the Sierra Club (down 60,000 members), the National Audubon Society (down 30,000), and the Wilderness Society (down 40,000).[60] By one estimate, total membership in the ten largest groups declined 6 percent in just three years, from 1990 to 1993.[61] Operating budgets of some groups also shrank commensurately.

The ideological tension among groups is somewhat different but equally important organizationally. A small conservative cluster of environmental organizations, including the so-called Wise-Use groups, has long existed, but for the most part the tension is between moderate, mainstream groups, such as the Audubon Society, and more aggressive and sometimes extreme groups, such as Greenpeace and Earth First,

---

[58] Christopher J. Bosso, "Seizing Back the Day: The Challenge to Environmental Activism in the 1990s," in Vig and Kraft, eds., *Environmental Policy in the 1990s*, pp. 53–74.

[59] Robert D. Putnam, *Bowling Alone: The Collapse and Revival of American Community* (New York: Simon and Schuster, 2000).

[60] Membership figures from Bosso, "Seizing Back the Day."

[61] Ronald G. Shaiko, *Voices and Echoes for the Environment: Public Interest Representation in the 1990s and Beyond* (New York: Columbia University Press, 1999).

which espouse "deep ecology," "radical environmentalism," and the like. Moderate and extreme groups differed on advocacy strategy, with the more extreme groups less inclined to engage in traditional lobbying because it so often entailed negotiation and what they saw as policy compromises. On occasion, environmental groups differed visibly over national policy, as in the case of the North American Free Trade Agreement, which was supported by the Environmental Defense Fund and opposed by Greenpeace.

Some groups, especially the Sierra Club, experienced a good deal of internal tension in the 1990s over their direction and ideological positioning. This tension reflects developments associated with the third characteristic of environmental organizations: increasing bureaucratization.[62] Most environmental organizations grew increasingly well institutionalized and professionalized by the late 1980s and 1990s. Changes occurred in organizational leadership, as management of many groups evolved from charismatic activists to more politically experienced, professional managers. Budgets grew, the number of permanent staff expanded, and larger-scale management techniques came into play. Political experts became more important to many groups, and increasingly slick techniques for mass mailing and marketing became common. In many groups, the classic features of institutionalization became apparent, and organizational preservation became increasingly important, alongside policy advocacy. This bureaucratization phenomenon has been shown in other interest groups in roughly the same period.[63] Within the environmental organizations, these developments were not seen as universally good, despite the apparently increased political capacity of the groups. Some members accused the mainstream groups of losing the energy and zeal of the 1970s as they grew more bureaucratic, risk-averse, and "mainstream."[64]

The fourth organizational characteristic of these groups is an impetus toward coordination and cooperation. This tradition extends back as far as 1946, when the Natural Resources Defense Council of America was formed by environmental and conservation organizations. Over the years, coalitions of environmental groups have taken on many forms, from information-sharing and technical working groups to strategic councils designed to coordinate lobbying activities by the organizations'

[62] See Bosso, "Seizing Back the Day," for more on this topic.
[63] Shaiko, *Voices and Echoes for the Environment.*
[64] On this issue, see Walter A. Rosenbaum, *Environmental Politics and Policy,* 3rd ed. (Washington, D.C.: CQ Press, 1995).

representatives.[65] By the 1990s, coalition building had become, along with "grassroots" mobilization efforts, one of the chief strategies of environmental organizations seeking to influence policy.[66] An increasing tendency over time to work in coalitions is by no means limited to environmental organizations, but has also been reported generally among interest groups.[67]

The fifth characteristic, an orientation toward information as a political resource, is intriguing and perhaps stronger among environmental groups than any other category of interest organization. As Samuel Hays has shown, from their origins most environmental groups have operated on an implicit premise that information must be assembled and distributed if the goals of environmental advocacy are to be achieved.[68] This premise is a foundation of many of their activities. It is manifest in public education campaigns, when groups attempt to inform the public about previously unacknowledged relationships, such as between fossil fuel use and global warming, electricity production and acid rain, or between pesticides such as DDT and a variety of complex effects throughout the ecosystem. It is manifest in organizations' efforts to monitor corporations and industrial activities for pollution, release of toxins, or compliance with rules. It is manifest further in the reports and studies the organizations produce, and in their publicizing of voting records and positions of public officials.

Hays calls this implicit and widespread orientation toward the flow of information an "environmental knowledge culture."[69] It is a consequence of the revelatory history of environmentalism even prior to the 1950s, involving the discovery and making public of information that activities generally presumed harmless by the public, such as spraying of DDT, were in fact damaging to the environment. A fundamental theme of environmental politics since has been revelations of this kind, in which new information is disclosed to the public about atmospheric warming, acid rain resulting from electricity generation hundreds of miles away,

---

[65] See Jacqueline Vaughn Switzer, *Environmental Politics: Domestic and Global Dimensions* (New York: St. Martins, 1994).

[66] Shaiko, *Voices and Echoes for the Environment.*

[67] Kevin Hula, *Lobbying Together: Interest Group Coalitions in Legislative Politics* (Washington, D.C.: Georgetown University Press, 1999); Kay Lehman Schlozman and John T. Tierney, *Organized Interests and American Democracy* (New York: Harper and Row, 1986).

[68] Samuel P. Hays, *A History of Environmental Politics since 1945* (Pittsburgh: University of Pittsburgh Press, 2000).

[69] Hays, *A History of Environmental Politics since 1945*, p. 101.

deforestation, the precarious existence of a species once unknown or previously abundant, and so on. Throughout the environmental movement, the premise that improved flows of information are central to good public policy is widespread.

Several of these five characteristics have made environmental groups particularly responsive to the changing information environment produced by new technology. Environmental Defense is a classic example of a traditional interest group, and its strategic and structural changes since 1999 exemplify organizational transformation in the contemporary information revolution. The Environmental Defense Fund (EDF), as it was then called, was founded in 1967 out of a scientific and legal effort to ban DDT. The formation of EDF was something of a milestone in the history of environmental politics in the United States because it was the first group dedicated exclusively to using litigation as a political strategy. When it was created, existing environmental groups such as the Audubon Society, the Wilderness Society, and the National Wildlife Federation were structured as membership lobbies and conservation organizations, using member fees to fund traditional lobbying or conservation activities. EDF supported a new strategy – the citizen lawsuit – and it led the way in expanding that strategy into a standard element of contemporary environmental politics. In this sense, EDF's position was somewhat analogous to the NAACP's in its decisions at the turn of the century to fight segregation using the courts, rather than Congress or the state legislatures. Although EDF did not rise to become as dominant in its policy area as did the NAACP, and although arguably no environmental decision was as significant as the NAACP's *Brown*, EDF's pioneering of a legal strategy toward public policy is akin to what the NAACP brought to the civil rights movement.

EDF called its main strategy "science and the law," and it took on issues as diverse as the listing of whales as endangered species and the adoption of unleaded gasoline. It continues to work toward the negotiation of voluntary policies by businesses and landowners, such as McDonald's abandonment of styrofoam food containers, and it occasionally works with other groups on traditional legislative lobbying. In 1998, EDF had a staff of 170, with a strong roster of scientists, engineers, and lawyers. It reported about 300,000 members, who provided about half of its operating budget of $24 million.[70] EDF was therefore not a "grassroots"

[70] Environmental Defense Fund, *Annual Report*, 1998, http://www.ed.org/pubs/AnnualReport/1998/AR1998.pdf.

organization, and had little skill or expertise in mobilizing citizens – so much so that one scholar observed in a study published in 1999 that since its beginning when "EDF had no real social network through which to build constituency support," the organization has viewed its supporters as donors rather than true members.[71]

In 1999, officials at EDF undertook a major change in strategy in an effort to exploit new possibilities for communication and information management made possible by the Internet. EDF leadership decided to "reorient all strategies to include an Internet component."[72] It dropped the word "Fund" from its name, and adopted a new logo, with a lowercase "e," which evokes the electronic "e" in e-mail and e-commerce, as well as the environment. On its web site, the executive director of the new ED proclaimed, "[W]e want to use the power of the Internet to take environmental activism to the next level."[73] ED would continue as a "science and the law" group, but would now become a grassroots lobbying firm using twenty to twenty-five full- and part-time staff.

The functional centerpiece of the new ED was data base–driven web sites aimed at attracting citizens, collecting information about their environmental interests, and then mobilizing them through calls for political action. The concept behind the change was a traditional one, even though the consequences would be dramatic and new. ED officials believed that a wealth of information existed about neighborhood pollution that could be of political value, if only it could be delivered to the right citizens. They understood collective action in Tocquevillian terms. Citizens have interests in the environment, they knew, but these tended to be highly particularistic. The key to mobilizing these citizens was delivering highly specific information to them about their particular concerns – not broad, information-poor calls to collective action in order "to protect the environment," but narrow, information-rich messages linking local events and issues with citizens' individual interests. The Internet, ED felt, seemed to promise new opportunities for that kind of information-intensive politics.

The change in strategy came at a time of challenge to ED and many other environmental organizations. The stagnation in environmental membership of the mid- to late 1990s had hit ED comparatively hard. After a period of expansion when membership had grown from about

---

[71] Shaiko, *Voices and Echoes for the Environment*, p. 81.
[72] Anonymous official, Environmental Defense, telephone interview by Joe Gardner for the author, April 18, 2000.
[73] "Environmental Defense, Director's Message," May 2000, http://www.ed.org.

60,000 in 1987 to 300,000 in 1995 – about 400 percent in eight years – membership was now actually falling.[74] Although it continued to report membership at 300,000 publicly, by 2001 the actual figure was 200,000, down a third in half a decade. In addition, the organization's overall intensity and richness of communication with those members was on the decline. As was true of many other major environmental groups, by the mid-1990s, ED was sending newsletters to its membership less frequently than it had in earlier years. The number of issues covered in each newsletter had also declined over time, from about fifty on average in the late 1970s to about thirty in the 1990s.[75] The median length of membership was three years, and about 18 percent of its members had belonged for less than one year.[76]

The only bright spot for ED in the resource arena was funding. Through growth in grants and nonmember-related funding sources, the late 1990s were a period of increasing financial resources that more than offset slipping membership revenue. Between 1995 and 2000, funding expanded from about $25 million to nearly $40 million. ED's success at attracting institutional support helped distinguish it among environmental groups in the 1990s. In 1996, ED spent about $27 for every $100 raised in donations and gifts, a figure substantially less than those of Greenpeace, the Sierra Club, the Audubon Society, and Defenders of Wildlife.[77] So ED had plenty of funds, all things considered, but an ailing membership to which it was less connected than in the past.

The change of strategy to embrace new technology represented a way to invest financial resources in a new approach to communication with citizens beyond its bounded set of dues-paying members. It targeted a variety of issues in its new web-based system: clean air, pesticides, national forest protection, and other issues. In a comparatively short time, the organization found that its efforts were attracting large numbers of citizens. These were not traditional donor-members, but what one official calls "a second type of membership."[78] These citizens visited the web site, expressed interest in some particular issue, and frequently left contact information. By 2001, ED had compiled a list of 120,000 interested citizens seeking information and communication from the organization.

---

[74] Source: Environmental Defense (Fund) Annual Reports, 1974 through 2000.
[75] Shaiko, *Voices and Echoes for the Environment*, p. 112.   [76] Ibid., p. 157.
[77] Only a few major groups had comparable or lower costs of funds. Source: AIP Charity Rating Guide, reported in ibid.
[78] Bill Pease, Environmental Defense, personal interview with Joe Gardner for the author, May 13, 2000, New York, New York.

This "second type of membership" did not pay dues, and did not consider itself attached to the organization in the way that traditional members did. But they were sufficiently interested to seek opportunities for political learning and engagement; they were a new resource to be exploited by the organization.

Other environmental organizations were making similar discoveries at the same time. Defenders of Wildlife designated the Internet a "high priority" by 2000, and one official reports that "every part of the organization is involved" in its Internet-based information system. Like ED, grassroots lobbying had also not been an important part of Defenders' strategy until the technological revolution of the late 1990s. The same was true of the World Wildlife Fund, which had little experience in grassroots political action prior to taking on Internet-based communication.

By 2001, ED, Defenders, and World Wildlife Fund were each operating with two distinct classes of membership. They used various terms for the new class, calling them "activists" or "in-kind members." These citizens would find a group's web site and express an interest in some particular issue the organization was working on, but would limit their association to that. In many cases, these loosely affiliated citizens are politically centrist and did not identify themselves even as environmentalists, let alone as formal members of the organization.[79] Instead of the kind of support for an environmental agenda that characterizes traditional members, these affiliates were often defined by a single concern. Because of their moderate political orientation and unwillingness to become involved in a sustained way, the potential pool of affiliated citizens are sometimes called "lite-greens."

An official of the World Wildlife Fund claims that his organization thinks of traditional members and the new class of affiliates as equals, even though the latter do not pay dues.[80] The fact that the affiliates can be mobilized in service of one of the fund's goals gives them their political standing. Defenders of Wildlife has made a strategic decision

---

[79] This thin form of membership is not entirely novel, especially at Environmental Defense. A large number of traditional "members" of the Environmental Defense Fund understood themselves chiefly to be donors, rather than formal members of a group or organization. See Putnam, *Bowling Alone*. The new form of membership is intriguing because it expands the size of the membership, removing the one historically important connection, namely, donations, but at the same time introducing more possibilities for actual political participation through the organization's mobilization efforts.

[80] Anonymous official, World Wildlife Fund, personal interview by Joe Gardner for the author, May 22, 2000, Washington, D.C.

to solicit these affiliates heavily, even though their attachments to the group are very weak. Referring to the organization's initial communication strategy using new information technology, one Defenders official says, "[W]e made a decision at the beginning not just to go after our membership."[81]

By 2001, ED had developed strategies aimed exclusively at recruiting the kind of lite-greens that it had discovered were visiting its original web site. The group hired advertising firms to develop and place online banner ads aimed at citizens sympathetic to an environmental issue but not otherwise self-identified as environmentalists. It also developed a dedicated lite-green web site in cooperation with the National Wildlife Fund, and directed citizens responding to its banner advertisements to the site.[82] ED now had multiple faces. To the dedicated traditional environmentalist, it was a committed, liberal defender of the environment working on a range of issues to improve the condition of the air, land, and water. To lite-green citizens, it was a friendly, nonstrident group who cared about whatever particular issue they cared about.

The economics of this redefined membership have yet to fully develop, but ED and Defenders of Wildlife approached affiliates in the following way. Compared with a traditional member, an affiliate offers less sustained value to the organization. An affiliate provides no material resources to the organization, and may respond only once or twice to appeals for action. In this sense, their political attachments are thin. On the other hand, affiliates are inexpensive to identify and contact, and represent a potentially very large pool of recruits. An official at Defenders reports that his group is not concerned that citizens may have provided the group with their electronic mail address only because they saw a picture of a cute animal at a commercial web site. His group is satisfied if a lite-green affiliate participates in only a single mobilization effort and then disappears. The group drops from its list any affiliate who has not responded to at least three calls for action in twelve months, so the list is constantly churning. The organization's approach is quite the opposite of attempting to extract extra yearly commitments from its dues-paying members on an annual basis. ED still makes little effort to mobilize its traditional dues-paying members into grassroots action; it reserves that class of politics for its affiliates. One organization official says, "The Internet

---

[81] Anonymous official, Defenders of Wildlife, telephone interview by Joe Gardner for the author, Feb. 28, 2000.
[82] The site is http://www.formyworld.com.

allows you to get at a centrist audience. That's where we're doing something different. We're hoping to cultivate people to act."[83]

ED and other organizations employ highly developed practices of selective mobilization for working with the new class of members. One element of information-intensive selective mobilization involves their profiling citizen interests. Web sites permit the groups to collect and update very readily records about quite specific environmental concerns, such as protecting dolphins in the Pacific, saving Caribbean turtles, or banning logging in the Cascades. Using these records, the organizations are able to target appeals for political action to just those individuals with particular interest in the issue at hand. This increases responsiveness and reduces appeal fatigue on the part of citizens, since turtle supporters do not receive messages about saving wolves, and for that matter neither do people interested in Minnesota wolves receive messages about an action that would affect Arizona wolves. ED also uses the zip codes it collects to target citizens whose representative or senator is a key player on a particular issue.

This is information abundance at its fullest: exploiting an information-rich environment to connect small groups of targeted citizens with specific officials in government who represent them and who play a role in a key decision. Other groups do the same. Defenders of Wildlife, for instance, reports that it *never* targets all members of Congress or even all members of a key committee when it mobilizes affiliates.[84] Instead, it targets only swing votes, which typically means something like ten senators and forty representatives. Unlike traditional, information-poor mass mail campaigns exhorting an entire membership to "write your congressman," this kind of information-intensive mobilization means that different members of the same group may receive dramatically different numbers of calls for action over the course of a year, aimed at different issues and different decision makers. It also means that the number of affiliates the groups attempt to mobilize varies dramatically across issues, from only a few hundred to thousands, and that in any one week or month, a particular environmental organization may constitute in effect many different environmental groups.

Response rates to this kind of action can be comparatively high. Defenders of Wildlife reports that its average response rate to calls for action is about 5 percent. Environmental Defense claims that as of mid-2000, it was averaging between 7 percent and 13 percent, with occasional peaks

---

[83] Defenders of Wildlife interview.   [84] Ibid.

as high as 20 percent on some issues. It set an internal record in March 2001, when about 60 percent of the select group of 8,000 Internet "members" it contacted responded to a call to express objections to the White House over a Bush decision not to implement new carbon dioxide emission standards. The group achieved this rate by exploiting what it knew about its affiliates, selecting only people who had expressed an interest in clean air and who had responded at least once before to a call for action.[85]

Not all groups pursued such strategies. World Wildlife Fund (WWF) eschews the lite-green approach in favor of working strictly with dedicated, self-identifying environmentalists. The fund also gathers information and operates a second level of affiliate members through the Internet, but it seeks to filter out citizens without a broad and dedicated commitment to the environment. As a result, WWF's affiliates behave more like traditional members, but they do not pay dues. As of spring 2001, WWF had a growing body of about 30,000 on-line activists, up 100 percent over the previous nine months. As a result of its selectivity, its average response rate on mobilization efforts among affiliates is 25 percent and sometimes reaches 30 percent.[86]

Because of these developments, it is no longer particularly helpful to compare environmental organizations as to membership size. The groups I studied had a difficult time answering questions about how many total members they had. The groups could report the number of traditional members, although they are sometimes reluctant to do so. But counting affiliates was another matter. Turnover is so high that overall numbers change very rapidly from month to month. Defenders of Wildlife reported 381,000 traditional members in May of 2000, and somewhere between 200,000 and 260,000 affiliates or "activists," as it calls them. When we spoke with them in mid-2001, a year after our initial interviews, ED had about 130,000 affiliates and claimed it would increase the figure to 1 million by the end of the year through sharing lists with other groups. More to the point, the effective number of members that any one group has under this new approach is a function of the issue at hand. On the same day, ED may have 5,000 effective affiliates on one issue, 1,000 on another, and 500 on a third.

[85] Ben Smith, Environmental Defense, telephone interview by Joe Gardner for the author, May 9, 2001.
[86] Anonymous officials, World Wildlife Fund, personal interview by Joe Gardner for the author, May 22, 2000, Washington, D.C., and telephone interview, April 26, 2000.

The new approach has proven especially useful for pursuit of public policy at the state and local level. An official at ED reported that since adopting its new strategy, the organization has found itself focusing its interactions increasingly on local issues, because those are most successful for the new mode of communication and mobilization. The group did not, however, set out to use the network that way. Referring to affiliates, he said, "The closer to home, the better. Ninety percent of action [requests] have to be in members' backyard" if they are to be successful. He said that "big national issues become background noise," because citizens who sign up with the group have specific interests that connect to their own life situations, and because many tend to believe that national issues are insurmountable.[87] An unintended consequence of the information-rich approach to membership and collective action has been this pull toward the local and a need for the organization to think like a network of local or regional organizations rather than a centrally managed, unitary structure. At Defenders of Wildlife, the combination of localism and selective mobilization has also created an opportunity for the organization to function as if it were a federation of local or regional units or as if it operated subnational chapters, neither of which was the case historically. By obtaining specific interests about citizen concerns in an inexpensive way and then targeting calls for action, this monolithic national organization can operate as if it were a network of more regionally focused organizations, each specializing in particular issues. Defenders believes that much of the value of sophisticated information systems is the flexibility it gives the organization to configure and reconfigure rapidly the subsets of its body of affiliated citizens.

In some cases, environmental organizations find that the difference between national and local issues is simply one of framing. In other cases, local or regional issues really are just that. ED mobilized about 100 local affiliates in 2000 to contact the New England Fishery Management Council regarding cod fishing in the Gulf of Maine. Because of public and scientific concern about the fate of the fishery, the council adopted a series of fishing restrictions aimed at reducing the cod harvest by 80 percent. Around the same time, the organization mobilized several thousand affiliates to contact the U.S. Secretary of Commerce and members of Congress from the Northeast asking for stronger protections for another species, the spiny dogfish.

---

[87] Azar Moulaert, Environmental Defense, personal interview by Joe Gardner for the author, May 13, 2000, New York, New York.

This kind of local focus also couples with the capacity to easily target citizen action at specific decision makers. Officials of the World Wildlife Fund believe that the selective mobilization of affiliates is most likely to succeed when there are few decision makers involved. The fund prefers to direct the energies of its affiliates toward individuals in the Forest Service, EPA, or international policy-making bodies. This means that fighting large-scale policy battles in Congress is a much less promising strategy for it than targeting specific agency actions or persuading regional or local policy bodies to act. One of ED's most successful efforts involved a response in early 2001 to an announcement by EPA Director Christine Todd Whitman that her agency was considering relaxing standards for diesel emissions. ED officials distributed a call for action the same day, and claim to have generated 12,000 faxes and electronic mail messages to Whitman in two days.[88] Along with the responses of many other organizations, this effort appears to have contributed to EPA's backing away from the proposal. Neither ED nor the other groups examined in this study have experienced a comparable level of effectiveness with Congress, lending support to WWF's assumption.[89]

One of the most interesting changes precipitated by these new approaches to communication and managing information about citizen interests is ongoing coordination efforts between ED and other environmental groups. Coalition formation among interest groups is generally a highly information-centric practice. Research by Kevin Hula has shown that receiving information from coalition partners is an important incentive for interest groups who are considering working with others. At the same time, groups in coalitions require an intensive flow of information in order to act in concert with one another.[90] Across interest groups of all kinds, therefore, lowered costs of information and communication make coalition-brokering tasks easier and less costly and provide potentially enhanced benefits from group participation in coalitions.

The new information and communication systems being employed by the environmental groups are having effects consistent with this

[88] Ben Smith, Environmental Defense, telephone interview with Joe Gardner for the author, May 9, 2001.

[89] Interviews with congressional staff confirm this fact. For example, one staffer of the Senate Environment and Public Works Committee reports that electronic mail advocacy directed at the committee is minimal, and that when electronic mail campaigns do hit Congress, they are almost always directed at individual members rather than the committees working on the bills. Duane Nystrom, Senate Environment and Public Works Committee, telephone interview by Joe Gardner for the author, April 27, 2000.

[90] Hula, *Lobbying Together*.

expectation, making it easier for groups to coordinate with one another and pool information. According to one ED official, his organization has "dramatically ramped up the amount of cooperation and coordination with other groups" because of its move onto the web and use of Internet-based communication.[91] The organization's start with this cooperation dates to its decision to permit a large group of mainly local and regional environmental organizations to use its information and communication system. Called the "Action Network," this system is a sophisticated software system for managing communication with interested citizens. Internally, ED used the Action Network to manage its new class of "activist" members. Beginning in 2000, ED shared the system at no charge with other environmental groups, establishing a broad and heterogeneous network of groups using similar strategies, from the New Jersey Chapter of the Sierra Club to American Lung Association of Texas. Many of those groups were themselves regional networks or collections of groups who could coordinate regionally, but otherwise faced large obstacles to broader collective action. These included at various points the Chesapeake Bay Action Network, the Wyoming Action Network, and the San Francisco Bay Area Transportation and Land Use Coalition. Through the Action Network mechanism, ED had spread the new approach to mobilization across a wide, loose, and shifting alliance of groups. The results were new opportunities for cross-group mobilization efforts as well as more traditional coordination of lobbying activities. Later in 2000, ED capitalized on the success of its Action Network tools by spinning off a for-profit business, Locus Pocus, with the software as its core product. In the assessment of an official of the World Wildlife Fund, the Internet generally has "increased dramatically" the extent of cooperation among environmental groups.[92]

ED took this flexible approach to membership sharing and coalition-formation process substantially further, by extending the effort across major national groups as well. In September of 1999, ED and fifteen other national environmental organizations announced the formation of yet another coalition called the "Save Our Environment Coalition." This effort at partnering included a number of major groups including the Sierra Club, Defenders of Wildlife, the Audubon Society, and World

---

[91] Smith, telephone interview.
[92] Deb Prybyla, World Wildlife Fund, telephone interview with Joe Gardner for the author, March 12, 2001.

Wildlife Fund.[93] The coalition was intended to reduce competition and boost coordination among the main players in national environmental politics. According to a staff person involved from the National Resources Defense Counsel, the chief purpose of the coalition is to "coordinate and collaborate appeals for action" by drawing on an enormous, pooled list of activists.[94] ED gave members of the coalition its Action Network technology for that purpose. The project's web site advertises itself as "a collaborative effort of the nation's most influential environmental advocacy organizations harnessing the power of the Internet to increase public awareness and activism on today's most important issues."[95] The policy aims of the network, according to an ED official, are national in scope. The network is intended as a way to amplify the efforts of the national groups in working with Congress and federal agencies.

As a novel organizational structure, the Save Our Environment Coalition is difficult to characterize in traditional terms. Technically, it is a metaorganization of about twenty national environmental groups. In 2000, the group claimed to have 3.5 million traditional members in its promotional material; however, it is impossible to characterize the actual size of the organization in traditional and affiliated members, since its configuration differs from issue to issue and because no central membership list exists. As of May 2001, it employed just one full-time paid staff person, who functioned as director. It otherwise has no job classifications or titles. It is guided by a board of directors comprised of the top officer of each member group. In this flexible, issue-driven organization, a lead staff person from a member group is identified for each issue, and that lead person manages the coalition's activities for that single issue. With funding from the Turner Foundation, the coalition exists to provide services and coordination to its member groups, all of which have equal status in the coalition, regardless of size. One of its central functions, according to its director, is assessing political engagement patterns, tracking how citizens respond to calls for action by the various member groups,

---

[93] The complete list of organizations is: American Rivers, the Center for Marine Conservation, Defenders of Wildlife, Earthjustice Legal Defense Fund, Environmental Defense, the Izaak Walton League, the League of Conservation Voters, the National Audubon Society, the National Resources Defense Council, the National Parks Conservation Association, the Sierra Club, the Wilderness Society, the State PIRGs, the Union of Concerned Scientists, and the World Wildlife Fund.

[94] Lisa Catapano, Director of Citizen Advocacy, National Resources Defense Council, telephone interview by Joe Gardner, April 11, 2001.

[95] Save Our Environment Coalition, "Who We Are," Save Our Environment Action Center, Feb. 15, 2000, http://www.saveourenvironment.org/about.

and returning this information to the groups. In 2001, it worked with the League of Conservation Voters to sift through voting records state by state to identify lists of which citizens voted. It then matched these lists with its own records of coalition "members" to identify which members were actually most politically engaged. This information-intensive exercise helped the coalition fine-tune its records about which "members" are the most promising targets of requests for action.[96] Especially where membership is concerned, the coalition serves to undermine the distinction between groups while also claiming to strengthen each group individually. In its internal mission statement, the coalition claims that "[b]y uniting their members and contributors on coordinated actions, the participating groups are creating a sum of citizen participation and advocacy greater than they could generate acting apart. The project is also serving to strengthen each group by providing information that can deepen its understanding and relationship with its own base of support."[97]

The organization of these groups is made even more Byzantine by the existence of another shadow group behind the coalition called "The Green Group." This network consists of another informal coalition of about thirty environmental groups. Membership in the Save Our Environment Coalition also confers membership in the Green Group, which engages in efforts to set priorities and goals for the environmental movement as a whole.

What all this means for a group like ED is that it is embedded in a dense and flexible network of organizations that attempt to coordinate and cooperate with one another in pursuit of public policy. The boundaries between these organizations and their memberships are often blurred, and the political resources ED and its allies can draw upon in policy making are a function of the particular issue and event at hand. To be sure, ED and other organizations still maintain formalized memberships and organizational structures, and they engage in traditional planning, priority setting, and resource allocation; however, on the ground, as ED actually engages in politics, these traditional bureaucratic structures mean less than ever for the ways that it operates. Within just two years of its decision to reorient itself to exploit new information technology, ED's Internet-based political action was

---

[96] Julie Waterman, Campaign Director, Save Our Environment Coalition, telephone interview by Joe Gardner, May 2, 2001.

[97] Save Our Environment Coalition, "Mission Statement of the Save Our Environment Coalition," n.d. (provided by Julie Waterman, Campaign Director, May 2, 2001).

"completely integrated" with all other techniques, in the words of one official.[98] The group still engaged in more traditional lobbying and "science and the law" activities, but these were now part of a very different political organization, one connected to an expanded but new kind of membership and engaged in new types of political organizing in concert with a loose network of other organizations. The language used by the ED official to describe how new technology affects his group reveals its transformative character. He says that the Internet is "not just a lobbying tool"; it affects the organization more deeply by altering its basic relationships.[99]

EDUCATION POLICY

The Telecommunications Act of 1996 constituted the first comprehensive overhaul of U.S. telecommunication policy since 1934, when the Communications Act originally established a regulatory framework for broadcast media.[100] As a result of dramatic technological and economic innovations since the days of radio, policy change on a large order was long overdue by the 1990s. Virtually every political actor with an interest in telecommunications sought some form of new regulatory framework. When the law passed in 1996, its provisions spanned telephone service, cable and other video services, broadcast, and telecommunications services in schools. The act qualified as one of the most complex policy packages of the 1990s, crafted as an omnibus bill balanced on a great variety of compromises. Its primary aim was to promote freer competition and remove outmoded barriers to technological innovation. In the official language of the law, it was "an act to promote competition and reduce regulation in order to secure lower prices and higher quality services for American telecommunications consumers and encourage the rapid deployment of new telecommunications technologies."[101]

In addition to providing for deregulation that would soon change telecommunications, Congress also established in the 1996 law a set of

---

[98] Smith, telephone interview.   [99] Ibid.

[100] This case is based chiefly on an examination of public records and twelve interviews. Interviews included staff of the American Association of School Administrators, the National School Boards Association, the National Association of Independent Schools, the Juno Advocacy Coalition, EdLiNC, the Federal Communications Commission, the American Library Association, the Universal Service Administrative Company, and the National Education Association. Most of the research and an initial analysis were conducted by Eric Patterson, doctoral student in the Political Science department at UCSB.

[101] Telecommunications Act of 1996, Pub. LA. No. 104-104, 110 Stat. 56 (1996).

"universal service principles." These principles called for a set of quality and affordability standards, expanded access to telecommunications in rural and high-cost areas, and subsidies for low-income consumers. Among the universal service provisions was a mandate that "elementary and secondary schools and classrooms, health care providers, and libraries should have access to advanced telecommunications services." This mandate was the result of efforts of a large number of education and library organizations, led by the National Education Association (NEA). It was inserted into the bill as the "SREK amendment," sponsored by Senators Olympia Snow, John Rockefeller, James Exon, and John Kerrey.[102]

The amendment stipulated that "all telecommunications carriers serving a geographic area shall, upon a bona fide request for any of its services that are within the definition of universal service . . . provide such services to elementary schools, secondary schools, and libraries for educational purposes at rates less than the amounts charged for similar services to other parties." The act authorized the Federal Communications Commission (FCC) to administer this provision, including setting the amount of the SREK discounts. The FCC issued its order implementing the lowered rates in May 1997, setting 20 percent to 90 percent discounts on telecommunications services to schools and libraries, depending on their financial circumstances. The commission provided for expenditures of federal funds up to $2.25 billion per year to subsidize part of the discounts by private telecommunications service providers.[103] The discounts and subsidy came to be known as the "E-Rate" program, named for the new educational rate that firms were directed to provide. Schools and libraries were invited to apply for discounts and federal subsidies for high-speed telecommunication lines, internal wiring, and infrastructure.

As an education provision in a telecommunications bill, E-Rate might seem out of place. It was, however, consistent with the typically oblique angle of federal education policy. Because the locus of U.S. education funding and policy making is the states and localities, federal policy has been for the most part supplemental and focused on the pursuit of particular national social goals, in particular, equality. Prior to the 1960s, the federal government played little role in education outside of

---

[102] Daniel Bennett and Pam Fielding, *The Net Effect: How Cyberadvocacy is Changing the Political Landscape* (Merrifield, Va.: E-Advocates Press, 1997).

[103] Federal Communications Commission, "Report and Order in the Matter of Federal-State Joint Board on Universal Service," FCC 97–157 CC Docket No. 96-45, May 7, 1997, http://www.fcc.gov/ccb/universal_service/fcc97157/97157pdf.html.

making land grants for universities and some public schools and providing supplemental grants to schools for operating costs.[104] The Elementary and Secondary Education Act of 1964, along with its amendments and reauthorizations, was the backbone of new federal education legislation. Its emphasis on assisting low-achieving children, supporting bilingual education, and funding educational technology is a reflection of its origins in the civil rights and social movements of the early 1960s.

It is revealing that at the federal level, the courts have been as important as Congress in establishing education policy, through decisions dealing with desegregation, school prayer, and equal access. The fact that the arguably most popular and successful federal education program, Head Start, is operated through the Department of Health and Human Services rather than the Education Department, is symbolic of the character of federal policy. Although the 1980s and 1990s witnessed a national dialogue about education and calls for national education standards under Presidents George H. W. Bush and Bill Clinton, for the most part the federal government's role in education is still channeled through equality and social welfare issues. As an effort to subsidize educational technology for disadvantaged schools and others through the FCC, E-Rate is generally consistent with this orientation in national education policy.

Another feature of E-Rate is also typical of education policy making in the United States: fragmentation among constituency groups and between constituency group leaders and members. Several major groups involve themselves in education policy making, most visibly the NEA and the American Federation of Teachers (AFT), but also the Parent Teachers Association (PTA), League of Women Voters, the NAACP, and others. In part because of the structure of education policy making, many organizations – especially the teachers' unions – sometimes operate as federations of state groups rather than unitary national organizations. The largest of the NEA's state organizations, the California Teachers Association (CTA), does not even directly bear the national group's name. On some issues, NEA and CTA operate quasiindependently; on others they act as a single organization. This makes educational organizations particularly effective at influencing state policies, but somewhat less so at coordinating policy advocacy across states. It also situates the unions to be particularly effective in electoral politics because they

---

[104] Sidney W. Tiedt, *The Role of the Federal Government in Education* (New York: Oxford University Press, 1966).

combine large memberships with national, state, and local organizational structures.

Unlike environmental organizations, which are typically tightly connected to policy preferences of members, the leaderships of educational organizations sometimes operate quite independently of member views. The lobbying activities of education groups, especially at the national level, typically represent elite actions in pursuit of goals and strategies set by group leaders who are comparatively insulated from the political activities of many members. In some cases, this means groups pursue policy that is actually at odds with member views. The leadership of the NAACP, for instance, strongly opposes school vouchers, despite the fact that polls typically show African-Americans favoring them.[105]

In addition to the major national organizations, education constituencies also include conservative and liberal groups that either advocate for particular education policies or include positions on education issues in their overall policy statements. The education issues include vouchers, tax credits, private schools, charter schools, testing and standards, bilingual education, and national education goals. By one count in the late 1990s, forty-five interest groups had taken official positions opposing private school tuition tax credits alone.[106] These diverse interest groups often align themselves with the political parties and institutional players such as school administrators and state education officials. The result is a complex and chaotic mix of organizations and interests that do not always fall neatly into opposing camps. Ideological fault lines generally divide those who seek a reduced federal role from those who support a stronger federal role in education; but from issue to issue, education policy does not have the organizational polarization of other issues, such as gun control. These features of education politics also mean that few national policy questions result in large-scale mobilization of grassroots groups and memberships. Except for the influence of teachers' unions in electoral politics, national education policy is not characterized by highly visible battles involving mobilization of citizens by organizations.

The origins of E-Rate also fit this general pattern. The SREK amendment was the result of traditional "inside" political advocacy by a few organizational elites. A number of groups with a particular interest in

[105] Quentin L. Quade, *Financing School Education: The Struggle between Government Monopoly and Parental Control* (New Brunswick, N.J.: Transaction Press, 1996).
[106] Frederick M. Wirt and Michael W. Kirst, *The Political Dynamics of American Education* (Berkeley: McCutchan Publishing, 1997).

educational technology advocated successfully for the policy in Congress, with little membership involvement or media attention. It did not involve a large-scale mobilization of groups or publicly visible battles involving grassroots action.

Once E-Rate became effective, however, its politics changed. The possibility of cost savings immediately appealed to a large number of potential beneficiaries. Applications to the FCC for discounts came in the tens of thousands from public and private schools as well as libraries. Opposition to discounts emerged no less rapidly from the telecommunications industry. The firms had not opposed the SREK amendment when it was inserted into the bill and passed, in part because of the complexity of the bill and in part because some firms underestimated how large the discounts set by the FCC would actually be. As the agency processed the flood of applications for discounts, AT&T, MCI, BellSouth, GTE, SBC Communications, and other telecommunications firms organized resistance directed at both the FCC and Congress. They argued that the agency had exceeded its congressional mandate by setting deep discounts that would apply to so many of their institutional customers. Southwestern Bell and Pacific Bell/Nevada Bell filed a petition on July 3, 1997, requesting that the commission stay its order for the program pending judicial review. When the FCC did not respond, the firms pressed the issue with Congress and filed suit to block the program. In their lawsuit, they took the eventually unsuccessful position that the program's requirements amounted to a tax on firms, and the FCC lacks the statutory authority to tax.[107]

The intention of bill sponsors had been that the telecommunications firms would absorb the basic cost of the discounts. However, as it became clear that E-Rate would be a substantial program, firms announced that they would pass on their costs to rate-paying customers in the form of an extra charge on telephone bills. This proved to be a shrewd maneuver. Allies of the firms in Congress, especially among Republicans, labeled the surcharges a "tax" imposed by the Clinton administration. Some blamed the surcharges directly on Vice President Gore because he had endorsed the SREK amendment and the FCC rules. In the mass media, E-Rate sometimes was called "the Gore tax."

Framing the new service in tax terms was enormously successful politically. Rush Limbaugh lampooned the administration's new "tax," and in May, the *Wall Street Journal* ran an editorial slamming the program.

[107] The federal courts eventually ruled against the firms in July of 1999, ruling that the program involved imposition of a "fee" rather than a "tax," and therefore fell within the authority of the FCC.

As attention to the increased phone charges grew, a number of influential members of Congress backed away, including House Speaker Newt Gingrich and Senate Appropriations Committee Chairman Ted Stevens. By late May, two major consumer groups also opposed E-Rate: the Consumers Union and the Consumer Federation of America. In its May 25, 1998, issue, *Time* magazine ran a story about the controversy over the program, choosing as a frame the idea of a contest between Gore's enthusiasm for government support of technology and Republicans' opposition to growth in the federal bureaucracy. The *Time* authors reported that E-Rate was "under assault from Congress as an out-of-control entitlement engineered by an out-of-control bureaucracy."[108] On June 2, the *Washington Post* ran an opinion piece by James Glassman, an economic commentator at the American Enterprise Institute, charging Al Gore with attempting to hide an expensive new entitlement program.[109]

All this obscured the fact that E-Rate was a congressional creation, passed in a bill supported by industry, and requiring businesses to charge educational institutions less than others for their services. But the damage was serious. By the first week of June, the fuss over phone surcharges extended to some of E-Rate's erstwhile supporters. On June 4, Senators John McCain and Ernest Hollings, along with Representatives Tom Bliley and John Dingell, wrote to FCC Chairman William Kennard demanding that E-Rate be suspended immediately. The lawmakers called FCC implementation of the program a "spectacular failure" because it had led to increased phone rates. They warned against any FCC efforts "tinkering with a fundamentally flawed and legally suspect program" and directed that the "[c]ommission should immediately suspend further collection of funding for its schools and libraries program."[110] The letter, which the authors released publicly, was apparently intended to mollify education groups as much as to persuade Kennard to change course. Representative John Dingell sent an individual letter on the same date, using the stronger language for which he is known. Dingell called FCC's stewardship of E-Rate "asinine," and asked that the commission "simply pull the

---

[108] Karen Tumulty and John F. Dickerson, "Gore's Costly High-Wire Act," *Time*, May 25, 1998, http://www.time.com/time/magazine/1998/dom/980525/nation. Gores_Costly_High1.html.

[109] James K. Glassman, "Gore's Internet Fiasco," *Washington Post*, June 2, 1998, p. A13.

[110] Letter from Senators John McCain and Ernest Hollings and Representatives Tom Bliley and John Dingell to the Honorable William E. Kennard, Chairman, Federal Communications Commission, June 4, 1998, http://techlawjournal.com/agencies/slc/80604let.htm.

plug" on the program.[111] In exchanges with Kennard throughout June, Dingell stated his support in principle for E-Rate, but objected to FCC's stewardship of the program and threatened new legislation to redirect the agency.[112] In what was likely a reply to the June 4 letters, President Clinton praised the E-Rate program in a commencement speech the next day at the Massachusetts Institute of Technology. Nonetheless, with members of Congress distancing themselves from a policy that had unexpectedly transmuted into a tax issue, E-Rate was in jeopardy. Though the average surcharge would be well under a dollar per month, citizens were reminded of the "tax" every month on their phone bill, and an industry with substantial resources was working to remind them of the cost.

In 1994, a group of education lobbyists had formed a coordinating coalition called EdLiNC, for Education and Library Networks Coalition. The group included representatives of the American Association of School Administrators, the National Association of Independent Schools, the National Catholic Educational Association, the National Education Association, the National School Boards Association, and the U.S. Catholic Conference. Between 1994 and 1996, representatives had met about twice a month to share information on policy activities. They operated loosely, without a regular chair, staff, or operating funds. The main function of the EdLiNC meetings, according to one member, was to move information from the groups to Congress, and from the groups' leaders to their members. When the Telecommunications Act passed in 1996, EdLiNC representatives had stepped up the intensity of their interaction by advocating for the E-Rate program. Representatives met weekly, and increasingly relied on electronic mail distribution systems to speed the flow of information.[113]

By spring of 1998, with the new E-Rate program in jeopardy, some of the organizations represented in the EdLiNC meetings decided to attempt an alternative form of advocacy focused on grassroots strategies. EdLiNC lobbyists had worked throughout 1997 and 1998, submitting legal filings to the FCC and meeting with members of Congress and the

[111] Letter from Representative John Dingell to the Honorable William E. Kennard, Chairman, Federal Communications Commission, June 4, 1998, http://www.house.gov/commerce_democrats/comdem/press/105ltr75.htm.

[112] House Committee on Energy and Commerce, Statement of Congressman John D. Dingell, Ranking Democrat, House Commerce Committee on the Federal Communications Commission "e-rate," June 12, 1998, http://www.house.gov/commerce_democrats/comdem/press/105nr24.htm.

[113] Hula, *Lobbying Together*.

commission, but it appeared these were likely to fail.[114] According to the representative to EdLiNC from the National School Boards Association, the group eventually realized that they "needed to be more aggressive" as organizations if their program was to be saved.[115] It was clear that the transformation of E-Rate into a high-salience tax issue attracting mainstream media attention required a broader and more intensive advocacy effort than the groups had mounted so far. They also felt a sense of urgency because of the pace of the agency rule-making process, which is faster and less flexible than the legislative process in which the groups were typically involved.

Two of the EdLiNC groups, NEA and the American Association of School Administrators, had worked previously with Capitol Advantage, the largest Internet-oriented political communications firm working in Washington.[116] EdLiNC representatives agreed that their organizations would individually contract with the consulting firm for a coordinated, fast-moving, Internet-based advocacy campaign aimed at persuading the FCC and Congress to keep E-Rate. The result was to be a meta-organization existing on the Internet, to be called the "Save the E-Rate Coalition." This metaorganization would present a single face on the Internet, but would effectively consist of the aggregate memberships of all the participating groups and any other citizens they could attract. As for funding, the coalition would be supported by the wealthier groups such as the NEA. The funding arrangements are intriguing because they were so obscure even to member organizations. In interview after interview, leaders of the smaller groups in the coalition were unable to describe in any detail precisely how the coalition was being funded. Most were aware that the NEA was putting up money for the effort, but few were sure of the amounts, how it was being spent, and whether other groups were also pitching in. Funding from the NEA's deep pockets clearly was very helpful in the coalition's success, but decision making and coordination on financial matters were not an important focus of leaders' attention. Staffing arrangements and the allocation of responsibility and tasks were similar. These, along with funding, occupied little of the groups' attention compared with the tasks of monitoring developments,

---

[114] The organization maintains an archive of filings at http://www.edlinc.org.

[115] Michele Richards, formerly of the National School Boards Association and representative at EdLiNC meetings, telephone interview by Eric Patterson for the author, March 27, 2001.

[116] Anonymous former staff member of the American Library Association, telephone interview by Eric Patterson for the author, June 19, 2000.

distributing information, and coordinating actions in pursuit of common goals.

The coalition employed two web sites, one for internal communication and coordination among member organizations and one for public use. The internal site, along with electronic mail networks, permitted members of the coalition to pool information and distribute it among themselves. As individual groups obtained information about developments on the Hill or at the commission, they could disseminate it to others without their traditional meetings and strategy sessions. The public web site provided a means for attracting citizens outside the memberships of the coalition groups. The coalition made it easy for citizens to contact public officials using a zip code look-up facility for identifying senators and representatives and their contact information.[117] Beginning on May 6, 1998, the coalition began distributing calls for citizens to contact Congress, the commission, and the firms. These messages went out through the web site and also filtered through the member organizations and from them outward to others with an interest in education or universal service. Citizens were directed to the coalition's web site, where forms were available for composing and sending original messages to public officials. Organizers claim that the campaign moved from concept to distribution of messages in forty-eight hours.[118]

By the end of the May, the coalition claims to have generated 10,000 e-mail messages to Congress, and another 10,000 by the end of June, during the most intense period of public attention to E-Rate.[119] It also reports that a substantial number of these messages came from people outside their own formal memberships, although this claim cannot be verified. In principle, the coalition had effectively merged the memberships of several groups into one, and at least in principle if not in practice had opened up the pool of recruitable participants who were outside those organization membership rolls.

An official of the NEA reports that the total cost of generating those messages was about $40,000.[120] At $2 per message sent to Congress, the cost of this campaign was a fraction of the cost of traditional direct mail,

---

[117] http://congress.nw.dc.us/e-rate.   [118] Bennett and Fielding, *The Net Effect*.

[119] Ibid.; also see the May 29, 1998, press release of the National Conference of Catholic Bishops/United States Catholic Conference, "10,000 E-Mails Swamp Government Officials, Telecommunications Companies Defending 'E-Rate' for Schools," http://www.nccbuscc.org/comm/archives/98-122.htm; and Rebecca Weiner, "It's Cheaper Than a Stamp," *National Journal's Technology Daily*, Aug. 4, 1999, http://nationaljournal.com/technologydaily?.

[120] Weiner, "It's Cheaper Than a Stamp."

which runs from a half dollar to a dollar per solicitation, with a response rate to Congress of 10 percent or less. Because their technology brokered mail coming from citizens, the coalition knew precisely how many messages each public official was receiving, and from whom – information not available to members of Congress or the media. This helped coalition lobbyists fine-tune their pitches to members of Congress.[121] When at one point FCC officials and some members asked the lobbyists to stop the incoming messages from citizens, coalition members knew they had officials' attention.[122] By early June, at the time of the exchange between members of Congress and Chairman Kennard, the coalition had successfully demonstrated to members of Congress that E-Rate had a public constituency.

On June 12, under pressure from the coalition and industry, and after a hearing before the Senate Commerce Committee with both sides aggressively represented, the FCC voted to "save" but also curtail E-Rate. The commission reduced federal funding from $1.67 billion to $1 billion, restricted qualifications for schools, and extended the initial distribution of funds from 12 months to 18 months. This move satisfied the bulk of the telecommunications firms, who withdrew their opposition, as well as the Save the E-Rate Coalition. The group had won what organizers called a "glass half full." Their program had survived, but was diminished in the process, at least in the short run. By all accounts, the capacity of the coalition to produce a large, active public constituency for E-Rate on short notice had been a key part of the outcome, more for its influence on members of Congress than the FCC itself.

In the longer run, the compromise by FCC worked to the advantage of the coalition. As the number of schools actually receiving discounts grew, E-Rate's natural constituency consolidated. According to a report by the Department of Education in September 2000, about 13,000 public school districts and 70,000 schools had applied for funds by the second year of the program, along with 5,000 private schools and 4,500 library systems. These applications represented about 75 percent of all public schools and districts in the United States, 15 percent of private schools, and 50 percent of libraries.[123] Not only was this constituency large, but

---

[121] Roger Stone, Vice President, Juno Advocacy Network, telephone interview by Eric Patterson for the author, May 16, 2000.

[122] Anonymous staff member, American Association of School Administrators, telephone interview by Eric Patterson for the author, June 20, 2000.

[123] Department of Education, "E-Rate and the Digital Divide: A Preliminary Analysis from the Integrated Studies of Educational Technology," prepared by the Urban

it covered most congressional districts around the nation. At the same time, the phone surcharges lost their novelty as a new "tax," and the spike in public awareness of the program faded rapidly.

E-Rate also developed an industrial ally: the producers of information technology being used in the schools and libraries. While E-Rate cost telecommunications firms money, or so they claimed, it meant additional sales to hardware and software firms and consulting operations involved in connecting computers to the telecommunication services being brought to schools. A number of computer companies eventually went on record in support of E-Rate. One firm, Corporate Networking, Inc., reported a 30 percent increase in its annual sales of networking equipment due chiefly to E-Rate.[124] In 1999, under pressure from supporters, the FCC voted to restore full funding to the program up to the maximum permitted by law, $2.25 billion. The telecommunications firms were not interested in another fight, and by its third year, E-Rate was safely in place as a public program, actually earning praise from many observers.[125]

The story of E-Rate bears similarity to both the Libertarian Party's efforts on Know Your Customer and developments in the environmental lobby. Like the Libertarian case, E-Rate organizers were able to exploit low-cost communication and information tools to form and mobilize a public constituency. To some extent the coalition probably reached outside its own memberships, which was the key to the Libertarians' success, but, more important, it drew together a far-flung set of memberships not accustomed to working together and often not tightly connected to lobbying efforts by the organizations themselves. And in both cases the organizations' efforts proceeded very rapidly in response to short-term policy events rather than long-term strategic plans. Like Environmental Defense and other environmental lobbies, the E-Rate coalition created a metaorganization connected by information technology in which the structure of funding and the organization of traditional resources was less important than the capacity to coordinate and to respond flexibly and quickly to

Institute for the U.S. Department of Education, Office of the Undersecretary, Doc 00-17, Sept. 18, 2000, http://www.ed.gov/offices/OUS/PES/erate_fr.pdf.

[124] Gail Repsher, "E-Rate's Success Silences Critics," *Washington Technology*, on-line edition, Oct. 9, 2000, http://www.wtonline.com/vol15_no14/cover/1851-1.html.

[125] For independent commentary on E-Rate, see Brian Staihr and Katharine Sheaff, "The Success of the 'E-Rate' in Rural America," *The Main Street Economist* (Center for the Study of Rural America, Federal Reserve Bank of Kansas City, Feb. 2001), http://www.kc.frb.org; and Carolyn Hirschman, "E-Rate OK for Now," *Telephony*, March 19, 2001, http://www.telecomclick.com.

unfolding events. The use of information technology drew closer together an existing coalition, EdLiNC, but not in traditional bureaucratic terms. As is true of the Save Our Environment Coalition and Green Group, the actual organizational structure of the Save the E-Rate Coalition was obscure in traditional terms, even to its members. When participants describe the Save the E-Rate Coalition as an organization, they talk about how information flowed rather than about how responsibilities were assigned or how relationships were structured by rules or procedures.

GUN CONTROL

The terrain of national gun control policy in the United States is among the most tightly defined policy areas organizationally.[126] The absolute dominance of pro-gun advocacy by the National Rifle Association (NRA) makes that side of the policy arena nearly a monopoly. Other groups, such as Gun Owners of America and the Citizen's Committee for the Right to Keep and Bear Arms, are much smaller and less influential in policy making.[127] To a large extent, opposition to gun control policy is defined by the strategies and resources of this one organization. The success of the NRA rests on several factors: a membership in excess of 3 million, very savvy lobbying campaigns of both the inside and outside variety, and an insistent and laser-like focus on framing gun control as a civil liberties issue resting in the Second Amendment.

The absence of opponents with comparable resources is another reason for the NRA's clout. Gun control advocacy is characterized by a number of vastly smaller groups. A few national gun control organizations exist, along with over a dozen state-level groups of note. Some organizations with primary missions in other areas also take stands in favor of gun control, such as the American Bar Association's Coordinating Committee on Gun Violence and the American Jewish Congress. At the national level, the most powerful group is the Brady Campaign to Prevent Gun Violence, formerly Handgun Control, Inc.[128] It was founded in 1974 and rose to prominence in the 1980s, when Sarah Brady became chair

---

[126] This case is based chiefly on news accounts and two interviews with participants in the Million Mom March. Most of the research for this case study and an initial written summary were prepared by Diane Johnson, doctoral student in the Political Science department at UCSB.

[127] For an analysis of groups' influence, see Laura I. Langbein and Mark A. Lotwis, "The Political Efficacy of Lobbying and Money: Gun Control in the U.S. House, 1986," *Legislative Studies Quarterly* 15, no. 3 (1986): 413–440.

[128] Handgun Control, Inc., renamed itself in June 2001.

of the group following the assassination attempt on Ronald Reagan that wounded her husband, James Brady. The Brady Campaign is dwarfed by the NRA, which is several times larger in membership and budget. During the 1984 election cycle when Congress considered the McClure-Volkmer bill, a major piece of gun legislation, the NRA outspent Handgun Control six to one in PAC donations.[129] This type of imbalance in resources is typical.

A key element in gun control policy dynamics in the United States is the fact that a number of the NRA's positions are at odds with public opinion. Survey data show that nearly 90 percent of the public favors a seven-day waiting period for gun purchases, about 80 percent favors a ban on assault weapons and handgun registration, and roughly 40 percent favors a ban on handguns.[130] Although they fluctuate a little, these figures are for the most part stable over time. Between 40 percent and 50 percent of Americans report owning a gun.[131] Not surprisingly, gun ownership is correlated with opposition to gun control measures, but the relationship is comparatively weak for gun-control policies other than an outright ban on handguns. Gallup data show that in excess of 60 percent of gun owners support registration, waiting periods, and banning of assault weapons and cheap handguns.[132]

The long-term, stable disparity between public policy and public opinion on gun control in the United States is almost certainly attributable at least in part to the effectiveness of the NRA's members and money.[133] The state of public opinion limits the general appeal of the NRA's message outside its own ranks, and so tends to push the organization toward internal mobilization of its own membership as a "grassroots" strategy. For that, the organization uses tactics that would likely not be particularly effective with the broader public. It uses strong appeals to patriotism and the

---

[129] Langbein and Lotwis, "The Political Efficacy of Lobbying and Money." The McClure-Volkmer bill became the Firearms Owners Protection Act of 1986, which weakened gun control measures.

[130] Robin M. Wolpert and James G. Gimpel, "Self-Interest, Symbolic Politics, and Public Attitudes toward Gun Control," *Political Behavior* 20, no. 3 (1998): 241–262; also see Robert J. Spitzer, *The Politics of Gun Control* (New York: Chatham House, 1995); Robert Singh, "Gun Control in America," *Political Quarterly* 69, no. 3 (1998): 288–296.

[131] Gregg Lee Carter, *The Gun Control Movement* (New York: Twayne Publishers, 1997); Wolpert and Gimpel, "Self-Interest, Symbolic Politics, and Public Attitudes Toward Gun Control."

[132] Reported in Carter, *The Gun Control Movement*, p. 51.

[133] See John M. Bruce and Clyde Wilcox, eds., *The Changing Politics of Gun Control* (Lanham, Md.: Rowman and Littlefield, 1998).

Second Amendment and avoids public debates over crime and violence in most cases. The organization is very effective with these techniques at mobilizing its traditional membership. Its campaign donations are also politically notorious. Research attempting to assess the influence of NRA donations has a history of producing mixed results, but it is likely that NRA giving does exert at least a marginal influence independently of legislators' ideology, prior positions on gun control, and other factors.[134]

The dynamics of public opinion may lead to differing strategies for donating versus lobbying by the NRA as well as by the Brady Campaign and other gun-control advocates. Research by Laura Langbein shows that the NRA's donations tend strongly toward supporting the most conservative, pro-gun legislators and often have the effect of reinforcing the allegiance of the groups' allies in Congress.[135] Historically, the donations of Handgun Control also tended toward the strongest gun control supporters. *Lobbying* efforts by both groups, on the other hand, have been more likely to target moderates and swing voters. Langbein speculates that the reason for this disparity is the greater visibility of donations, the groups' need to bolster and support their own memberships through their donations, and the difficulty of explaining to their members donations to legislators with a moderate record. Public strategies of influence tend to exacerbate polarization and policy conflict, while private strategies tend to diminish them.

In light of these features of gun control politics in the United States, the circumstances of the largest rally in U.S. history about gun control come as a surprise.[136] On May 14, 2000, a group probably in excess of a 100,000 converged on the Washington Mall in support of stronger gun control, along with a much smaller group that met as a countermarch.[137] Not Handgun Control, other gun control groups, or the NRA played a role in these events. The May 14 march and countermarch took place literally outside the influence of the dominant gun control organizations. The main event, called the Million Mom March, was successful in attracting many participants – if not a full million – precisely *because* it occurred outside the traditional organizational structure and policy

---

[134] The same effect has been shown for Handgun Control. See Langbein and Lotwis, "The Political Efficacy of Lobbying and Money."

[135] Laura I. Langbein, "PACs, Lobbies, and Political Conflict: The Case of Gun Control," *Public Choice* 77, no. 3 (1993): 551–572.

[136] I find no reports of major gun control marches or rallies in Washington in the academic literature.

[137] Reliable counts of participants are not available.

framework for gun control lobbying. It was premised on a fundamental reframing of gun policy as a motherhood and family issue. Mothers and others concerned with the health of children should care about gun control, the march claimed. This reframing, along with low-cost communication techniques and, eventually, coverage by mass media, proved enormously successful at mobilizing citizens not engaged in the traditional contest over crime and the Second Amendment. This fact made the Million Mom March unusual, not only in the gun control arena but more generally in the history of political marches.

Research shows that two phases have existed in the evolution of American political marches and rallies. The first major march on Washington did not occur until 1894, when "Coxey's Army" rallied over economic issues. Between the Coxey march and the early marches involving civil rights and social policy in the 1960s and 1970s, marches tended to attract citizens who were not participants in traditional, institutional politics and who felt that their interests were not adequately represented through traditional means.[138] Marches on Washington typically constituted an outlet for those who felt disenfranchised, and as a result marches and rallies were often viewed as illegitimate acts with the potential to undermine democracy. For many political elites and members of the public, marches carried with them the aura of potentially violent discontent, constitutional threat, and even revolution.[139]

During the period of heightened political activity of the 1960s and '70s, this view of marches and protest activities changed, as public demonstrations moved from the periphery to the mainstream of politics. These events increasingly engaged citizens who were otherwise well enfranchised and active in traditional institutionalized politics.[140] Rather than being an extreme act on the boundaries of democratic acceptability, the march became a mainstream and even routine feature of normal politics, especially by the 1980s.

Contemporary survey research conducted in the 1990s shows a positive correlation between participation in traditional institutional politics and participation in protest and rally activity, as well as a positive

---

[138] Norman T. Gilbert, "The Mass Protest Phenomenon: An Examination of Marches on Washington," Ph.D. diss, Northern Illinois University, 1971.

[139] Lucy Grace Barber, "Marches on Washington, 1894–1963: National Political Demonstrations and American Political Culture," Ph.D. diss., Brown University, May 1996.

[140] Jerome Skolnick, ed., *The Politics of Protest and Confrontation: A Staff Report to the National Commission on the Causes and Prevention of Violence* (Washington, D.C.: Government Printing Office, 1969).

correlation between march participation and socioeconomic status.[141] As a general rule, participants in contemporary marches tend to be strongly ideologically committed to the cause and knowledgeable about it, as well as deeply embedded in community organizations and networks. Marches as a form of political expression have lost their taint of radicalism and alienation.

They still tend to be polarizing events, however. Moderates and the uncommitted do not attend marches. By drawing from and activating citizens who tend to be knowledgeable and strongly committed ideologically, they typically contribute toward the strengthening of opposing positions on policy.[142] Also, leaders of national marches typically have experience in subnational political organizing. They are political veterans with access to material and organizational resources, and they draw on their networks of activists and their political experience to rally the most committed citizens. This means that most marches draw heavily from the memberships of established groups.[143] To a substantial degree, the modern political march is a manifestation of established civic and political organizational structure.

The Million Mom March did not fit this pattern. Not only did it occur outside the memberships and boundaries of the traditional pro– and anti–gun control groups, it was organized by people inexperienced in political marches and it made moderate, centrist appeals to action for citizens not otherwise engaged in the politics of guns. The Million Mom March was intended precisely as a protest of moderates and centrists.

It originated in efforts of a single political entrepreneur, Donna Dees-Thomases. According to her own public statements, Dees-Thomases was moved to political action in August of 1999 by two events: televised news coverage of a shooting of children at the North Valley Jewish Community Center in Granada Hills, California, and an encounter on the Long Island Railroad with a menacing man wearing a swastika tattoo. She reports having formulated the idea on the train that gun control was an issue of salience to mothers, and resolved to attempt to mobilize other

---

[141] Rory McVeigh and Christian Smith, "Who Protests in America: An Analysis of Three Political Alternatives – Inaction, Institutionalized Politics, or Protest," *Sociological Forum* 14, no. 4 (1999): 685–702; Raymond Arthur Smith, "Overcoming the Collective Action Dilemma: Political Participation in Lesbian-Gay-Bisexual Pride Marches," Ph.D. diss., Columbia University, 1999.

[142] Gilbert, "The Mass Protest Phenomenon."

[143] Barber, "Marches on Washington."

mothers in a political effort.[144] Adapting the name of the Million Man March, a rally in 1995 sponsored by the Nation of Islam, Dees-Thomases's first political action was to register "Million Mom March" as an Internet domain name. Her second was to obtain a permit for a march on the Capitol Mall. Symbolic of the speed of political action in the new information environment, she notes wryly that securing the domain name that would serve as the Internet "location" of the mobilization effort took just one day, while obtaining permission for the physical location at the Mall required a week of effort.

Dees-Thomases's original intent was to initiate the march and then hand off the organization building and management of the event to acquaintances in Washington familiar with political advocacy. She could find no takers for her brainchild, however. Left largely on her own, she recruited volunteers among friends, formed a steering committee, and then organized a set of state coordinators who in turn recruited more volunteers.[145] She and the volunteer network framed their efforts as a mothers' issue, adopting the slogan "We're Looking for a Few Good Moms" and featuring a "Mom's Apple Pie Award" for officials who supported tougher gun control laws as well as a "Time Out Chair" for pro-gun officials – a designation monopolized by Majority Whip Tom Delay. In their public rhetoric, march organizers used phrases such as: "Getting some lawmakers to act reasonably is about as difficult as getting our kids to clean their rooms. If we've told them once, we've told them a hundred times."[146] March organizers also pointed out that Mother's Day, the date of the march, originated during the Civil War to remind women to care for each other's wounded sons.[147] At a press conference on Labor Day, Dees-Thomases pointed out that it was nine months until Mother's Day, saying, "If we mothers can make babies in nine months... surely that's enough time for Congress to make tougher gun laws to protect them."[148] March organizers sought mandatory safety locks, a limit of

[144] Million Mom March, press kit, May 8, 2000, http://www.millionmommarch.com; George James, "Mothers Hope They're One in a Million," *New York Times*, Oct. 31, 1999, p. A8.

[145] Maria Newman, "March for Gun Control Starts with One Worried Mother," *New York Times*, March 27, 2000, p. B5.

[146] Home Page, Million Mom March, May 26, 2000, http://www.millionmommarch.com.

[147] Million Mom March, "Million Mom March Held in Washington, DC on Mothers Day: Mothers across the Country Call for Gun Licensing and Registration," press release, March 1, 2000, http://www.millionmommarch.com.

[148] Quoted in James, "Mothers Hope They're One in a Million."

one handgun purchase per month, background checks at gun shows, the licensing of handgun owners and registration of all handguns, and improved enforcement of existing gun laws.

In September 1999, the march as an organization constituted one phone line and two volunteer grandmothers transcribing messages from an answering machine, as well as the steering committee and network of volunteer coordinators. It used electronic mail to communicate and coordinate internally throughout the network, and ran a web site to distribute information and volunteer instructions publicly. It also aggressively sought donations and media coverage. Vickie King, a volunteer for the Million Mom March, reported that in the beginning "almost everything [was] done on-line" and added, "I don't think we could have done it without the Internet."[149] In a pattern consistent with the efforts of gay activists to support Tim McVeigh, the new information technology permitted the rapid, inexpensive development of a wide network of participants in the absence of traditional political organization; the existence of that network then validated the project as newsworthy and permitted the organizers a forum in the mass media. As news stories grew, the march attracted donations and additional volunteers.[150] By late April 2000, the march was operating seventy-five phone lines and receiving tens of thousands of visits per day to its web site.[151] It opened an office in Washington, took on paid staff, and hired professional organizers and public relations experts.[152] The cycle of fund raising, organizing, and media attention continued to snowball throughout the fall and winter. The *Washington Post* in particular provided extensive coverage, especially as Mother's Day approached.[153] In mid-March, an article

---

[149] Vickie King, staff member, Million Mom March, telephone interview by Eric Patterson for the author, April 17, 2000.

[150] According to a report in the *Washington Post*, the Million Mom March raised $2.3 million as of May 11, 2000, a few days before the event. Andrew McGuire, Executive Director of the Bell Campaign, oversaw the Million Mom March's finances. More than $200,000 was raised through T-shirt sales and individual contributions; the balance came from foundation and corporate underwriting. The largest single donation was from an anonymous New York City business executive who gave $1 million; other large donors included CIBC World Markets Corp. ($250,000), Dannon Yogurt ($150,000), the Barbara Lee Family Foundation ($200,000), and the Funder's Collaborative for the Prevention of Gun Violence ($500,000). Reported in Susan Levine, "A Roster of Gunfire's Next of Kin," *Washington Post*, May 11, 2000, p. B1.

[151] Megan Rosenfeld, "A Force of Nurture Readies for Battle: Born on Labor Day, Gun Control Rally Is Set for Mother's Day," *Washington Post*, March 23, 2000, p. C1.

[152] Ibid.

[153] On May 11 alone, for example, the *Post* ran nine articles about the march or the marchers.

entitled "Marching Mums Take Aim at the Gun Lobby" also appeared as far away as the *Sydney Morning Herald*.[154] On television, the march won an announcement on *CBS This Morning* and an appearance by a participant on the *Rosie O'Donnell Show*. The fact that Dees-Thomases was herself a media professional helped a great deal, with experience as a part-time publicist for the David Letterman show, former employee of CBS News, and former staffer of Senator Russell Long. Her sister-in-law, Susan Thomases, was also a veteran political campaigner. In the media frame that Dees-Thomases successfully sought, her lack of prior experience in gun control policy played to her advantage. The story of a political novice (if not a media novice) organizing volunteer women around the country made for great copy. As funding grew, the media campaign eventually culminated in televised ads featuring actresses Susan Sarandon, Whoopi Goldberg, and others.

By the time of the march, organizers claimed its web site had received about 5 million visits as a result of this publicity, and by May, the web site listed eighty-one sponsors and endorsements from 105 national organizations, including the U.S. Conference of Mayors, the League of Women Voters, the National PTA, the NAACP, and Handgun Control.[155] The Million Mom March was endorsed by fifty-two national religious organizations and hundreds of state organizations, as well as President Clinton and First Lady Hillary Rodham Clinton. An organization of considerable dimensions politically had been built in the span of months in a way that no one involved in gun control policy could have predicted. Its supporters were an ad hoc coalition, and its internal structure reflective of no existing organization.

The march attracted for the most part only muted opposition, since its premise – mothers protecting children – was difficult to attack directly. The NRA was critical of the march, but for the most part kept a low profile and went so far as to decline to comment on it for an article in the *New York Times* in October 1999. With its own members, the NRA relies on very aggressive rhetoric and has been aptly characterized by one scholar as "polemical, ideological, and zealous."[156] But its typical crisis- and threat-based appeals were clearly not right for a mothers' group. Only as the march drew near did the NRA launch a soft countercampaign

---

[154] Mark Riley, "Marching Mums Take Aim at the Gun Lobby," *Sydney Morning Herald*, March 15, 2000, http://www.smh.com.au.
[155] Mary Leigh Blek, Memo to Million Mom Marchers, Million Mom March, May 19, 2000, http://www.millionmommarch.com.
[156] Spitzer, *The Politics of Gun Control*, p. 113.

emphasizing gun safety and children, attempting to direct some of the potential energy of the march away from itself. It announced a $1 million contribution to its "Eddie Eagle" program for children, and ran print ads the Sunday before the march, which read, "This is one week to put politics aside and put kids first. Because whatever our disagreement over gun politics, we all want gun safety. We all want safe kids."[157] The NRA had been pulled from its standard Second Amendment position. Finally, on the day of the march itself, the NRA finally stopped pulling its punches and returned to its traditional line of polemicism. NRA Executive Vice President Wayne LaPierre appeared on NBC's *Meet the Press*, claiming that education of children and more aggressive prosecution of criminals was the way to reduce gun violence among the young. "Setting fire to freedom should never be the answer," he said.[158]

Aside from NRA rhetoric, the countermarch planned for the same day was the only organized opposition to the march. Called the Armed Informed Mothers' March (AIMM), it was organized by a group first calling itself Moms 4 Guns. Eventually renamed the more palatable "Second Amendment Sisters," the group advocated tougher sentencing for violent criminals, the "absolute right to self-defense," safety education, and more involved parenting.[159] The Sisters claimed to be independent of other pro-gun organizations, in particular the NRA, from which it claimed to accept no funds or endorsement.[160] Even more so than the Million Mom March, the Second Amendment Sisters/AIMM event was Internet-based. It was founded in January 2000 in an Internet chat room by five women, each from a different state. The group organized participants through a web site and toll-free number, and grew modestly as a virtual organization throughout the winter and spring. The Sisters stated their mission as follows: " ... There is a group of women who want to take away, or severely infringe on your right to protect yourself and your family. They call their effort the Million Mom March. We need you to

---

[157] Susan Levine, "Marching Moms Hope to Recast Gun Debate," *Washington Post*, May 10, 2000, p. A1.

[158] Susan Levine, "Many Moms' Voices Are Heard on Mall," *Washington Post*, May 15, 2000, p. A1.

[159] Rosenfeld, "A Force of Nurture Readies for Battle," p. C1.

[160] Melinda Gierisch, a member of Second Amendment Sisters, reported to *Washington Post* journalist Megan Rosenfeld that both the NRA and the Gun Owners of America had turned down their requests for underwriting. See ibid. Other organizers reported the same to *Post* writer Susan Levine. See Susan Levine, "Pro-Gun Women to Counter 'Million Mom' Message," *Washington Post*, May 9, 2000, p. B1.

help us send a Million Moms of our own, to let Congress know that these women do not speak for all mothers!"[161]

The structure of the Sisters group was similar to that of the Moms, but it was unable to attract a comparable level of public support and media attention. An important reason was the Sisters' violence-tinged, revenge-oriented message. One photo appearing at their web site pictured a well-dressed businesswoman with a phone in one hand and a rifle in the other, with a caption that said: "Two shots to stop. One to make sure. Reload. Call 911."[162] Another depicted a woman in casual attire pointing a gun straight at the camera, with the words "As seen by a would-be rapist (for about 0.2 seconds)."[163] These extreme images characterized the group's approach to organizing. The Sisters' concept of armed self-defense was doomed to failure as a broad counterpoint to the Moms' message of keeping children safe.

The Million Mom March and AIMM countermarch on May 14, 2000, unfolded as dueling events organized independently of traditional gun control groups and reliant heavily on information infrastructure in place of traditional organizational resources – more so initially than at the climax of the campaign, in the case of the Moms.[164] The Moms' march was a standard large-scale Capitol Mall event, with an Interfaith Service and a "children's village" with face painting, juggling, storytelling, and soccer clinics. It included a memorial wall listing the names of 4,001 Americans who had died of gunshot wounds between the shooting spree at Columbine High School in Littleton, Colorado, and the march; voter registration tables; music; and speeches by a variety of public figures hosted by Rosie O'Donnell: Martin Luther King III, Lieutenant Governor of Maryland Kathleen Kennedy Townsend, Kerry Kennedy Cuomo, and Sarah and Jim Brady. Organizers claimed 750,000 participants in Washington, and "tens of thousands" more at several dozen local marches around the country. Although no disinterested measurements of the size of the Washington crowd were made, it is reasonable to assume that attendance was smaller than organizers' estimate of 750,000 but still substantial.[165] A few blocks away, the AIMM event

[161] Home Page, Second Amendment Sisters, Inc.
[162] Levine, "Pro-Gun Women to Counter 'Million Mom' Message," p. B1.
[163] Home Page, Second Amendment Sisters, Inc., May 11, 2000, http://www.sas-aim.org.
[164] Levine, "Many Moms' Voices Are Heard on Mall"; Rosenfeld, "A Force of Nurture Readies for Battle."
[165] The Park Police no longer estimate the attendance at events on the Capitol Mall, so the organizers' estimate was the only one available. Other estimates of the attendance were lower than those of the march organizers. Reports in the *Washington Post* estimated

was of far more modest proportions. It featured none of the prominent speakers of the march, with the keynote address given by Texas State Representative Suzanna Gratia-Hupp. The Sisters claimed to have raised $40,000 and communicated with about 35,000 people, and on event day they reported 1,000 to 3,000 attendees.[166] A *Washington Post* journalist estimated that half of these were men.[167] Interaction between the two opposing marches was limited to a few verbal confrontations.

Impressive as the size of the Moms' march was, especially in comparison with the Sisters' countermarch, the aim of persuading Congress to pass tougher federal gun laws was a tall order, even following on the heels of the Columbine shooting that had left fifteen dead in April 1999. The number of major gun control laws passed by Congress in the last fifty years can be counted on the fingers of one hand with a single digit to spare, and these occurred in clusters: two major laws in 1968, and two again in 1994.[168] Following the Columbine shooting, a number of public officials made predictable public gestures in favor of stronger gun legislation. A bicameral study group of women in the House and Senate formed, issuing calls for new legislation and endorsing the Million Mom March effort.[169] President Clinton called for stronger gun legislation in his State of the Union Address in January 2000, proposing national licensing of gun owners. On May 9, shortly before the march, Senator Dianne Feinstein introduced a registration bill that had no chance of success.

"tens of thousands." Also, estimates of the number of local Million Mom March rallies throughout the country vary according to the source; on May 9 – a few days before Mother's Day – a report in the *Washington Post* said that there would be events in sixty-three cities. See Levine, "Pro-Gun Women to Counter 'Million Mom' Message."

[166] Afterward they cited a police estimate of 5000. See Second Amendment Sisters, Inc., "Rally Reports," undated (2000), http://www.sas-aim.org/rallyreports/WashingtonDC.html; Levine, "Pro-Gun Women to Counter 'Million Mom' Message."

[167] Carol Morello, "Victims Aim to Save Rights and Themselves," *Washington Post*, May 15, 2000, p. A15.

[168] The Omnibus Crime Control and Safe Streets Act of 1968, the Gun Control Act of 1968, the Violent Crime Control and Law Enforcement Act of 1994, and the Brady Handgun Violence Protection Act of 1994.

[169] U.S. House of Representatives, "Congresswoman Morella and the Million Mom March Call for Passage of Gun Safety Legislation," press release, Sept. 23, 1999, Washington, D.C.; U.S. Senate, "Senator Mikulski, Other Women in Congress Get Tough on Guns: House, Senate Women Gather to Coordinate Gun Control Strategies," press release, May 20, 1999, Washington, D.C.; statements were also posted at the web sites of Senators Barbara Boxer, http://www.senate.gov/~boxer, and Diane Feinstein, http://www.senate.gov/~feinstein.

The best chance for real legislative change was a crime bill that was under consideration in 1999 and 2000 called the Violent and Repeat Juvenile Offender Accountability and Rehabilitation Act of 1999. By spring of 2000, the bill had passed both the House and Senate. It provided for trial of certain juveniles as adults, authorized funds for state law enforcement and prevention, and included other law enforcement and prevention measures. The Senate version of the bill, known informally as the Juvenile Crime bill, included a set of gun control amendments added after the Columbine shooting spree. These amendments, including one passed on a tie-breaking vote by Vice President Gore, called for mandatory background checks, a waiting period of up to three days, bans on the importation of high-capacity ammunition clips, requirements for child-safety devices on handguns, a ban on firearms possession by people convicted of violent crimes as juveniles, and a bar to juveniles acquiring assault weapons. In the House, members had defeated gun control amendments, and so their version of the Juvenile Crime bill that landed in conference lacked the Senate measures. Republicans had refused throughout the spring to schedule the Conference Committee, which was to be chaired by Orrin Hatch, and Senate Democrats supporting the amendments had failed to force conference action. As the date of the Million Mom March approached, its organizers increasingly turned their attention to this bill as a vehicle for achieving their goals. By the day of the march, it was clear that if organizers were going to succeed, it would be through somehow passing the Juvenile Crime bill gun provisions.

The struggle over those provisions proved anticlimactic given the energy and momentum of the march. On May 16, two days after the event on the Mall, Senate Minority Leader Tom Daschle attempted to bring a vote on attaching such provisions to the military construction appropriations bill. His effort was blocked by Republicans, and instead he offered a nonbinding resolution endorsing the Million Mom March and calling for action on the stalled conference report. This resolution was to be the denouement of the march. Following two days of especially acrimonious debate in the Senate, the Senate voted 50 to 49 in favor of the Daschle resolution, and 69 to 30 for a competing Republican resolution endorsing milder proposals. This vote ended action on the gun control amendments for the 106th Congress, providing nothing more than an opportunity for gun control legislators to vote their positions and endorse the march. The Moms had succeeded at the immediate goal of mobilizing a large number of citizens into political engagement on gun control, but had failed at the ultimate goal of changing public policy.

The Juvenile Crime bill votes represented a classic policy-making window: clear policy instruments and well-defined decision points, willingness to invest effort on the part of leaders inside the institution, and attention from the public and mass media. It also fit a classic pattern in gun control policy: the rapid closing of the policy-making window as public attention temporarily aroused by an event turns elsewhere. Research on protests and Washington marches shows that throughout the twentieth century, groups typically have not won immediate policy concessions or contributed directly to short-term changes in public policy. The common effects of marches are more diffuse than immediate policy change: They appear to contribute to the strength of social movements, influence public opinion, and elevate the status of issues under discussion in the public sphere.[170] Measured against that historical standard, the Million Mom March is by no means a failure.

Like marches historically, it was a case of event-centered politics. But unlike most marches of recent decades, it was largely disconnected from traditional political organizations – unions, civil rights organizations, and interest groups – especially at the outset, and it mobilized citizens in the political middle as a result. Abundance of information and communication opportunities were an important reason the March occurred as an event, especially at the beginning. As one participant put it, until February, the organization "existed largely in cyberspace."[171] It was not that information technology permitted organizers to wholly bypass the media; on the contrary, it provided a means for an organizationless group eventually to attract the attention of the mass media. As in the McVeigh case, the new information environment lowered the resource requirements for an organizer to identify and mobilize a core of participants. Once in place, their efforts garnered the kind of mass media attention that permitted the group to reach the national policy agenda.

CAMPAIGNS FOR OFFICE IN 2000

More attention has been paid to the role of the Internet in election campaigns than in any other aspect of American politics.[172] For the most

---

[170] Barber, "Marches on Washington."

[171] Quoted in Susan Levine, "Fight Against Guns Gives Moms a Cause," *Washington Post*, April 19, 2000, p. B1.

[172] This case is based chiefly on about two dozen interviews with officials and candidates of the following campaigns. For President in 2000: Pat Buchanan, George Bush, Bill Bradley, Al Gore, John Hagelin, John McCain, and Ralph Nader. For President in other years: Bill Clinton (1996); Bob Dole (1998), Steve Forbes (1996). For Senate:

part, the attention has centered on campaign web sites and their use as a means of external communication that supplements television advertising. Campaign web sites have evolved from a novelty to a standard element of campaigns in less than ten years, and a great deal of discussion has ensued about what that means. Opinions vary, even among campaign staff and political consultants. One official of a 1998 California Senate race who was interviewed for this study claims that information technology "changes the dynamics of politics" by creating a twenty-four-hour candidate presence, combined with speed and new forms of interaction.[173] Another official for a different California Senate candidate called new technology "irrelevant" because the Internet, with its self-selection effects, cannot substitute for television.[174] Yet another Senate campaign staffer said, "You can't not go online these days; you have to have e-mail and a web site."[175] An official at Stanton Communications, a Washington-based public relations firm, claims that "the Internet is totally changing how [public relations] practitioners work."[176] An official of Votenet, the Internet-specific advocacy firm with more than a little self-interest at stake, describes new technology as "the great equalizer" that can "make one person as powerful as a big company."[177] These disparate views constitute the first impressions of political professionals experimenting with a new medium for political communication.

Given the manifest importance of mass media for the evolution of campaigning in the second half of the twentieth century, the hypothesis that contemporary changes in communication technology should affect elections is plausible in general terms. It is important, however, to be specific. One of the major lessons of the third information revolution

John Ashcroft (2000), John Brown (2000), Tom Campbell (2000), Matt Fong (1998), and Ray Haynes (2000). For governor: Gray Davis (California 1998), Jim Talent (Missouri 2000), and Matt Holden (Missouri 2000). Most of the interviews were conducted by Diane Johnson and Eric Patterson, doctoral students in the Department of Political Science at UCSB. Some were conducted by the author and, where noted, by Professor Richard Davis of Brigham Young University for a related research project.

[173] Joe Wierzbicki, consultant to Matt Fong, telephone interview by Eric Patterson for the author, Aug. 28, 2000.

[174] Darry Sragow, Public Strategies, telephone interview by Eric Patterson for the author, Aug. 16, 2000.

[175] Darryl Ng, Assistant Press Secretary for Tom Campbell, telephone interview by Eric Patterson for the author, Aug. 22, 2000.

[176] Anonymous staff member, Stanton Communications, telephone interview by Eric Patterson for the author, Aug. 1, 2000.

[177] Jason Dell and Mike Tuteur, Votenet, telephone interviews by Eric Patterson for the author, July 20, 2000.

in the United States was that new channels for communication between candidates and voters undermined the dominance of parties as campaign organizations. In terms of mass communication, this meant that the functions of communicating with voters on a large scale could be managed by organizations other than parties. In organizational terms, it meant that party organizations, polling firms, communications consultants, and other political advisers could form temporary networks centered on the candidate organization and existing only for the duration of an electoral campaign. This feature of the third information revolution can be thought of as the specialization and diversification of organizations involved in campaigns. The questions raised by the Internet in contemporary election campaigns should be cast in these terms.

The brief history of the Internet in national campaigns begins in 1992, prior to the development of the web as a large-scale means of communication. Political organizations such as the Democratic Senatorial Campaign Committee had used electronic mail for internal communication as far back as the 1980s, but 1992 was significant not only for the greater intensiveness of information technology but for its emergent potential as a means for communicating outside the campaign organization.

In the 1992 races, a few candidates employed electronic mail networks and distribution lists to coordinate participation in their campaigns and inform supporters about their progress. One of the most prominent experiments was an electronic mail–based campaign information system created by the Artificial Intelligence Laboratory at MIT that was provided by the university to the major candidates. The system permitted citizens to volunteer for a presidential campaign, debate issues with other citizens, and request news and issue papers from participating candidates. George H. W. Bush, Bill Clinton, John Hagelin, Andre Marrou, and Ross Perot participated.[178] The Clinton campaign made the most extensive use of the system, assigning a staff person reporting to George Stephanopoulos to develop content and coordinate the distribution of information from campaign headquarters using the MIT system. After the election, the Clinton administration adapted the technology into a White House electronic mail distribution system that provided subscribers with press releases, copies of executive orders, press briefing transcripts, and presidential proclamations.[179] That system proved long-lived, operating

[178] Kenneth D. Campbell, "AI Lab Initiates Electronic Presidential Town Meeting," MIT *Tech Talk*, Oct. 28, 1992, http://web.mit.edu/newsoffice/tt/1992/oct28/27118.html.
[179] Lee Ridgway, "The Web, Politics, and the 1996 Presidential Campaign," *i/s* 11, no. 8 (1996), http://web.mit.edu/is/isnews/v11/n08/42074.html.

175

throughout the entire Clinton administration until it was terminated in January 2001 by the Bush administration.

None of the 1992 experiments had any plausible bearing on election outcomes. They amounted to nothing more than minor experiments in campaigning, conducted apart from the main business of campaign politics. The story was largely the same in 1994, and again in 1996, though by that time, the web had come into use by a number of campaigns and experimentation by candidates was much broader. In 1996, all major presidential candidates used web sites, as did about three-quarters of U.S. Senate candidates.[180] A few citizens visited these web sites, although campaign staff could not be sure who they were. A few citizens signed up for electronic mail–based news and information, but in no campaign did these activities rise to the level where they might potentially affect the outcome of a race.[181] For most candidates in 1996, use of new information technology to communicate with citizens amounted to little more than joining an inexpensive bandwagon with few costs and little risk. The best examples are the Dole and Forbes campaigns. Dole's web site was operated in Tempe, Arizona, by two Arizona State University students.[182] Forbes's own Internet manager describes his web site as a novelty item in the campaign, added as an "afterthought" to the campaign plan.[183] Although the Internet had yet to become meaningful in political campaigns in 1996, optimists began predicting that in the next cycle or the one following, new communication techniques would prove decisive in a race for the first time, as television had apparently been in the Kennedy-Nixon race of 1960.

The 1998 elections did see several substantive developments in Internet use, although expectations comparing the Internet to television were premature, to say the least. One of the most important developments was higher production values in web sites and generally more sophisticated

---

[180] Robert Klotz, "Virtual Criticism: Negative Advertising on the Internet in the 1996 Races," *Political Communication* 15, no. 3 (1998): 347–365.

[181] Reliable counts of use of web sites in House races and by candidates for state offices are not available, but it appears that experimentation with the new media was correlated with level of office: the higher the office, the more likely the candidate to experiment. A number of nonpartisan voter-information operations such as Project Vote Smart also opened Internet-based operations in 1996, providing a variety of voter guides, town-hall functions, and other civic information.

[182] John Whalen, "A Doleful Mission: Two Guys from Tempe Aim to Force Virtual Vigor into Bob Dole's Official Web Page," *New Times*, Aug. 24–Sept. 4, 1996, http://www.newtimes.com.

[183] Mike Low, Internet consultant to the Forbes campaign, personal correspondence with Eric Patterson for the author, Sept. 15, 2000.

technology-based efforts by professional political consultants and public relations firms. Yet for most candidate organizations, the new technology still remained largely symbolic, a mechanism for signaling technological progressivism at a time when engineering culture was becoming "cool." A few candidate organizations began to gain the first real political traction from using information technology, however modestly. Their experiments demonstrated four major principles of political communication on the Internet. The first was that a fundamental difference exists in the nature of broadcast political communication and Internet-based political communication: audience self-selection. Although little systematic polling data was available, it became clear that Internet-based audiences were vastly different from the citizens exposed to broadcast campaign commercials. Not only were Internet-using citizens socioeconomically selective, but citizens viewing candidates' web sites and signing up for electronic mail messages had passed through a filter of intentionality: They were sufficiently interested in the campaign to seek out information and interaction. That made web sites fundamentally different from television advertising and news coverage. The emergent wisdom among campaigns in 1998 was that the audience for a candidate web site was likely comprised chiefly of supporters, a few undecided voters, and journalists.

The second lesson of 1998 was that as a means for communicating with citizens and journalists, effective information technology was not cheap. In earlier election cycles, low levels of sophistication meant that operating internal communication systems and web sites was comparatively inexpensive. By 1998, larger numbers of candidates on line, more sophistication about the technology, and a fading novelty effect among citizens resulted in greater competition among candidates for attention of citizens through the Internet. As a result, production values at web sites rose substantially, as did the sophistication of customized messages and interactive techniques. Running an effective Internet-based campaign operation was far less expensive than mounting a broadcast advertising campaign, but it still required a substantial investment. Any candidate could create a web site for $5,000 or less, which was certainly less costly than television. But really competitive web sites in 1998 cost ten times that much, and so better-endowed candidates again had the advantage. By 2000, the cost of top web sites would be yet another order higher than that, running in the hundreds of thousands of dollars. These new economics of web sites solidified the relationship between level of office and use of new media. One analysis for 1998 estimates that about 86 percent of campaigns with total budgets exceeding $1 million had

campaign web sites, while only 54 percent of those with budgets under
$50,000 had them.[184] Something similar to the traditional relationship
between financial resources and communication capacity had emerged.
The new media had a far lower threshold for entry than television, since
almost any candidate could afford at least some form of web site and
electronic mail system; but money still bought apparently more power
and efficacy in this new medium.

The third lesson of 1998 was that in the area of interaction with supporters, the Internet offered real value. The new communication channels offered novel ways for campaigns to engage interested citizens. What
many candidates found to be a weakness of the web – namely, the inability to reach the broad, nonselective audiences of television – more
sophisticated candidate organizations exploited as an advantage: a direct
channel for sustained communication with selective groups of supporters who might be turned into donors or volunteers. One of the most
successful campaigns in this regard was that of Barbara Boxer for Senate
in California. Her site provided what amounted to a changing interactive
exhibit about the candidate, which was designed to keep interested voters
engaged and coming back to the site right up until election day. Rather
than attempting to persuade voters who were undecided or inclined toward her opponent, the Boxer site was intended to boost turnout among
supporters – not unlike precinct-walking immediately before an election.
Her campaign also helped pioneer ways for supporters to make campaign
donations by credit card, raising about $25,000 this way.[185] That was a
paltry amount for a California Senate race, but enough to constitute
proof of the viability of a new means for moving campaign funds.

The fourth lesson of 1998 came from the idiosyncratic campaign of
Jesse Ventura for the governorship of Minnesota. Lacking the traditional
organizational support of a major party and the financial resources
of his opponents, Democrat Skip Humphrey and Republican Norm
Coleman, Reform Party candidate Jesse Ventura relied almost exclusively on comparatively inexpensive information technology in lieu of
the traditional campaign organization. His campaign initiated its web

[184] The study was conducted by *Campaigns and Elections* magazine, a publication of
Congressional Quarterly, Inc. It relied on a sample of 270 campaigns drawn during
July and August of 1998. It was reported at the time on the Campaigns and Elections
web site, http://www.camelect.com/survey.html, but has since been removed. For
information, see www.campaignline.com.
[185] David A. Dulio, Donald L. Goff, and James A. Thurber, "Untangled Web: Internet
Use during the 1998 Election," *PS: Political Science and Politics* 32, no. 1 (1999):
53–59.

presence in February 1998, and never opened a traditional campaign headquarters. It had no paid employees until the final two months, when it took on a single paid staff person as campaign manager.[186] Instead, the Ventura campaign relied on its web site and e-mail distribution list as well as fax technology and telephones to solicit and organize volunteers, run campaign events, direct the volunteer campaign, and raise funds. According to his campaign manager, the on-line fund-raising efforts produced about one-third of Ventura's total of $600,000 in donations.[187] What funds the campaign did raise could go almost exclusively to broadcast advertising and travel for the candidate, since Ventura was not paying salaries, rent, or other traditional campaign costs.[188] Internally, the Ventura campaign consisted of an almost entirely "virtual" organization, while externally it was represented by a modest broadcast advertising presence connected to a network of volunteers.

Observers of the Ventura campaign, as well as its campaign manager, have widely credited information technology for being instrumental to Ventura's victory – the first case where the presence of a new means of political communication materially altered an election outcome. Without the Internet, some said, Ventura would not have won.[189] While it is clear that the successful Ventura campaign relied more heavily on information infrastructure in place of traditional political infrastructure than any major campaign to date, this claim is problematic and its comparison with Kennedy in 1960 is not useful. Ventura brought enormous name recognition to his candidacy, won a three-way race with just 39 percent of the vote total, and ran in a state with a history of support for nontraditional candidates. These features of the 1998 Minnesota governor's race are more important than the Internet in explaining the

---

[186] Phil Madsen, "Notes Regarding Jesse Ventura's Internet Use in His 1998 Campaign for Minnesota Governor," Dec. 7, 1998, Jesse Ventura for Governor Volunteer Committee, http://www.jesseventura.org/internet/netnotes.htm.

[187] Phil Madsen, "Notes Regarding Jesse Ventura's Internet Use"; Bill McAuliffe, "Ventura Riding the Web," Star Tribune, March 1, 1999, http://www.startribune.com.

[188] Dennis Cass, "'The Body' Rocks Minnesota," ABC News, Nov. 4, 1998, http://abcnews.go.com/sections/us/DailyNews/pn_jesse981104.html.

[189] Phil Noble, "Jesse Watch: The PoliticsOnline Summary," 1998, http://www.politicsonline.com/jv/summary.html; Jon Katz, "The Morning After: Digital Democracy II," Slashdot, Dec. 12, 1998, http://www.slashdot.org/features/98/12/20/1210224.shtml; Diane Lynch, "Being There," Christian Science Monitor, on-line edition, Jan. 5, 1999, http://www.csmonitor.com/atcsmonitor/cybercoverage/media/p-media010599.html; Rebecca Fairley Raney, "Former Wrestler's Campaign Got a Boost from the Internet," New York Times Cybertimes Edition, Nov. 6, 1998, http://www.politicsonline.com/coverage/nytimes2/06campaign.html.

outcome. It is more useful to say that the Ventura campaign, like Boxer's, established proof of principle, namely, that under the right circumstances, it is possible to operate a successful campaign organization with little traditional campaign infrastructure. As a tool of internal communication and coordination, information infrastructure has the potential to reduce campaign costs.

These four lessons of the 1998 races summarize much of the state of information technology in political campaigns at the end of the century. By the time of the 2000 primaries, virtually every candidate for national and statewide office in the United States employed new channels for external political communication based on information technology, about two dozen national political consulting firms were offering election campaign services focused on information technology, and of course virtually every campaign relied heavily on information infrastructure for its internal operations.[190] In various ways, most campaigns had absorbed the lessons about new media from the elections of 1992 to 1998. The 2000 election would see these lessons put into more widespread practice and would reveal where campaigns' use of the new technology was similar to that of interest groups and where it differed.

During the 2000 primary season, the most significant uses of new media in campaigns involved fund raising and the organization of volunteers for major underdog candidates, especially Bill Bradley and John McCain. Bradley himself made on-line activities a fundamental part of the campaign from his earliest stages of planning, hiring a leading Internet consultant to head the effort. The Bradley campaign was one of only two major presidential campaigns in 2000 to designate its Internet manager a "senior adviser," reporting directly to the campaign manager and equivalent in access and rank to the television and polling consultants.[191] The initial objective of the Bradley campaign's adoption of

[190] A partial list of political consulting firms offering Internet services as of October 2000 is CampaignAdvantage, CampaignOffice.com, Campaign Zone, Capitol City Consulting, Capitol Online, Casey Dorin, Democrats.com, Digital Gear Internet Industries, GO-GOP Internet Consulting, Grassroots.com, Hathaway Group, Integrated Web Strategy, iPolitics.com, Mindshare Internet Campaigns, New Media Communications, Net Politics Group.com, Patriot Campaign Consulting, Politics Online, U.S. Elect 2000, USPolitics.net, and Votenet.com.

[191] The other was the Buchanan campaign, which otherwise placed little emphasis or resources into its effort. Sources are Lynn Reed, Internet manager for Bill Bradley, telephone interview by Diane Johnson for the author, Nov. 17, 2000; Tim Haley, campaign manager for Pat Buchanan, telephone interview by Diane Johnson for the author, Nov. 20, 2000; Jan Braswell, webmaster for Pat Buchanan, telephone

information technology was symbolic. Given his standing as underdog to the incumbent Vice President, the campaign's first goals were to convince a network of donors that Bradley was a serious candidate, just as Dees-Thomases had persuaded the mass media that her efforts were serious and had the potential to be successful. The Bradley campaign relied substantially on the web site for that job, displaying photographs of Bradley on the campaign trail and other documents designed to signal his viability. Lynn Reed, his Internet director, describes the tactic as follows: "People were asking us, 'Are you crazy? How can you take on the sitting Vice President?' In order to raise enough money, we had to convince potential fundraisers that we were for real. They could look at the web site and see pictures of Bradley out on the campaign trail. So at the beginning, we were trying to persuade a select group of people that this was a real campaign."[192]

As the campaign matured, strategy for the site shifted toward attempting to engage supporters and potential supporters, along the lines of the Boxer and Ventura models. In particular, campaign officials hoped to create a mechanism for interested citizens to become involved. Reed says that the campaign attempted to provide Bradley supporters "as much additional information as possible . . . so that we can communicate with them and have a longer conversation than just that 30 second chunk of television time."[193] An archive of documents, issue papers, and biographical information at the web site therefore had a different focus than television advertising, which was aimed at attracting citizens' attention to the campaign. Bradley's strategy was to use television to attract the attention of the public, and then to use the web to engage those who proved interested.

Bradley collected electronic mail addresses of citizens through its web site, and eventually amassed a list of about 85,000 "volunteers" this way.[194] During the campaign, Reed said, "[T]he biggest lesson that all of us learned was from the success of the Jesse Ventura campaign last year. That wasn't so much the web site but their use of e-mail to organize folks, to get them to come out to campaign events, to communicate with

interview by Diane Johnson for the author, Nov. 20, 2000; and Rebecca Fairley Raney, "Campaign Lessons from the Bradley Camp," *Inter@ctive Week*, July 3, 2000, pp. 26–27.

[192] Reed, personal interview.

[193] Published interview with Lynn Reed, Freedom Channel, December 9, 1999, http://www.freedomchannel.com.

[194] Reed, personal interview.

them on an on-going basis. We in the Bradley campaign now send out probably eight or ten e-mails a day, not always to our full list, sometimes to subdivided portions of the list."[195] For Bradley, the advantage of this channel for communication was its vastly greater speed and lower cost than mail and phone trees.

Collecting donations through the Internet was a high priority for Bradley, who led a successful effort to change Federal Election Commission (FEC) rules on credit card donations. Prior to 2000, individual donations to candidates by credit card – which meant all Internet-based donations – did not qualify for federal matching funds under FEC rules. The commission rules were the result of concern about fraud and illegal donations from corporations and foreign citizens. At the urging of candidates in the 2000 primaries, most notably Bradley, the FEC changed its rules in June to permit credit card donations to qualify. According to the campaign, about 1 percent of visitors to Bradley's campaign site made a credit-card donation.[196]

John McCain's campaign and organization were similar to Bradley's. The plan for making use of the Internet in the campaign began with the organizers of McCain's exploratory committee, based again in part on the success of Jesse Ventura.[197] In the months before the New Hampshire primary, McCain proved he could organize and manage volunteers using electronic mail exclusively, and that he could raise funds the same way. In an interview with the author, McCain attributed much power to the Internet, claiming that his web site "kept [them] alive" during the primary campaign.[198] He rejected my devil's advocate proposition to him that campaign sites – especially his – are useful only for managing donations. He argued that the new technology permits campaigns to communicate with a network of supporters and volunteers, and that this adds meaningfully to campaign strategy and success. At the end of the year, long after his unsuccessful primary run was over, McCain claimed he was still maintaining a database of 30,000 e-mail addresses.

One of the most interesting aspects of the McCain campaign was the immediacy it revealed in the psychology of campaign donations.

---

[195] Reed, published interview.   [196] Reed, personal interview.
[197] Source is Max Fose, McCain campaign official, cited in *Inter@ctive Week*, July 3, 2000, p. 60, and reported by PoliticsOnline.com. See *Net Pulse* 5, no. 1 (Jan. 2, 2001); *Net Pulse* 4, no. 9 (May 2, 2000); *Net Pulse* 2, no. 13 (July 1, 1998); *Net Pulse* 4, no. 4 (Feb. 16, 2000), http://netpulse.politicsonline.com.
[198] John McCain, personal interview with the author, Dec. 9, 2000, Phoenix, Ariz.

After winning the New Hampshire primary on the first of February, the campaign received a surge of donations in a very short period, about $1 million in two days. The capacity for citizens to respond immediately with their wallets to news events appeared to stimulate donations, a finding consistent with the results of survey analysis of donations. According to a McCain campaign official, nearly half of those giving money through the Internet were first-time donors to a political campaign, and a large majority were younger than forty-five.[199] In the two-week period following the New Hampshire victory over George Bush, McCain's campaign signed up about 26,000 volunteers through the Internet and received another $2.5 million in donations on top of the million from the first two days. By April, McCain had raised about $6.4 million through his web site and collected a self-reported 142,000 electronic mail addresses of volunteers.[200] The McCain campaign exploited the on-line donation surge itself as a newsworthy event, and was successful at generating beneficial media stories about the rush to donate.

Most journalists covering the on-line donations phenomenon missed an important subtlety. Some of the "Internet money" was simply traditional donations that candidates steered through their web sites in lieu of accepting checks or telephone pledges.[201] Across the board, reports of "Internet donations" in the 2000 races included both funds that would have been secured by telephone or fund-raising events and "new" money that was likely stimulated directly by the Internet option for making donations. By mid-February of 2000, the top four presidential candidates had received a total of about $7.5 million on line, which constituted 5 percent of fund-raising totals. By the end of the campaigns in 2000, the extent to which the candidates' funding came through Internet-based channels varied substantially. McCain reported a little over $6 million, which represented about 20 percent of his total of $31 million, but it is unclear what fraction of that amounted to funds steered from traditional mechanisms for donating. Gore, on the other hand, received about $10

---

[199] Quoted in Glen Warchol, "Web Becomes Player in Presidential Race," *Salt Lake Tribune*, Feb. 2, 2000, p. A1.

[200] Figures from Max Fose, *Inter@ctive Week*, p. 60.

[201] According to a campaign official, in the race to report Internet donations to the media, several campaigns taking donations by telephone and at traditional fund-raisers had staff enter these donations through the campaigns' web sites, and then reported the funds as "Internet donations" as an indicator of swelling interest in the campaign. This practice of steering funds aside, a nontrivial amount of funding did flow directly into the campaigns' web sites.

million through the Internet, half of which was steered and half "organic" Internet funds.[202]

Use of information technology by minor-party candidates running in 2000 had more in common with Bradley and McCain than with Bush and Gore. The rhetoric of minor candidates is often overly enthusiastic about information infrastructure as a means for overcoming resource disadvantages. A spokesman for Natural Law Party candidate John Hagelin claimed that "the Internet has been the single most important tool that John Hagelin's campaign has had in getting the word out in brief, and in depth, about the issues and platforms that he proposes."[203] His campaign reported receipts of $5,000 to $10,000 per day in donations through the Internet as of June 2000. Voters can go right to the web site and get the party platform."[204] The Green Party also reports that it "does almost all its business on the Internet," because it is so modestly funded.[205]

Inside the Ralph Nader organization, the primary objective of the five-person external Internet campaign was to raise money, and secondarily to sign up volunteers.[206] The Nader staff did not solicit requests for funds by electronic mail until the end of the campaign, when it sent "four or five" electronic mail requests and received about $100,000 that it used toward its final media buys. It also signed up electronically about 40,000 volunteers.[207] Nader's chief web strategist reports that information technology was the "ultimate means of communication with people" specifically because the campaign lacked the resources of the major candidates."[208]

The Pat Buchanan organization made even less use of new information technologies, except for communication and coordination within the organization.[209] It dedicated only one staff person to managing the web-based external communication effort. In an interview for this project immediately following the general election in 2000, Buchanan's campaign manager was aware that some funds had come in through the campaign's web site, but he did not know the amount or even whether the site

---

[202] Anonymous official, Gore campaign, personal interview with the author, March 1, 2001. Sources for McCain are: Max Fose, *Inter@ctive Week*.

[203] Quoted in Nate Brown, "Seeking a Level Playing Field for Third Parties," *Inter@ctive Week*, July 3, 2000, p. 40.

[204] Quoted in David Ross, "The Internet – Kingmaker for Small Parties?" *The Standard*, April 6, 2000, http://www.thestandard.com/article/display/0,1151,13887,00.html.

[205] Quoted in ibid.

[206] Jonah Baker, webmaster for Ralph Nader, telephone interview by Diane Johnson for the author, Nov. 17, 2000.

[207] Ibid.   [208] Ibid.   [209] Braswell interview.

had paid for itself.[210] Buchanan's organization also made some use of information technology for communicating with the press, but made little use of the Internet to turn out supporters or persuade undecided voters. Instead, the Buchanan organization relied much more heavily on using electronic mail to organize staff and volunteers. According to the campaign manager, "[M]ore than anything, we used [information technology] for keeping the troops in the field informed."[211]

There is little evidence that these efforts by minor party candidate or-ganizations to exploit new information infrastructure are having much bearing on their viability. To be sure, the number of minor-party can-didates running for President shows signs of growing, but information technology is hardly the cause of this trend. Between 1900 and 1960, an average of around five minor party candidates ran for President nationally every four years. By the election of 1980, the figure was up to ten, and it averaged thirteen in the 1990s.[212] So the trend is an old one. In the early days of the Internet, major party candidates were actually more likely than minor party candidates to use the Internet. In 1996 and again in 1998, for instance, only about a third of minor party candidates for House and Senate had web sites, compared with all of the major party Senate candidates and over half of major party House candidates.[213] Moreover, the number of minor party candidates receiving more than 5 percent of the vote for President or winning seats in Congress has not improved over time, even since the rise of the Internet. While the contemporary information revolution may help some resource-poor minor parties get their message out, it has yet to affect vote totals, let alone outcomes.

The greater sophistication of major candidates' use of new technology was especially evident in the 2000 campaigns. Front-runners Bush and Gore mounted elaborate web- and e-mail–based operations, although for both the Internet was at best a complement to the vastly more important traditional media campaigning. Bush eventually committed substantial resources to the Internet, including at peak about a dozen staff, but the

---

[210] Haley, personal interview.   [211] Ibid.

[212] Steven J. Rosenstone, Roy Behr, and Edward Lazarus, *Third Parties in America: Citizen Response to Major Party Failure* (Princeton: Princeton University Press, 1984); Foun-dation for Public Affairs and Congressional Quarterly, Inc., *Congressional Quar-terly's Guide to U.S. Elections*, 3rd ed. (Washington, D.C.: Foundation for Public Affairs, 1994); Richard M. Scammon, Alice V. McGillivray, and Rhodes Cook, eds., *America Votes: A Handbook of Contemporary American Election Statistics, 1996*, vol. 22 (Washington, D.C.: CQ Press, 1996).

[213] Elaine Kamarck and Joseph S. Nye, Jr., *Democracy.com: Governance in a Networked World* (Hollis, N.H.: Hollis Publishers, 1999).

organization placed comparatively little emphasis on the Internet as a means for fund raising or organizing volunteers. The Internet campaign staff were compartmentalized, disconnected from policy and press operations, and granted little authority over the messages distributed through the Internet. In the Bush organization, the Internet was never more than a modest supplement to traditional media. A Bush campaign official explained the approach by saying that since an increasing number of people use the Internet, "it just makes sense to start pushing your message that way. In campaigns in the past you had your three mediums – your print, your TV, and your radio – and that was it. That was how you got your message out there, and now the Internet has blossomed into a very viable source for distributing your message."[214] Still, not all media were equal in the view of the Bush organization, and clearly the Internet was at the bottom of the stack.

The Gore campaign was more ambitious in its efforts to exploit new communication channels. The five-person Internet staff was well integrated into the rest of the campaign, reporting directly to the campaign's communication director. According to Ben Green, Gore's Director of Internet Operations, the campaign's strategy was to use the Internet in three ways: as a general means for distributing the candidate's evolving message, as a way to raise funds, and as a way to "establish a one-to-one relationship" with supporters.[215] The campaign made a concerted effort to include Gore's web address visibly in each televised appearance on the campaign trail. Where possible, the campaign displayed the address on each side of podiums and speaking stands, so that photos or video from any camera angle would be likely to include it. The purpose of this strategy was to "drive" interested citizens who might see Gore on television to visit the web site, where the campaign could engage them and possibly obtain contact information and other specifics. More than any other campaign to date, the Gore organization attempted to use "new" and "old" media together.

Data on traffic to the Gore site shows two elements of citizen use of the web site. The first is a steady base of activity accelerating gradually over the course of the campaign, reflecting steadily increasing attention to the race as election day neared. In addition, citizen use of the

---

[214] Cliff Angelo, e-campaign manager for the Bush campaign, personal interview by Professor Richard Davis of Brigham Young University, for a related research project, Oct. 18, 2000, Austin, Texas.

[215] Ben Green, director of Internet operations for the Gore campaign, personal interview with the author, March 1, 2001, Santa Barbara, Calif.

web site experiences periodic spikes associated with news events. There were about a dozen such spikes, associated with news about the campaign's move to Nashville, the Bradley-Gore debate, the Iowa caucuses and New Hampshire primary, Super Tuesday, and the conventions. In some cases, spikes in use of the site came from events in other campaigns, including McCain's win in Michigan and Bush's announcement of his running mate. Even the Columbine school shooting was correlated with a surge in attention to Gore's site. The surges tended to bring with them increases in the flow of campaign funds. The highest of these was about $150,000 in donations that came through the web site on the day following Bush's selection of Dick Cheney as a running mate. About half of that was in response to an e-mail solicitation, and half unsolicited.

Like the Bush official, Green says that the Internet provides "an opportunity you don't have with television and its fifteen-second sound bites." The opportunity is not to attract disengaged or undecided voters, but to recruit interested supporters on the basis of information-intensive communication. One technique was to tailor messages seen by citizens returning to the site, based on records from their previous visits. The campaign solicited information on citizens' location and interests, and then customized what the citizen saw on return visits as well as distributing tailored messages by electronic mail. According to Green, the campaign's aim was to permit a citizen visiting the site to say, "I'm from Pennsylvania and I'm interested in civil rights," and from then on receive a tailored political experience accordingly. The campaign amassed a collection of 400,000 electronic mail addresses in this way. Green says for a marginal cost of essentially nothing, he could send a message "to women in New York who are interested in the environment." The Gore organization also experimented with "instant messaging technology," which permitted citizens who had visited the site to identify and communicate directly with other citizens who had compatible interests and who might be located near one another.

Although Gore's campaign was among the most serious and intensive efforts of any campaign so far in the United States to exploit new channels for communication, in the end the effort did not come close to displacing the fundamental importance of traditional media. In almost every way, the Gore campaign, like Bush's, McCain's, and Bradley's, employed precisely the same strategies that have dominated campaigns for several decades. The Internet served as a useful and often profitable side activity in this strategy, but altered neither strategy or organizational structure. As Lynn Reed of the Bradley campaign reports, "[t]he rules of campaigning since the beginning of the TV era are still in play."[216]

SUMMARY OF THE CASES

What do the cases of the Libertarians, Environmental Defense, Save the E-Rate Coalition, the Million Mom March, and the 2000 campaigns suggest about the state of postbureaucratic political organization? It comes as no surprise that none of the cases involves a purely postbureaucratic organization. Few organizations or populations of organizations respond to changed environments by transforming themselves *in toto* in the space of a few years. Yet all five cases exhibit some of the features of postbureaucratic organization, and together they provide suggestive support for the thesis that a relationship exists in contemporary politics between the evolution of information abundance and changes in organizational structure.

Evidence in the cases about the effects of information technology on staff and resource requirements is intriguing. For small organizations with few resources, the infrastructure of information technology appears to substitute in certain cases for money and staff, permitting modestly or poorly endowed groups to behave as if they had greater resources. The Libertarian Party and, at the outset, the Million Mom March, offer the best illustration. The Libertarians avoided the costs of a major mass mailing or media campaign by using electronic mail and the web. Although the cost was still substantial and limited their ability to repeat the effort, it was far lower than the cost of traditional techniques of communication. Organizers of the Million Mom March exploited the low cost of information and communication differently. Its founders used the technology to build a viable, network-based organization with very

---

[216] Reed, personal interview. The 2000 elections also saw the first important experiments with banner advertising, the closest equivalent to broadcast advertising because of its inadvertency. For instance, the Bush campaign spent a total of about $100,000 for banner ads, including an ad about Bush's tax cut proposal in the finance section of Yahoo, where citizens viewing financial information would see a notice about Bush's plan to reduce income taxes. For the most part, banner ads such as these were not very successful, however. Banner advertising proved for some candidates to be either ineffective or more costly than broadcast advertising. The Bradley campaign had poor success with a set of ads, and the Buchanan campaign found that a petition campaign to place the Reform Party on state ballots cost about $80 per signature through banner ads, which is far more than the $5 or so per signature charged by political consulting firms. Sources: Angelo interview; Braswell interview; Haley interview; Reed, personal interview; Reed, published interview; Pamela Parker, "Political Campaigns Discover Online Advertising," *InternetNews*, Feb. 4, 2000, http://www.Internetnews.com.

little funding. They then used that organization to attract media attention, funding, endorsements, and more volunteers.

The larger, richer organizations also exploited low-cost information and communication to expand their reach. Environmental Defense and some of the other environmental organizations, and to a lesser extent the NEA and its allies in the E-Rate campaign, were able to lower their marginal cost of identifying interested citizens and mobilizing them into political action. Doing so, however, required substantial investments of resources that raised net costs. The cost of the technological infrastructure necessary to realize lowered marginal costs of communication was typically high, so those organizations best able to invest in new techniques reaped the largest benefits.

Increased fixed requirements in resources is especially clear in the case of the electoral campaigns. Several of the campaigns remarked at how inexpensively they could communicate with supporters through the Internet. Lynn Reed of the Bradley campaign says, "In the summer, we decided to canvas in New Hampshire . . . so we e-mailed about 5,000 people who were within driving distance. . . . About 300 replied, and of those, about two thirds showed up. We could never have afforded to make the phone calls with that rate of return."[217] Tim Haley, campaign manager for Pat Buchanan's Reform Party race in 2000, goes so far as to say that by using new technology, "It doesn't cost anything to get people to events."[218] It did, however, cost the campaigns to establish their Internet-based systems. For most of the campaigns, operating Internet-based tools added to the cost of running for office. The fact that the better-funded campaigns made the most sophisticated use of the technology drives home the point that the new information environment does not necessarily advantage the underdog.

The pattern suggested by the five cases is that larger and more well-established political organizations invest in expensive information systems that raise the cost of doing business on the whole but that permit them to project political influence under the right conditions even further than before. Smaller, poorly endowed organizations tend to use new information technology to substitute for resources they do not have, which creates new opportunities for exercising political influence. In terms of the hypothesis represented in Figure 3.1, the diminution of the threshold effect finds support in these cases. The relationship farther up the curve is less clear on the basis of these cases. Clearly, information

---

[217] Reed, personal interview.   [218] Haley interview.

technology expands capacity to organize collective action, so the dotted curve is positioned above the solid curve, as shown in the figure. But it may be that capacity to organize collective action actually accelerates as resources go up, with the curve growing more steep across the horizontal axis as greater investments in information technology produce ever larger marginal gains in organizing power. The case of ED and the major election campaigns supports this interpretation. On the other hand, some of the cases suggest that information abundance simply makes the relationship between resources and political influence less predictable. In any event, the overall effect of information abundance is neither a simple "leveling of the political playing field," as some observers have speculated, nor a reinforcement of traditional patterns of influence and power. In the new information environment, both wealthy and poor political groups may each find their hand strengthened, in different ways. Traditionally powerful groups can exploit low-cost communication and new levels of control over information to strengthen what they do, just as traditionally weak groups may find that on occasion they can use new technology to become players in a political game that is otherwise largely closed to them.

Changes in boundary conditions in some of the cases are related to these resource considerations. Information abundance does appear to offer the potential for more porous organizational boundaries in at least two ways. Especially in the case of Environmental Defense and the E-Rate coalition, the rapid, intensive movement of information between organizations strengthened opportunities for forming coalitions. In these coalitions, sharing of material resources and the costs of political action is far less important than moving pertinent information. As a result, the particular distribution of traditional resources among organizations may in some cases be less important to the structure of collective action that results when organizations join together. Second, at the low end of the resource scale, lack of institutionalization and diminished costs may induce some groups to exert comparatively little effort at defining and controlling their boundaries. Groups that invest few resources in their efforts, like the Libertarians and the Million Mom March at the outset, may be more likely to take a laissez-faire approach to who participates and to how information is controlled and managed. In general, as information becomes abundant and inexpensive, it moves more readily throughout the political system and is less constrained by the boundaries of organizations. As information becomes less well institutionalized in this way, the boundaries of some organizations themselves become less important.

Resource and boundary dynamics in the cases suggest two conclusions. The number of "elite" voices in politics is likely to rise, along with the overall level of competition for citizen attention and engagement. Whether traditionally powerful interests or previously peripheral groups prevail under these new conditions is likely to be a function of the structure of political conflict in any particular case.

The dynamics of political membership show some of the most striking developments in these cases, and they are related to cost and boundary issues as well. For some of the organizations, changes in the nature of membership are related to increased permeability of organizational boundaries. Among the five cases, three involve traditional membership organizations: Environmental Defense, the E-Rate groups, and the Libertarian Party. The case of ED and its sister environmental organizations shows the strongest shift in the direction of postbureaucratic membership, and this shift is manifestly tied to low-cost communication and information. The new category of members at ED, as well as at the World Wildlife Fund and Defenders of Wildlife, is the most substantial departure in the cases from any element of traditional political organization. This new form of "member" does not follow the principles of collective action theory in which "side payments" are needed as inducements to membership or participation. These "members" do not consider themselves as such, and indeed many would likely be surprised to learn that ED considers them part of its organization.

In the case of the E-Rate coalition, use of information technology by the education and library groups likely permitted the organizations temporarily to reach outside their own memberships to identify citizens with an interest in education, but, more important, it helped them mobilize an ad hoc collection of memberships not accustomed to this kind of political action, certainly not together.[219] The Libertarian Party exhibits the most dramatic temporary extension in reach. Low-cost, decentralized, self-organizing communication techniques permitted the leaders of an organization in the space of a few weeks to mobilize nearly ten times more citizens than belonged to its own membership.

If a universal postbureaucratic phenomenon appears in the cases, it is the tendency toward speed, opportunism, and event-driven political organization. Many of the informants interviewed for this project volunteered the observation that political processes have been accelerated

---

[219] Anonymous staff member, National Education Association, telephone interview by Eric Patterson for the author, May 30, 2000.

by information technology. What that means varies a great deal by organization, but the general trend is toward increased opportunities for organizations to respond rapidly to unfolding events around them. That capacity means more than simply greater efficiency at pursuing goals. As rapid responsiveness becomes more viable alongside long-term strategic planning, it appears to consume a greater fraction of organizations' attention. As the organizations in this study enhanced their capacity to make tactical decisions and follow up with political action on a daily and even hourly basis, the orientation of some showed an increased emphasis on short-range planning and event-based political action.

An important part of this phenomenon is the splitting of traditional memberships and citizen groups into submemberships on the basis of better information about interests and location. Especially in the case of ED and the electoral campaigns, organizations have come to understand the public in terms of vastly more specific information than in the past. As a result, these organizations are more inclined toward highly specific efforts at mobilization rather than blanket calls for participation by entire lists of memberships or supporters. This contributes to a kind of shape-changing phenomenon in which organizations draw on what are effectively different "memberships" from issue to issue and event to event. As information grows more abundant, the boundaries and membership of a political organization are increasingly a function of the particular event in which it is involved.

These are some of the possibilities and implications of postbureaucratic political organization suggested by the case studies. They endorse the theory from Chapter 3 that information abundance leads to a decay in traditionally bureaucratic forms of political organization and collective action, but they also illustrate quite clearly constraints on the postbureaucratic shift. The organizations in all the cases confronted in one way or another the limited capacity of new information technology to attract or direct the public's attention as effectively as broadcast and print media.[220] Literally every organization operated on the assumption that in an environment of information abundance, efforts to communicate political messages using new technology would mainly reach those citizens already interested in an issue or cause. None made the mistake of attempting to replicate the influence of television advertising

---

[220] I am especially indebted to Russ Neuman for helpful conversations and advice on the nature of political attention in the interaction between "new media" and "old."

using the Internet, and the shrewdest used "new" and "old" media in complementary ways. For the Million Mom March, effective use of low-cost information and communication proved a way to win the media coverage required to create public attention; for the Gore campaign, the presence of public attention to mass media provided a way to steer interested citizens to the Internet.

Several of the cases also illustrate the inability of communication mediated by technology to substitute for personal relationships between political elites who know and trust one another. None of the organizations abandoned its efforts at traditional lobbying, and only in the case of the Libertarians and the Million Mom March, which had little lobbying apparatus, did a group pursue major policy change without a strong element of traditional, relationship-based political influence. This dependence on traditional "inside" lobbying is most evident in the E-Rate case, where the organizations that mobilized citizens integrated the resulting public response into their lobbying efforts in Congress. This practice is consistent with research on the traditional outside lobbying behavior of groups. As Ken Kollman has shown, groups typically do not change aggregate public opinion favoring or opposing policies on various issues through their outside lobbying efforts. Instead, those efforts alter the public salience of the issues on which they lobby, thereby affecting elected officials' judgments about which issues are likely to be a factor in the next election. That process in turn enhances their capacity to persuade public officials through their "inside" lobbying efforts.[221]

The case studies illustrate how postbureaucratic forms of organization can lack the capacity to project political influence over time. The traditional, bureaucratic political organization can advocate a position, back it up with money, monitor an elected official's actions, and pose a credible threat of withholding donations in the future or of mobilizing voters against the official. Postbureaucratic organizations may be less able to connect advocacy at the most public stage of policy making to the rest of the policy process. This limitation may also draw organizations away from complex issues of national scope that require sustained efforts.

In the case of the Million Moms, leaders recognized that they did not possess the means to continue their pursuit of policy change after their day on the Washington Mall, because they lacked sufficient organizational structure. Immediately following the march, they formed an alliance with

---

[221] Ken Kollman, *Outside Lobbying: Public Opinion and Interest Group Strategies* (Princeton: Princeton University Press, 1998).

the Bell Foundation of San Francisco, a victim-based gun control group, in order to better institutionalize themselves. A year and a half later, in October 2001, they were still in operation and announced a merger with the Brady Campaign and Brady Center to Prevent Gun Violence, formerly Handgun Control. This meant that the march gained some of the advantages and resources of the traditional political organization, while the Brady organization gained the new "membership" and network-based structure of the march. The consequences of this hybridization of organizational types remain to be seen, but it represents a recognition of the limitations on extreme postbureaucratic political association.

Cheap-talk effects are the final form of constraint, and they appear in the cases in several ways. Many of the organizations found that in the absence of cost limitations on sending messages to "members," they had to self-regulate the number of solicitations they distributed. Organizations now have the capacity to distribute mass mail *more than once per day*, and a few did so – especially the campaign organizations. All feel the need to be selective and careful, however. The Gore campaign in particular sought to avoid overcommunicating with supporters up until the frantic final days of the campaign. The environmental groups sought to avoid "activist fatigue" by carefully rationing their outgoing messages.

Most of the organizations were sensitive to the need to avoid stimulating "junk" electronic correspondence to public officials. This was especially true of the established organizations such as ED. In early 2001, for example, Defenders of Wildlife undertook a campaign to persuade the Bush administration not to overturn a Clinton executive order banning road building in roadless National Forests. In addition to their sophisticated electronic network, called DEN (Defenders Electronic Network), the group also employed direct mail and a telephone campaign in which it called members and then transferred interested citizens directly to the White House, where they could register their views. The group recognized that this very expensive means of communication would signal public officials more powerfully than a mass electronic mail campaign. Perhaps the single most powerful strategy by the groups examined here is the use of low-cost Internet-based techniques to identify and organize citizens, followed by more costly efforts by mobilized citizens to communicate with public officials by phone, postal mail, fax, or in person.

Data on communication with Congress via electronic mail reveals the magnitude of the cheap-talk problem. By one estimate, the number of electronic mail messages directed at the House of Representatives in 2000 was about 48 million, up from 20 million in 1998.[222] This comes to an average of nearly 2,000 messages per week for each representative, and clearly presents problems for an institution accustomed to managing correspondence by hand. It was obvious by at least the year 2000 that members of Congress paid little or no attention to the junk electronic mail in this flood. For Congress, junk mail includes messages sent from citizens not resident in a member's state or district and impersonal, mass messages obviously composed by an organizer and simply forwarded along by citizens without effort. As an official of Hill and Knowlton puts it, "[i]f it is Spam, or e-mail from beyond their constituency, they don't care."[223]

On the other hand, it was also clear by 2000 that many members of Congress were attentive to personal messages that appeared to signal real political intent. Legislators are indeed solicitous of relevant information about constituents' interests and the possible course that various issues might take in the future. Many members were finding that electronic messages can, under the right circumstances, convey such information. Stephanie Vance, former Chief of Staff for a member of Congress and now an official at an on-line advocacy firm, confirms that members are indeed looking for relevant information in the flood of e-mail. She describes a form of cheap-talk funnel, estimating informally that 90 percent of electronic mail to members of Congress was being discarded in 2000, because it failed to identify the author as a constituent. Most of the rest of the electronic mail, she says, is form letters and mass mailings that are noted by members' offices but not treated as terribly important. The remainder constitutes thoughtful, original letters sent by constituents at some effort; these provide useful information to legislators. A staff person for Votenet, another firm with an obvious investment in electronic mail, reports roughly the same story, namely, that congressional staff they work with distinguish serious from nonserious electronic mail, treating serious electronic mail largely like letters by printing it out and providing counts by issue.[224]

A survey of congressional members' offices in 1998 found that many separate communications from citizens fall into three tiers: letters,

---

[222] Kathy Goldschmidt, "E-Mail Overload in Congress: Managing a Communications Crisis," the Congress Online Project, a joint project of the George Washington University and the Congressional Management Foundation, March 19, 2001, http://www.congressonlineproject.org/email.html.

[223] Anonymous staff member, Hill and Knowlton, telephone interview by Eric Patterson for the author, July 25, 2000.

[224] Dell and Tuteur interviews.

personal visits, and telephone calls at the top in importance; followed by faxes and serious electronic mail; and, in a distant third place, petitions, postcards, and form-letter campaigns, whether in electronic form or sent by mail.[225] In 2000, members of Congress adopted a policy aimed at helping them filter nonserious electronic mail from constituent communications of relevance. Under the new policy, members stopped accepting electronic mail sent directly from citizens, and instead required that constituents who wanted to send mail fill out web-based electronic mail forms. This mechanism made mass mailings difficult technically and provided a control on constituency status through zip code requests. From the members' perspective, potential advantages of messages communicated this way include the capacity to create flexible analyses of constituent comments and interests readily and automatically.

These efforts by public officials and political organizations to deal with new, low-cost communication techniques constitute a search for balance and proportion that is still in its initial stages of development. Political organizations know that the capacity to distribute messages cheaply guarantees that one can neither persuade citizens to become engaged nor convince elected officials that engaged citizens should be taken seriously. This fact limits the occasions in which low-cost alternative forms of collective action can be successful.

The cases suggest that a tension exists between new postbureaucratic political structures made possible by the latest technology and the set of traditional political structures and processes that in many ways remain dominant, at least so far. As they have in the past, bureaucratic organizations contribute to classical political pluralism in the United States, in which group politics is structured and organized by a set of traditional organizations. This is pluralism in Weberian and Olsonian terms. The consequence of new technology is evolution toward a kind of pluralism less easily recognizable in those terms. The cases suggest that it is too soon to identify in any detail the features of the information regime that will one day condense out of this latest information revolution. But, as past regimes do, it will surely feature new organizational structures adapted to the state of information and communication.

[225] OMB Watch, "Speaking Up in the Internet Age: Use and Value of Constituent E-mail and Congressional Web Sites," December 1998, http://http://www.ombwatch.org/ombpubs.html.

5

Political Individuals in the Fourth
Information Revolution

THE INFORMED CITIZEN?

The value of an informed citizenry is a well-established tenet of American popular culture.[1] At the core of good citizenship, so the belief goes, is the reasoned consideration of political information by citizens with an interest in civic affairs. To be informed is to fulfill part of one's civic duty, not only because information is a gateway into political engagement, but because being informed is itself virtuous. In short, the informed citizen is the responsible citizen, and the responsible citizen an informed one.

The story of information revolutions up through the rise of contemporary information technology raises an interesting question about this ideal of informed citizenship. If the evolution of media and the changing characteristics of information across time lead to changes in the nature of political intermediaries, what about levels of citizen engagement? Is the rise of information abundance and new postbureaucratic structures for collective action in the contemporary period linked to broader engagement in politics? Some of the case studies of the last chapter may seem to imply that the answer is yes. The Million Mom March, the Know Your Customer protest, and the new "lite-green" environmental affiliates might suggest that altered organizational structures are broadening participation in politics. As the nature of membership and the boundaries of organizations are altered, it may be that larger numbers of citizens are being drawn into politics – unless organizational changes simply mean new patterns of alliance and engagement by the

---

[1] This chapter expands on the theoretical argument and evidence from the 1996 and 1998 elections that appeared in an article by the author, "Information and Political Engagement in America: The Search for Effects of Information Technology at the Individual Level," *Political Research Quarterly* 54, no. 1 (2001): 53–67.

same body of citizens engaged in politics in the past. Direct evidence about the backgrounds of participants in most events such as the Million Mom March and the Know Your Customer protest is not available, so it is not possible to assess directly whether they were citizens newly mobilized into politics. Other, broader, forms of evidence are available, however, and these present an interesting picture. They show substantial differences between organizational-level and individual-level effects of information.

The history of previous information revolutions provides mixed clues about whether engagement expands or contracts (or neither) as changes in political information and communication occur. For one thing, it is important to note that the idea of a link between information and engagement is as much a product of politics as a source. Despite its apparently deep Madisonian resonance, the familiar belief in the necessity of informed citizenship did not originate in the nation's founding. It arose during the time that the second American information revolution was under way, as attacks on patronage and party power led to the evolution of a new ideal of citizenship and as the rise of new policy problems and processes created new informational demands on citizens and public officials. As Michael Schudson shows, the idea of the informed citizen as the good citizen owes more to Progressive politics than to Federalist ideas or the successes of nineteenth-century mass politics.[2] The ideal of the informed citizen was to the Progressive citizen what the rise of policy experts, rationalized bureaucracy, and technocracy was to the Progressive government institution. The new ideal displaced nineteenth-century norms of citizenship rooted in social association, which were manifest in bedrock partisan loyalties, torchlight processions, brass bands, spoils, and so on.

The norm of informed citizenship was not associated with increased levels of citizen engagement, however, at least in the voting booth. Between 1852 and the 1896, voting participation in presidential elections had fluctuated between 70 and 80 percent of eligible citizens. By 1904, it dropped to about 65 percent, and by 1912 was under 60 percent. By 1920, when the Twenty-second Amendment passed, participation in presidential elections was in the neighborhood of just 50 percent, comparable to current levels.[3] The reasons for this decline are multiple

---

[2] Michael Schudson, *The Good Citizen: A History of American Civic Life* (New York: Martin Kessler, 1998).

[3] Harold W. Stanley and Richard G. Niemi, *Vital Statistics on American Politics 1997–1998* (Washington, D.C.: CQ Press, 1998).

and have been explored thoroughly elsewhere. The realignment of 1896 reduced political competition in both the North and the South.[4] The disenfranchisement of African-Americans and poor whites, at least in the South, contributed further.[5] The destruction of party machines removed an important mobilizer of citizens, and the spread of more stringent registration rules also decreased participation in some places.

On top of these and other factors, the rationalized, informational approach to citizenship that emerged also likely contributed. As Schudson, Philip Converse, and others have argued, the new politics was simply less compelling to some voters than torchlight processions, brass bands, and other features of highly partisan contests that focused on emotional appeals and loyalty.[6] The new emphasis on policy, pamphlets, and scientific government over parades and patronage seems to have sapped citizen enthusiasm on election day.[7] The newly forming associations and interest groups of this era did a great deal to alter how political information was organized and how it moved throughout the political system, but the overall trend was not toward increased voting participation. The second information revolution encompassed political intermediaries, elites, and entrepreneurs, but certainly it did not sweep the mass public into the electoral process.

Later in the twentieth century, the third information revolution had roughly similar consequences for voting behavior. The capacity of broadcasting to focus enormous mass attention on political events was more than countered as any kind of stimulus to engagement by the effects of television on political parties as organizers and mobilizers of the electorate, and by its effect on political trust and the nature of citizens' attachments to the political process. Having climbed back up to 60 percent by the early 1960s, voting participation was back down to the mid-50 percent range by the '80s and actually reached the 50 percent mark by the '90s. Trends in other forms of traditional engagement varied during the third information revolution and regime. Donating money rose, working for a party fell, and contacting elected officials remained largely stable

[4] William H. Flanagin and Nancy Zingale, eds., *Political Behavior of the American Electorate,* 8th ed. (Washington, D.C.: CQ Press, 1994).

[5] Stanley and Niemi, *Vital Statistics on American Politics.*

[6] Schudson, *The Good Citizen;* Philip E. Converse, "Change in the American Electorate," in Angus Campbell and Philip E. Converse, eds., *The Human Meaning of Social Change* (New York: Russell Sage Foundation, 1972), pp. 263–337; Flanagin and Zingale, *Political Behavior of the American Electorate.*

[7] On this point, see, esp., Schudson, *The Good Citizen.*

until the end of the '80s, after which it fell.[8] On the whole, such activities certainly did not receive any major boost from the new information
environment. No consequential gains in overall citizen knowledge occurred during the 1960s and '70s, either.[9] Like the second information
regime, the third was a time of political disengagement by citizens from
the voting booths, while fundamental changes in the nature of political
intermediation were under way.

The first information revolution, on the other hand, was different in
this regard. The rise of the newspaper and the creation of a national system
of political communication in the 1820s and '30s was clearly a factor in
soaring political participation rates. The sweep of citizens into the voting
booths was faster and more abrupt than either of the great withdrawals
would be in later periods. In this one case at least, a dramatic change in
communication and information contributed both to a transformation
in the nature of political intermediation and an impetus for citizens to
become better engaged in democracy.

None of these prior information revolutions provides a particularly
strong case for what might happen in the contemporary period. There
are precedents in the prior developments for information expanding,
growing more complex and more widely distributed, but none where
information and communication also became less costly and so very
widely accessible and controllable by citizens. The kind of information
abundance evolving now is new, and history does not provide clear
precedents where questions about individual behavior and engagement
are concerned.

THEORETICAL CONSIDERATIONS

The classical approach to framing theoretical expectations about
information and individual levels of engagement might be called
"instrumental." This approach is dominated by rational choice theory,
but not limited to it. In this tradition, *changes in the cost and variety of
sources of information directly affect levels of political participation.* As information grows less costly and is provided by a greater variety of sources
over which individuals have control, more citizens are likely to become

---

[8] Steven J. Rosenstone and John Mark Hansen, *Mobilization, Participation, and Democracy in America* (New York: Macmillan, 1993); Stanley and Niemi, *Vital Statistics on
American Politics.*
[9] Michael X. Delli Carpini and Scott Keeter, *What Americans Know about Politics and
Why It Matters* (New Haven: Yale University Press, 1996).

engaged with politics. The centerpiece of this approach is the Downsian model of political rationality. As a classic of political science, *An Economic Theory of Democracy* is indeed as much a theory of political information as it is a theory of political behavior. In Anthony Downs's work, and in most of the work in the rational tradition, information is central to behavior because uncertainty is central. If one assumes as Downs does that uncertainty is a basic force in human affairs, then the acquisition and use of information to reduce uncertainty is an elemental feature of all human activity as well.[10] In the classical formulation, "coping with uncertainty is a major function of nearly every significant institution in society"[11] as well as a major activity of the political individual. At the same time, "most uncertainty is removable through the acquisition of information."[12]

Another feature of the rational model is the observation that information is costly. In the Downsian view, information costs are of two types: those associated with the acquisition of information – namely, the time, effort, and material resources needed to learn information relevant to a political goal – and those associated with its evaluation in the mind of the individual. The role of information in political activity is therefore subject to a law of diminishing marginal returns. In theory, "the information-seeker continues to invest resources in procuring data until the marginal return from information equals its marginal cost."[13] In practice, though, the situation is made slightly more complex by the fact that citizens' strength of preference varies. A citizen who is highly committed to a particular candidate or issue has little incentive to acquire information, since it is unlikely that any new information would alter his or her preferences. At the same time, Downs argues, a citizen who is uncertain and indifferent and who therefore could learn the most from a marginal increase in information may nonetheless be held back from obtaining it by ex ante indifference over outcomes.

Interestingly enough, a good deal of political science outside the rational choice tradition also approaches the relationship between information and participation in ways that are generally consistent with the rational approach, if not so explicit and well developed. The claim that the cost of political information could directly affect levels of participation

---

[10] Anthony Downs, *An Economic Theory of Democracy* (New York: Harper and Brothers, 1957).
[11] Ibid., p. 13.   [12] Ibid., p. 77.   [13] Ibid., p. 215.

is not an uncommon subtext in behavioral political science. Most closely allied, and spanning the boundary between rational and behavioral theories, are models of informational satisficing that posit that certain forms of behavior can be interpreted as efforts to avoid the need to acquire costly information by employing various short-cuts and heuristics.[14] The concept of information as a cost of political action is also echoed in one of the explanations of the relationship between education and engagement. In such explanations, information is often understood as a prerequisite to active participation; therefore, those with more education are more likely to have both prior information relevant to an action and the capacity to acquire new information.[15] Similarly, explanations of the mechanisms by which elites and social networks mobilize citizens often are based on the assumption that mobilization involves the subsidization of information costs.[16]

One of the most important features of the classical Downsian model for understanding the implications of the instrumental approach to information is dealing with the dilemma of a priori attention. The central feature of this dilemma is that it is apparently impossible for an individual to know which pieces of information are most relevant to a political choice without first knowing the content of all information. That is, for the would-be rational actor to calculate the marginal return from gathering additional information apparently requires first knowing the content of the information. To escape this dilemma, Downs argues, individuals establish "a few gatherers and transmitters [of information] and mold them into a personal information-acquisition system" that can be trusted to focus attention and select information that is relevant and trustworthy

---

[14] Paul M. Sniderman, Richard A. Brody, and Philip E. Tetlock, *Reasoning and Choice: Explorations in Political Psychology* (Cambridge, Eng.: Cambridge University Press, 1991); Herbert A. Simon, *Models of Man: Social and Rational* (New York: Wiley, 1957).

[15] Robert C. Luskin, "Explaining Political Sophistication," in Richard G. Niemi and Herbert F. Weisberg, eds., *Controversies in Voting Behavior*, 3rd ed. (Washington, D.C.: CQ Press, 1993), pp. 114–136; Sidney Verba, Kay Lehman Schlozman, and Henry E. Brady, *Voice and Equality: Civic Voluntarism in American Politics*, (Cambridge, Mass.: Harvard University Press, 1995); Raymond E. Wolfinger and Steven J. Rosenstone, *Who Votes?* (New Haven: Yale University Press, 1980).

[16] Allan J. Cigler and Burdett A. Loomis, eds., *Interest Group Politics*, 5th ed. (Washington, D.C.: CQ Press, 1998); Rosenstone and Hansen, *Mobilization, Participation, and Democracy in America*; Jan Leighley, "Group Membership and the Mobilization of Political Participation," *Journal of Politics* 58, no. 2 (1996): 447–463; Jeffrey M. Berry, *The Interest Group Society* (Boston: Little, Brown, 1984); Wolfinger and Rosenstone, *Who Votes?*

given the objectives of the individual.[17] This "system" of information acquisition is carefully tailored to select the information most likely to reduce uncertainty for each individual.

Among the many sources of information available to citizens are professional experts, interest groups, parties, mass media, government, and other individuals. Individuals therefore may delegate some of the task of acquiring and organizing information to others who are likely to use the same selection criteria that they would themselves. Downs argues that this means that obtaining one's political information from a knowledgeable and politically compatible neighbor may be rationally superior to systematically reading the newspaper until one feels adequately informed. This also means that a polity in which each individual is equally well informed is irrational, since it is frequently more efficient to delegate to others the task of becoming informed about any particular choice, provided the right information agents can be located.

In light of this general approach and especially the problem of a priori attention, we can turn to questions of the contemporary information revolution. What should be the consequences from the instrumental perspective of information abundance? In the Downsian formulation, the answer depends on the extent to which individuals can improve upon their personalized information-acquisition systems. If technological changes that reduce the objective cost of information also permit individuals to find information providers whose selection criteria are congruent with their own, then Downsian theory predicts that individuals will realize gains from the technological changes. If they are unable to locate compatible providers of information and must yield control over the way that information is selected and constructed by others, even if that information is essentially free, then this compromise may offset any gains from reduced objective costs of information. The realized cost of information to an individual is therefore a function of both its objective cost and its political loading – the ways that it is selected and the individual's perception of the congruence of that selection with his or her own approach to acquiring information.

The selection problem inherent in solving the dilemma of a priori attention creates what Downs calls a "major drawback" of mass media as a source of political information requisite to action.[18] Traditional mass media – Downs is thinking here chiefly of radio and newspapers – provide political information whose marginal costs to citizens are virtually zero,

---

[17] Downs, *An Economic Theory of Democracy*, p. 219.   [18] Ibid., p. 230.

but their potential congruence with any one citizen's selection criteria is low. Downs writes that "the selection principles embodied in the data [provided by mass media] may differ from those of the decision-maker in such a way that he may be led into wrong decisions."[19] Citizens are aware of this problem. Faced with choices among a comparatively small number of print and broadcast information channels, they recognize that the editorial policies and journalism practices that produce the information from those channels are not likely to comport well across many issues and choices. Even if one assumes that media exhibit a perfectly rational Hotelling effect and shift toward the median viewpoint, the multiplicity of issues and the distribution of citizens around the statistical median imply that no citizen may find information from the media to be reliably congruent with his or her own selection criteria on any particular issue. Downs argues that the most widespread and systematic failure of selection congruence between members of the public and the mass media takes place along class lines. Citizens at the lower end of the socioeconomic scale are likely to perceive a systematic incongruence between their interests and the mass media, which are owned and operated by those at the upper end of the socioeconomic scale. Downs writes that in general, "[T]he cost of information acts in effect to disenfranchise low-income groups relative to high-income groups when voting is costly."[20]

Although Downs's articulation of the problem of information selection in mass media predates the rise of television as a major force in American politics, the theory provides a plausible explanation for why citizen knowledge and participation rates did not rise as broadcast media apparently increased the flow of information to citizens in the 1960s and 1970s. That is, broadcast television provided information from a limited number of sources that gave citizens little control over selection. To the extent that citizens perceived television as a poor delegate for selecting personally congruent political information, this technological development did little to lower the real costs of information for citizens, despite the fact that the marginal cost of political information available on television is virtually zero.

Contemporary information technology may be different. Clearly, new information technology differs in important ways from traditional print and broadcast mass media. It offers a vastly greater volume of information than other media, often at comparably low or lower marginal costs, from a virtually limitless number of competing sources. More important, it

[19] Ibid., p. 230.   [20] Ibid., p. 261.

provides a higher degree of purposiveness and selectivity by permitting citizens to control what information they acquire, where they acquire it, and when they acquire it. From the instrumental perspective, the evolution of information abundance has created the most potentially important change in citizens' information environment so far, by reducing the cost of information, multiplying channels, and providing possibilities for greater purposive control and selection. Subject to a law of diminishing marginal returns, information abundance should lead to greater information consumption and at least marginal increases in participation rates. Specifically, as information costs fall, those who will benefit the most from it are those with the highest uncertainty *and who also exhibit a strong preference over outcomes*, all else being equal. Those with low uncertainty stand to gain little from additional information, as do those with high uncertainty but low interest or preferences over outcomes.

Instrumental conceptions of information and behavior confront many problems empirically, especially in laboratory experiments. When people's learning and "consumption" of information is observed directly, it frequently deviates from predictions of the theory. A large body of theoretical work and empirical evidence suggests a different set of expectations. For convenience, I use the label "psychological" to describe this approach, although it encompasses theories both inside and outside the field of political psychology. Unlike the instrumental approach, which is rooted in the theory of rational behavior, the psychological approach encompasses many theories and models from the literature on media, public opinion, political communication, and political psychology. While these theories are disparate, they share a common premise and for this reason can be classified together. The point of departure of the psychological approach from the instrumental can be traced to Downs's view that "the term rational is never applied to an agent's ends, only to his means," and therefore the process of acquiring information must be held theoretically distinct from the goals or normative ends to which the information will be put.[21] One foundation of the psychological tradition is the rejection of this separation of means from ends and information from values. If one accepts the premise that normative processes of choosing goals and ends may be intertwined with processes of learning and acquiring information, then a new theory and new set of expectations is required. In the

---

[21] Delli Carpini and Keeter, "The Internet and an Informed Citizenry," p. 13.

psychological approach, information does not move directly from the political environment into the mind of the political individual without undergoing transformations, irrationally biased selection, affective loading, and other transformative psychological effects. These effects, broadly speaking, demolish the thesis that people seek political information in order to reduce uncertainty before acting.

The psychological approach can be summarized in three basic tenets. The first is that *as information costs fall and information sources multiply, the information-rich get richer, and the information-poor stay poor.*[22] This tenet is analogous to a law of *increasing* marginal returns, because it suggests that the most energetic acquirers of new information are likely to be those already best informed. It has been supported in one form or another in a wide array of studies. Research on public opinion and political behavior show that those with more education and higher levels of political sophistication are more likely to assimilate new information than those with less education and less sophistication.[23] From the analysis of political cognition comes a similar result. Schema theory and research shows that well-informed and knowledgeable people learn and recall more from new information, while less well-informed people learn and recall less.[24] More readily accessible information therefore tends to widen knowledge gaps rather than diminish them. "Uses and gratifications" research in the field of media studies shows that citizens seek out one medium over another because it provides a particular form of gratification, not simply because it better informs them in an objective sense.[25] Past research has shown that newspapers prove more gratifying

---

[22] James H. Kuklinski, Robert C. Luskin, and John Bolland, "Where Is the Schema? Going Beyond the 'S' Word in Political Psychology," *American Political Science Review* 85, no. 4 (1991): 1341–1356.

[23] Sniderman, Brody, and Tetlock, *Reasoning and Choice;* Douglas M. McLeod and Elizabeth M. Perse, "Direct and Indirect Effects of Socioeconomic Status on Public Affairs Knowledge," *Journalism Quarterly* 71, no. 2 (1994): 433–442. One exception is the proposition from social learning theory that less interested (and therefore less informed) citizens are more likely to be affected by the interaction between new information and social context because they are more likely to discover that their preferences or opinions are discordant with their social environments. See Robert Huckfeldt and John Sprague, *Citizens, Politicism and Social Communication: Information and Influence in an Election Campaign* (Cambridge, Eng.: Cambridge University Press, 1995).

[24] In Downsian terms, this effect might be explained if the total costs of information are dominated not by the cost of acquiring it but by the cost of assimilating and evaluating it.

[25] Steven H. Chaffee and Stacey Frank Kanihan, "Learning about Politics from the Mass Media," *Political Communication* 14, no. 4 (1997): 421–430; W. Russell Neuman,

to citizens with greater sophistication and prior knowledge, because papers provide control and permit greater purposiveness.[26] That desire for control and purposiveness are particularly associated with greater knowledge, and are less important for citizens who are less politically sophisticated or knowledgeable. As Scott Althaus and David Tewksbury argue, this finding suggests that the new information environment created by information technology is likely to appeal differentially to those with more sophistication, because it provides and requires an even greater degree of control and intentionality.[27]

The second tenet of the psychological approach is that *the acquisition of new information does not necessarily make citizens better informed in a rational or objective sense.* This apparent paradox turns on the fact that citizens acquire and learn information in ways that are biased toward reinforcing previously held beliefs and mental constructs. In other words, research in political psychology shows that citizens tend to search for information that reinforces what they already believe about political choices, and they tend to avoid information that conflicts with existing beliefs. When confronted with balanced information that both supports and undermines their prior beliefs, experimental research has shown that citizens are likely to judge information that is consistent with their prior beliefs to be stronger or better than information that is inconsistent.[28]

Research on selective exposure shows that a complex body of factors shape which messages individuals attend to in an information-rich environment, and uncertainty is not among the most important. The rational model predicts that those with more uncertainty would be more solicitous of new information than those with less uncertainty; however, empirical research shows this to be false. Dolf Zillman and Jennings Bryant illustrate the fallacy in that prediction with an analogy from the study of television effects. If one posits that watching comedy on television reduces anger and hostility in viewers, does it follow that the presence of a large volume of television comedies reduces societal

Ann N. Crigler, and Marion R. Just, *Common Knowledge: News and the Construction of Political Meaning* (Chicago: University of Chicago Press, 1992).

[26] Chaffee and Kanihan, "Learning about Politics from the Mass Media," pp. 421–430.

[27] Scott L. Althaus and David Tewksbury, "Patterns of Internet and Traditional News Media Use in a Networked Community," *Political Communication* 17, no. 1 (2000): 21–45.

[28] Milton Lodge, Charles Tabor, and Aron Chase Galonsky, "The Political Consequences of Motivated Reasoning: Partisan Bias in Information Processing," paper prepared for the Annual Meeting of the American Political Science Association, Atlanta, Ga., Sept. 2–5, 1999.

anger and aggression? The answer is "not necessarily." Angry, hostile citizens may choose not to watch television comedy. Similarly, citizens with low levels of knowledge and political sophistication, who stand in principle to benefit most from an information-rich environment, are less likely to take advantage of new information resources.[29] In addition, research shows that among a variety of possible contributors to news recall, background knowledge is the strongest predictor of an individual's ability to recall current news – more so than education or level of news media use, which are also strong predictors.[30]

Schema research comes to a similar conclusion. When people have well-developed schema about an issue, they tend to be the most selective in assimilating information that reinforces existing ideas. Where they have the least well-developed prior schema, they are most influenced by the ways that elites frame and present information. Uses and gratifications research generally supports this view. Because citizens often feel most gratified when information reinforces existing knowledge, preferences, or world views, they are selective in their attention and assimilation of information. This means that they do not necessarily acquire information in ways that optimally identify alternatives and reduce objective uncertainty about them.[31] A purposive search for information is equally likely to reinforce a misperception as to correct it.

Media research also suggests that exposure to conflicting sources of information may legitimate opposing perspectives and views, which is desirable from a normative perspective, but which may be associated with less inclination to participate. As Mutz and Martin show, when citizens are given greater capacity to select among multiple media sources, they are more likely to make selections that expose themselves to narrower and more compatible viewpoints. That is, citizens do not use a richer and more diverse media environment to better inform themselves about conflicting ideas and positions, but instead to select a narrower and more parochial set of sources. Paradoxically, then, the more heterogeneous and controllable the information environment, the more homogeneous will be citizens' exposure to information. These various

---

[29] Dolf Zillman and Jennings Bryant, eds., *Selective Exposure to Communication* (Hillsdale, N.J.: Lawrence Erlbaum Associates, 1985).

[30] Vincent Price and John Zaller, "Who Gets the News? Alternative Measures of News Reception and their Implications for Research," *Public Opinion Quarterly* 57, no. 2 (1993): 133–164.

[31] From Doris A. Graber, *Mass Media and American Politics*, 5th ed. (Washington, D.C.: Congressional Quarterly, 1997); Zillman and Bryant, eds., *Selective Exposure to Communication*.

theories suggest that citizens behave as if they do not seek information chiefly in order to reduce uncertainty, but in order to bolster their prior beliefs.[32]

The third tenet of the psychological tradition is that *the processes by which information in the political environment is translated into knowledge and eventually political engagement are highly contingent.* In particular, these processes are contingent upon social context and the nature of the stimulus. Research on political learning, for instance, shows that the ways individuals assimilate information and convert it into knowledge can be contingent upon the approval or disapproval of those around them.[33] In this way, social structure interacts with information, so that two individuals with identical beliefs and values who are exposed to the same political information may assimilate different knowledge and may consequently act in different ways, depending on their social environment. The fact that political knowledge tends to be episodic and stratified also supports the tenet that what is learned from information is contingent. The strategies of elites and the contingencies of political events affect the salience of issues, direct public attention toward one body of information and away from another, and also affect which citizens acquire what information. Constructivist approaches to political knowledge go several steps further, claiming that political knowledge is not so much carried around in the mind of the individual as a function of past experience and exposure to information as it is constructed "on the spot," when an individual is prompted or stimulated to provide a view or preference about an issue.[34]

These three tenets of the psychological approach lead to theoretically superior expectations about political engagement in the contemporary period. They imply that new information resources are likely to be used mainly by the most well informed, who are already most likely to be engaged. For this reason and because information is likely to reinforce existing preferences and predispositions, it should exert little stimulus effect on engagement. In the contemporary information revolution, the informed citizen may indeed be more likely to engage in the practices of

[32] Lodge, Taber, and Galonsky, "The Political Consequences of Motivated Reasoning"; Charles G. Lord, Lee Ross, and Mark R. Lepper, "Biased Assimilation and Attitude Polarization: The Effects of Prior Theories on Subsequently Considered Evidence," *Journal of Personality and Social Psychology* 37, no. 11 (1979): 2098–2109; Diana C. Mutz and Paul S. Martin, "Facilitating Communication Across Lines of Political Difference," *American Political Science Review* 95 (2001): 97–114.

[33] Huckfeldt and Sprague, *Citizens, Politics, and Social Communication.*

[34] Zaller, *The Nature and Origins of Public Opinion.*

democracy than the uninformed. But increased availability of low-cost information is not likely to change greatly who is informed and who is not.

DIFFUSION OF INFORMATION TECHNOLOGY
AMONG INDIVIDUALS

In a short period of time, a good deal of new evidence about information technology and political engagement has become available from surveys. Ideally, panel designs or quasiexperimental evidence tracking individuals' knowledge over time could be used to test for effects of the information revolution, but such data are not available. Instead, several useful cross-sectional surveys repeated every year or two can be used to provide repeated snapshots of the public's use of the Internet. A number of inferences can be made from such evidence. For my analysis, I rely on several sources. The first is data I gathered through the Omnibus Survey Program administered at the University of Maryland in 1996, 1998, 1999, and 2001, with funding from the National Science Foundation and the Center for Information Technology and Society at the University of California, Santa Barbara. These random digit–dial probability samples each produced about 1,000 responses, and they employed design-effect weighting and poststratification weighting for sex, education, and region.[35] The data include demographics and responses to a set of questions about Internet use, including the kinds of political use, although cost limitations prevented asking a complete set of questions about political participation. The second source of data is the 1996, 1998, and 2000 American National Election Studies (NES) surveys. These surveys included very limited questions about Internet use, but are useful for their data on political participation and use of other media. The two sources of survey data are therefore complementary. I also supplement these surveys with evidence from other sources, as noted.

Examining how citizen access to the Internet has grown in the United States is a good starting point for considering all this data. Figure 5.1 shows growth in the percentage of adults in the United States who report having access to the Internet from home, school, or workplace, based on time series data from NES, the Pew Center for the People and the Press, and my own surveys. As the figure shows, in mid- to late 1996, around

---

[35] The sampling error is about 3.5 percent in each survey.

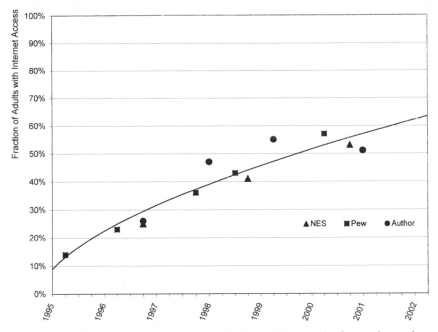

Figure 5.1. Diffusion of the Internet in the United States. The figure shows the fraction of adults reporting access to the Internet from home, school, or workplace. Sources are author's surveys, Pew Research Center for the People and the Press, and American National Election Studies (NES), 1996–2000.

a quarter of American adults had access to the Internet. By mid-1998, access was over 40 percent, and by mid-2000 it was over 50 percent.[36]

For comparison, Figure 5.2 shows curves for prior communication media. The growth of radio and television followed paths similar to each other. Both reached 90 percent of the population within two decades of crossing the 10 percent mark. These curves represent the standard mass diffusion model of technology adoption, starting with very slow growth for a period of several years, followed by extremely rapid expansion, and, theoretically, ending with asymptotic saturation.[37] Also shown in Figure 5.2 are the growth curves for telephones and newspaper

---

[36] The curve represents an equation of the form $y = ax^b$ and provides a rough average of the three underlying data sets. This provides a slightly better fit ($r^2 = 0.94$) than linear, polynomial, or logarithmic equations.

[37] For more on the diffusion of technology and of information technology in particular, see Pippa Norris, *Digital Divide: Civic Engagement, Information Poverty and the Worldwide Internet* (Cambridge, Eng.: Cambridge University Press, 2001); and Everett Rogers, *Diffusion of Innovation* (New York: Free Press, 1962).

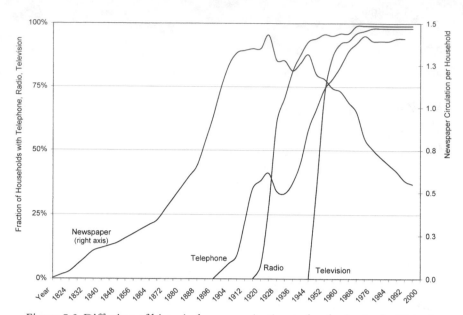

Figure 5.2. Diffusion of historical communication technologies in the United States. The left vertical axis shows the fraction of households with telephone, radio, and television; the right vertical axis shows newspaper circulation per household. *Sources:* For radio and television, U.S. Census Bureau; for telephone, U.S. Census Bureau and Milton Mueller, "Universal Service in Telephone History," *Telecommunications Policy* 17, no. 5 (July 1993): 352–369; for newspaper circulation, U.S. Census Bureau, and Michael Schudson, *Discovering the News: A Social History of American Newspapers* (New York: Basic Books, 1978).

subscriptions. Note that neither of these technologies adheres to the standard mass diffusion model. Telephone growth was linear and non-monotonic; its rate of growth was kept in check by the need for massive centralized infrastructure and was interrupted by the Great Depression. Newspaper growth during the nineteenth century was very rapid, but peaked in the first decades of the twentieth century and then declined.

It is too soon to know which of these experiences in technology diffusion the Internet will most closely resemble over time. Reliable data about Internet access prior to the mid-1990s is unavailable, but presumably from the beginnings of the Internet in the early 1970s through at least the late 1990s, growth in access fits the standard mass diffusion model. Growth in Internet access after the turn of the century is far less clear. Some data sources, including my own, show a slowing in the growth rate of the Internet, which might either turn out to be temporary or the

Table 5.1. Changing Demographics of Internet Users

	Internet users			
	October 1996	April 1999	February 2001	U.S. population
Mean age	38	40	38	43
College degree (%)	48	39	35	25
Female (%)	36	45	47	51
Caucasian/White (%)	88	86	84	75

Notes: An "Internet user" is defined as someone who reports using the Internet more than once per week. All data include only persons 18 years and older, except for U.S. education figures, which show the fraction of those 25 years and older with a four-year college degree. Race values follow census bureau practice, showing the fraction Caucasian/white compared with black/African-American, American Indian and Alaska Native, Asian, and Native Hawaiian or other Pacific Islander, independent of ethnicity. Source for Internet users is author's surveys; source for U.S. population figures is U.S. Census Bureau 2000 census (note that national population values change little over the period from 1996 to 2001).

beginning of a new, more sluggish period of growth like radio after the mid-1940s and television after 1960, or like telephony across much of its history.

Access to the Internet is only part of the story of the changing information environment. The frequency of use of the Internet as well as the ways people access it are also changing. In October 1996, only about 3 percent of all American adults used the Internet daily. In February 1998, the figure was up to 13 percent, and in April of 1999 it had reached 18 percent. By February 2001, about 23 percent of adults were using the Internet daily. Much more so than access, this is the behavioral phenomenon of interest.

Demographically, Internet users look increasingly like the rest of the U.S. population, which is to be expected as access and use expand into larger fractions of the population. In 1996, when only a few percent of adults used the Internet regularly, Internet demographics differed substantially from the demographics of the rest of the United States on most variables. Then, nearly half of regular Internet users had a college degree and nearly two-thirds were men. By 2001, only a third of Internet users had a college degree, drawing closer to the U.S. population figure of 25 percent, and women had almost drawn even with men, as Table 5.1 shows.

The term "digital divide" has come into wide use to describe differences at the individual level between those who are "on line" and those who are not. (No comparable attention is paid to gaps at the level of political organizations, perhaps in large part because few such gaps exist.) Since the individual-level digital divide mirrors traditional socioeconomic gaps in the United States, many observers, including agencies of the federal government, have rightly expressed concern that new information technology may tend to exacerbate inequality in American society.[38] These concerns have driven a number of federal and state policies aimed at bringing the Internet to poor areas and underprivileged schools, as is also happening in Europe and other places around the world.[39]

In practice, several "divides" are associated with information technology at the individual level. One involves simply access to the Internet. Another involves gaps in the kinds of habits and skills that lead to regular use of the technology, while yet another involves systematic differences across nations in access and use of the technology.[40] Problems of social inequality are no less complex in matters of technology than in other areas, and it is beyond the scope of the present study to assess the nature of digital divides in detail. Nonetheless, it is possible to provide a rough assessment of their structure here. Comparing the last two columns in Table 5.1 suggests that the most important differences between Internet users and nonusers involve education and race. Since these variables are themselves correlated, it is important to analyze matters of the digital divide using a multivariate approach. Table 5.2 presents the results of logistic regression analysis predicting two variables: access to the Internet and daily use of the Internet among adults with access.[41] The independent variables measure education, age, household income, sex, ethnicity, race, whether the respondent is employed full-time, whether the respondent is married, and whether the respondent is a full-time homemaker. The factors predicting variation in access are education, income, age, Latino ethnicity, and homemaker status. The model is reasonably strong, indicating that demographic information is moderately useful

---

[38] U.S. Department of Commerce, National Telecommunications and Information Administration, *Falling Through the Net: Defining the Digital Divide* (Washington, D.C.: Government Printing Office, 1999), http://www.ntia.doc.gov/ntiahome/fttn99.

[39] Norris, *Digital Divide.*   [40] See ibid.

[41] The most useful units for measuring frequency of Internet use have shrunk over time, as citizens have made greater use of new information technology: Between 1996 and 1999, I measured frequency of Internet use using days as units of measure; beginning in 2000, I changed to hours per day.

Table 5.2. Analyzing the Digital Divide: Access and Daily Use, 2001

	Have access to the Internet		Use the Internet daily	
	B	Standard error	B	Standard error
Education	0.68**	0.10	0.31**	0.11
Age	−0.06**	0.01	0.02*	0.01
Income	0.53**	0.07	−0.04	0.08
Sex	−0.01	0.19	−0.26	0.20
Latino/a	−0.89**	0.35	0.18	0.46
Race	−0.18	0.24	0.15	0.28
Employed	−0.25	0.21	−0.17	0.24
Married	0.30	0.20	−0.16	0.23
Housekeeper	−1.16*	0.52	0.38	0.65
Constant	−1.45**	0.54	−0.96	0.62
	$N = 704$, chi-sq. $= 221$;		$N = 429$, chi-sq. $= 15$;	
	$p = 0.00$, Nagel. $r^2 = 0.34$		$p = 0.00$, Nagel. $r^2 = 0.04$	

Notes: Table shows unstandardized logistic regression coefficients for models predicting whether respondents have access to the Internet from home, school, or work, and whether respondents with access use the Internet on a daily basis. The sex variable is coded 0 for men and 1 for women; the Latino/a variable follows census bureau practice by measuring ethnic self-identification independently of racial self-identification; the race variable compares white/Caucasian with other racial categories.
** = significant at .01 level.
* = significant at 0.5 level.
Source: Author's survey, Feb. 2001.

in predicting who has access to the Internet and who does not.[42] Those with more education and income are more likely to have access, while older people, women, Latinos, and housekeepers are less. However, race as defined by the census bureau does not have an independent effect.

Things change substantially for daily use of the Internet. First, predicting daily use from demographic characteristics is nearly futile. While the model is statistically significant, substantively it explains almost none of the variance in daily use. Only two factors have any bearing whatever: education and age. Income, ethnicity, and housekeeper status have no influence. The most striking effect involves age, where the direction of the effect is reversed from the model for access. On average, younger

[42] Nagelkerke $r^2 = 0.34$.

Table 5.3. Extent of Political Use of the Internet, as a Fraction of Those with Access (%)

	October 1996	February 1998	April 1999	February 2001
To find out what government or an official is doing	26	28	30	41
To contact a public official or candidate for office	10	9	9	14
To express views about politics or government	12	12	13	20
To learn about political issues	30	29	32	37
To browse for political information with no specific purpose	32	31	33	34
Total for any action as fraction of adults with access	47	43	52	56

Notes: Figures show fraction of adults with access to the Internet who report having used the Internet at least once in the last year for each activity. For 1996, $N = 259$; for 1998, $N = 471$; for 1999, $N = 550$; for 2001, $N = 508$. Note that 1996 and 2001 figures capture the effects of presidential elections. Source is author's surveys.

people are more likely than older to have access, but among those with access, younger people are just slightly less likely than older ones to use the Internet every day.

The data confirm the obvious impression that rates of expansion in Internet access and use have been rapid, but they also show that rates vary by category. Among the fastest rates of growth is daily use of the Internet, while the slowest are some categories of political use. As Table 5.3 shows, in 1996 about 10 percent of people with access to the Internet reported they had contacted a public official or candidate over the prior year using the Internet; in 2001 this figure had grown only to 14 percent. For comparison, about 25 percent of adults typically contact government annually using traditional means.[43] The number who report having used the Internet to learn what government or a public official was doing grew from 26 percent to 41 percent in the same period. Overall, people using the Internet for any political purpose grew from

[43] Verba, Schlozman, and Brady, *Voice and Equality.*

47 percent of those with access to only 56 percent between late 1996 and early 2001.

INFORMATION TECHNOLOGY AND
POLITICAL ENGAGEMENT

The diffusion of Internet technology during the fourth information revolution has reached a point where more people have access to the Internet than vote in presidential elections, and where roughly half of these use the technology in political ways. According to the psychological approach to explaining how people absorb political information, the wide accessibility of this new technology should not be altering overall levels of engagement. Data on the factors that influence attention to political information across different media begin to build the empirical case for this broad hypothesis. To examine media choice, I drew on data from the 2000 NES. To begin, I examined the correspondence between use of the Internet for political information and attention to the campaigns on television and in newspapers. The theory predicts that overall associations between different media should be high. In both cases, this expectation is supported by the data. The more people read about the campaigns in newspapers or watch shows on television, the more likely they are also to use the Internet for political information. There is scant evidence for a substitution effect of new media for old in which respondents use the Internet exclusively. Instead, Internet use is additive, and in a general way, the media-rich do seem to get richer.

To see what common underlying factors might influence people's use of the Internet, television, and newspapers for political information, I built a statistical model using logistic regression predicting people's attention to the campaigns that year. The model includes independent variables for education, age, sex, race, level of trust in the news media, level of trust in other people, belief in the helpfulness of others, and overall interest in the campaigns. I ran this model using dichotomous dependent variables for whether respondents obtained campaign information from the Internet, whether they watched at least one television show about the campaign, and whether they paid at least a little attention to the campaigns in newspapers.[44] I hypothesized that, in general, education,

---

[44] Unfortunately, the NES measures use of the Internet for campaign information only as a dichotomous variable, so a good deal of useful information about frequency or intensity is not available.

Table 5.4. Attention to Campaigns across Media, 2000

	Saw campaign information on the Internet		Watched a television program about the campaigns		Paid some attention to the campaigns in the newspaper	
	B	Standard error	B	Standard error	B	Standard error
Education	0.38**	0.12	0.20	0.11	0.37**	0.09
Age	−0.04**	0.01	0.01*	0.01	0.03**	0.01
Sex	−0.34	0.20	−0.46*	0.20	−0.60**	0.17
Race	−0.15	0.36	0.48	0.34	−0.92**	0.28
Trust news media	−0.48**	0.14	0.19	0.13	0.01	0.11
Trust other people	0.38	0.23	−0.14	0.23	−0.23	0.19
Other people helpful	−0.47*	0.24	0.13	0.22	0.36	0.19
Interest in campaigns	0.73**	0.17	1.03**	0.16	1.01**	0.13
Constant	0.67	0.41	−0.18	0.37	−3.07*	0.35
	$N = 518$, chi-sq. $= 78$, $p = 0.00$, Nagel. $r^2 = 0.20$		$N = 849$, chi-sq. $= 88$, $p = 0.00$, Nagel. $r^2 = 0.17$		$N = 850$, chi-sq. $= 206$, $p = 0.00$, Nagel. $r^2 = 0.30$	

Notes: Table shows unstandardized logistic regression coefficients for models predicting whether respondents obtained campaign information from the Internet, watched at least one television program about the campaigns, or paid at least a little attention to the campaigns in newspapers. The sex variable is coded 0 for men and 1 for women; the race variable compares white/Caucasian with other racial categories combined.
* = significant at 0.05 level.
** = significant at 0.01 level.
Source: American National Elections Studies, 2000.

age, trust in the media, and interest would be predictive of media use, but that differences would appear among newspapers, television, and the Internet, especially for age and trust in news media.

The results are presented in Table 5.4. They show expected differences between television and newspapers, such as the fact that education influences newspaper reading about political information but not television watching. The model for the Internet shows that it is possible to predict use of this new medium about as well as use of television and slightly less well than use of newspapers.[45] In the Internet model, education is significant. As one would expect, the more education, the more likely one is to use the Internet for political information. Age works in the negative direction, which is also not surprising. Younger citizens are more likely to obtain political information through the Internet than older citizens. Neither race nor sex is significant in the Internet model, whereas women are less likely than men to use traditional media for political information and whites are more likely than others to pay attention to newspapers.

Another intriguing departure from patterns of traditional media use involves the trust variables. People using the Internet for political information are more likely to be mistrustful of traditional media, and are more likely to report feeling that other people are not helpful in a general sense. These variables suggest an element of cynicism influencing media choice. People using the Internet for political information are well educated, somewhat younger users of traditional media who have an interest in politics and who tend to be skeptical of what they read and see in other media. They are not outwardly mistrusting of other people, but may feel somewhat more independence and self-reliance with respect to others.

What about voting and other forms of participation? My approach to this issue was to develop a model of engagement with politics using standard predictors of participation – many of which are correlated with Internet use – and also a variable for using the Internet for obtaining campaign information. In this model, I included independent variables for education, age, income, sex, ethnicity, race, contact by a mobilizing organization, interest, trust in others, and sense of efficacy.[46] The Internet variable measured whether the respondent had obtained information about the campaigns through the Internet. A finding of significance for this variable would indicate a correlation between Internet use and political engagement that is not simply the result of other factors, such as general political interest. Such a correlation would not necessarily show causation, since other factors might still contribute to both Internet use and engagement, but it would be suggestive. At the very least, a positive finding would indicate that use of the Internet is connected to participation-related factors not identified here and in most standard

---

[45] Nagelkerke $r^2 = 0.20$.
[46] The efficacy variable comes from level of agreement with the statement "People like me don't have any say about what the government does."

Table 5.5. The Internet and Political Engagement, 1998

	Voted		Displayed message		Attended event		Worked on campaign		Donated money	
	B	Standard error	B	Standard error	B	Standard error	B	Standard error	B	Standard error
Education	0.22**	0.05	−0.27**	0.09	−0.03	0.09	−0.08	0.16	0.25**	0.08
Age	0.05**	0.01	0.01	0.01	0.00	0.01	−0.01	0.02	0.03**	0.01
Income	0.04**	0.01	0.03	0.02	0.04	0.02	0.08	0.05	0.06**	0.02
Sex	0.11	0.14	−0.21	0.26	−0.55*	0.28	0.17	0.46	0.09	0.22
Latino/a	0.06	0.23	0.07	0.41	0.63	0.40	0.50	0.64	0.24	0.38
Race	0.16	0.20	−0.01	0.40	0.70	0.36	−6.97	19.98	−0.46	0.40
Contacted	0.75**	0.17	1.12**	0.26	0.90**	0.28	0.69	0.48	0.31	0.23
Interest	0.89**	0.11	0.84**	0.20	1.20**	0.23	1.16**	0.40	0.70**	0.18
Trust others	0.52**	0.15	0.07	0.27	0.02	0.29	0.24	0.49	0.09	0.23
Efficacy	0.07	0.06	0.09	0.10	0.11	0.11	−0.08	0.19	0.07	0.09
Used Internet for political information	0.21	0.26	0.51	0.40	0.45	0.40	0.34	0.63	0.98**	0.30
Constant	−5.05**	0.38	−3.91**	0.62	−5.48**	0.70	−6.49	1.25	−7.10**	0.65
	$N = 1,190$, chi-sq. = 425, $p = 0.00$, Nagel. $r^2 = 0.40$		$N = 1,190$, chi-sq. = 60, $p = 0.00$, Nagel. $r^2 = 0.13$		$N = 1,190$, chi-sq. = 75, $p = 0.00$, Nagel. $r^2 = 0.18$		$N = 1,190$, chi-sq. = 28, $p = 0.00$, Nagel. $r^2 = 0.15$		$N = 1,190$, chi-sq. = 127, $p = 0.00$, Nagel. $r^2 = 0.22$	

Notes: Table shows unstandardized logistic regression coefficients for models predicting whether respondents voted in the elections for the year shown; wore a campaign button or displayed a campaign sticker or yard sign; attended a meeting, rally, speech, or dinner in support of a candidate; did any work for a party or candidate; or donated money to an individual candidate, party, or group. The sex variable is coded 0 for men and 1 for women; the race variable compares white/Caucasian with other racial categories combined; the contacted variable measures whether the respondent was contacted by a party during the campaign; the efficacy variable measures level of disagreement with the statement, "People like me don't have any say about what the government does."

* = significant at 0.05 level.

** = significant at 0.01 level.

Source: American National Election Studies, 1998.

models of engagement. A null finding, on the other hand, would be more conclusive. If Internet use exerts any positive influence, it is likely to appear in this variable.

I ran this model for five political acts: voting; displaying a campaign button, sticker, or yard sign; attending a meeting, rally, speech, or dinner in support of a candidate; working on a campaign in some other way; and donating money to a candidate, party, or group. Since information technology is changing so rapidly over time, I ran these models both for 1998 and 2000. The results, which are shown for 1998 in Table 5.5, provide for a comparison across political acts for each variable. Political interest is the most consistently significant variable, followed by education and contact with a mobilizer. The strongest model is for voting, where the expected factors show up as significant: education, age, income, whether the respondent was contacted by an organization and asked to participate, political interest, and trust in others.[47]

Use of the Internet for political information is not significant in the 1998 voting model. While more Internet users (for political purposes) voted than non-Internet users, this difference is accounted for by these other factors, especially education and interest. Similarly, use of the Internet has no significant effect on displaying a political message, attending a political event, or working on a campaign.

However, in the case of donating money, the Internet variable is significant. People who obtained political information through the Internet were more likely to donate money than those who did not in 1998. There are several possibilities for why this occurred. One is that the kind of people who are likely to donate money in an election year are also likely to obtain political information through the Internet. The reasons for such a relationship are unclear and cannot be inferred from the model at hand. Another explanation is the novelty effect of Internet-based donations and solicitations for money. These were pioneered by candidates for the most part in 1998, although they were not heavily pushed by candidates until 2000. General enthusiasm for financial transactions on the Internet and the stimulation of new means for soliciting and donating may explain some of the effect. In any event, this is a somewhat surprising finding though substantively very modest.

Results for the year 2000 are similar, but also contain a few unexpected findings. In these models, the Internet variable is significant again for donating money, but also for attending a political event and for voting.

[47] $r^2 = 0.40$.

Table 5.6. The Internet and Political Engagement, 2000

	Voted		Displayed message		Attended event		Worked on campaign		Donated money	
	B	Standard error	B	Standard error	B	Standard error	B	Standard error	B	Standard error
Education	0.55**	0.12	0.03	0.16	0.47	0.25	−0.04	0.33	0.23	0.18
Age	0.02**	0.01	−0.01	0.01	−0.01	0.01	−0.01	0.02	0.02*	0.01
Income	0.07*	0.03	0.04	0.04	0.03	0.05	0.05	0.07	0.11**	0.04
Sex	0.13	0.20	0.03	0.27	0.33	0.38	−0.90	0.56	−0.46	0.29
Latino/a	−0.10	0.38	−0.87	0.94	0.07	1.02	0.18	1.30	0.53	0.78
Race	0.38	0.31	0.60	0.41	0.51	0.59	1.05	0.71	0.27	0.50
Contacted	1.31**	0.25	1.07**	0.28	1.14**	0.41	1.53**	0.61	1.10**	0.30
Interest	0.76**	0.16	0.51*	0.22	0.95**	0.34	0.66	0.46	1.27**	0.26
Trust others	0.52*	0.21	0.57	0.31	0.16	0.41	0.30	0.60	0.34	0.32
Efficacy	0.24**	0.08	0.04	0.12	0.15	0.17	0.16	0.24	−0.05	0.13
Used Internet for political information	0.61*	0.26	0.11	0.31	0.88*	0.41	0.69	0.59	0.79*	0.33
Constant	−3.46**	0.46	−3.91**	0.65	−6.93**	1.10	−6.17	1.41	−6.93**	0.86
	$N = 759$, chi-sq. = 245, $p = 0.00$, Nagel. $r^2 = 0.40$		$N = 759$, chi-sq. = 44, $p = 0.00$, Nagel. $r^2 = 0.13$		$N = 759$, chi-sq. = 55, $p = 0.00$, Nagel. $r^2 = 0.23$		$N = 759$, chi-sq. = 24, $p = 0.00$, Nagel. $r^2 = 0.17$		$N = 759$, chi-sq. = 121, $p = 0.00$, Nagel. $r^2 = 0.33$	

Notes: See Table 5.5.
Source: American National Election Studies, 2000.

The finding for attending a political event is more readily explained, since many candidates in 2000 used the Internet to attempt to organize and announce campaign events, as we saw in the last chapter. The voting effect suggests either that Internet-based information was a factor in turnout or that some other factor not captured directly in the model influenced both voting and use of the Internet for political information. Either way, the act of seeing political information on the Internet is associated in a very small way with voting.[48] The magnitude of this influence is tiny, even though statistically significant. In the voting model, which is similar to the others, the Internet variable improves overall predictive power by a little under 1 percent. Among 726 people included in the analysis, data on whether each had seen political information on the Internet improves the number of correct predictions in the model about who reported voting for just eleven individuals.[49] (See Table 5.6.) This hardly counts as a revolution in political engagement, but it is just large enough to be difficult to dismiss entirely without further evidence from future elections.

In interpreting this finding, it is important to note the NES data suffer from several limitations. For one, the Internet measure is dichotomous. By measuring only whether people obtained any information from the Internet, the survey failed to capture useful information about frequency or intensity of use. Second, the data lump together all forms of Internet use, so it is impossible to differentiate among the huge number of ways that people use the Internet politically: to read news from traditional sources, to read alternative sources of political information, to watch video of candidates, to communicate with others, to receive messages and solicitations of various kinds, and so on. The problems with this technique are obvious in data from the 2000 General Social Survey (GSS), which was fielded in the spring. This study was the first major scholarly survey to recognize that different forms of "Internet use" might be conceptually distinct. The designers of the Internet module in the GSS employed about a hundred Internet variables. These differentiate activities such as number of hours per week spent using a home computer for commerce from hours spent using a work computer for electronic mail. The GSS data show that the bivariate correlation between the two major categories of Internet use – time spent using electronic mail and

---

[48] Also since 1996. The author's analysis of 1996 data was consistent with the 1998 results here. See Bimber, "Information and Political Engagement in America: The Search for Effects of Information Technology at the Individual Level."

[49] The Nagelkerke r^2 value goes from 0.399 without the Internet variable to 0.404 with it, and the chi-square value from 241 to 245.

time spent using the web – is moderately strong, but they hardly vary precisely together across individuals ($R = 0.43$).[50] Time spent in chat rooms, one of the most interactive forms of Internet use, is weakly correlated with e-mail use ($R = 0.20$) but more strongly correlated with time spent on the web ($R = 0.54$). Unfortunately, the 2000 GSS was conducted before the general election got into full swing and so does not contain the kinds of political variables needed to resolve further the puzzles left by the NES data. It does suggest that as better data about different aspects of Internet use become available, new inferences will be possible about political behavior. It may be that the Internet variables in the NES are simply capturing the efforts of parties and candidates to mobilize citizens through e-mail and web appeals, which would not be a particularly new or theoretically important development. On the other hand, this finding may reflect a substantively new effect of the changing communication environment on a handful of citizens' sense of efficacy or on the relationship between interest and action. The message here is clear: As the Internet has evolved to become a rich and varied environment for communication and information, Internet use has become a multidimensional phenomenon best treated as a set of variables involving related but often quite divergent activities.

Analyses of Internet use in politics must be designed with this in mind. One important task will be to differentiate among information sought by citizens in purposive ways; information they encounter unintentionally, such as at a news site on the web; and information distributed to them by a political organization.

The bottom line in this analysis is consistent with the psychological approach to information and behavior: The new information environment has not changed levels of political engagement in any substantial way. This analysis does leave the door open, though, to possible refinements as more data become available about the Internet and political behavior. In 2000, but not in 1998 (or 1996[51]), a tiny number of those who obtained political information on line were more likely to vote, donate money, and attend a meeting or rally than politically and demographically similar people who did not use the Internet in that way. A better understanding of what this means will have to await improved survey measures that disaggregate forms of Internet use.

[50] All values are Pearson's R; $p = 0.01$.
[51] See note 46 above.

These largely null findings about use of the information technology and political participation lead to the question of the ultimate "on line" political act: Internet voting. A few remarks about this question are in order. In the United States, experiments with use of the Internet as a polling mechanism were under way even prior to the 2000 presidential election problems with the machine counting of physical ballots. The most important public election in which voters were permitted to cast ballots through the Internet was the Arizona Democratic primary in 2000. In that election, about half the ballots were cast through the Internet rather than using traditional means, and of those, over three-quarters were cast from computers located in voters' homes.[52] The expansion of this practice has important implications, especially if taken from traditional desktop computers to handheld electronic devices, which might permit voting from literally any location around the globe.

A set of important technical and constitutional matters at present limit that expansion. In January 2000, a commission appointed by the California Secretary of State that was expected by many to endorse Internet voting in the state most responsible for the development of Internet technology, recommended otherwise. The California Internet Voting Task Force found that "technological threats to the security, integrity and secrecy of Internet ballots are significant."[53] While optimistic – probably unduly so – about the long-term possibilities of the Internet for reducing barriers to voting, the commission urged "evolutionary" rather than "revolutionary" changes in balloting practices. To the surprise of many, given the strong representation of the computer industry

---

[52] Internet straw poll voting was also permitted for selected precincts in the Alaska Republican caucuses in 2000, but only about three dozen votes were cast this way. See James Ledbetter, "Net Voting Experiment Leaves Alaskans Cold," *The Standard*, Jan. 26, 2000, http://www.thestandard.com/article/display/0,1151,9163,00.html. Other minor Internet experiments were also contemplated and conducted between 1998 and 2000. For instance, as of early 2000, the Federal Assistance Voting Program, an absentee ballot system for overseas U.S. military personnel set up by the Defense Department in 1986, was being modified to permit a pilot group of 350 military personnel to vote by Internet. See Fred Solop, "Digital Democracy Comes of Age in Arizona: Participation and Politics in the First Binding Internet Election," paper prepared for the annual meeting of the American Political Science Association, Washington, D.C., Aug. 31–Sept. 3, 2000; Deborah M. Phillips, "Are We Ready for Internet Voting?" (Arlington, Va.: The Voting Integrity Project, Aug. 12, 1999), http://www.voting-integrity.org/projects/votingtechnology/internetvoting/ ivp_title.shtml.

[53] California Internet Voting Task Force, *A Report on the Feasibility of Internet Voting, Executive Summary* (Office of California Secretary of State, January 2000), p. 1, http://www.ss.ca.gov/executive/ivote/final_report.htm#final-1.

on the task force, the group concluded, "At this time, it would not be legally, practically or fiscally feasible to develop a comprehensive remote Internet voting system that would completely replace the current paper process used for voter registration, voting, and the collection of initiative, referendum and recall petition signatures."[54]

About a year later, a major study initiated by the Clinton administration and commissioned by the National Science Foundation came to roughly the same conclusions. A distinguished panel of political scientists and others concluded in a March 2001 report that "remote" Internet voting or registration from homes or workplaces would not be viable in the immediate future, chiefly for security reasons. Instead, the group advised in favor of experiments using Internet-based voting technology that would be situated in traditional polling places under the direct control of election officials and, more cautiously, in nontraditional voting kiosks located elsewhere.[55] The first major academic study of voting technology following the 2000 election problems in Florida, which was a joint institutional effort of MIT and Caltech, largely concurred on the need to solve substantial security problems before shifting to Internet-based voting.[56]

In addition to the security concerns of the California and NSF studies, Internet voting raises problems concerning federal and constitutional requirements for equal access. Those questions were addressed directly in the Arizona experiment. The Voting Integrity Project (VIP), a national voting watchdog group, applied unsuccessfully first for Justice Department intervention, then for a federal court injunction against Internet voting in Arizona, on equal access grounds.[57]

The resolution of security and equal-access matters will be among the chief factors regulating the rate of adoption of Internet voting. However, in the long term, these matters are unlikely to prevent eventual abandonment of mechanical and optical ballot machines in favor of electronic mechanisms with far greater flexibility and far less place-dependence.

---

[54] Ibid.

[55] Internet Policy Institute, *Report of the National Workshop on Internet Voting: Issues and Research Agenda* (sponsored by the National Science Foundation, conducted in cooperation with the University of Maryland, and hosted by the Freedom Forum, March 2001), http://www.netvoting.org/Resources/E-Voting%20Report_3_05.pdf.

[56] Caltech MIT Voting Technology Project, "Voting: What Is, What Could Be," California Institute of Technology and the Massachusetts Institute of Technology Corporation, July 2001.

[57] Voting Integrity Project, "The Arizona Primary" (Arlington, Va.: Voting Integrity Project, March 1, 2000), http://www.voting-integrity.org/projects/votingtechnology.

The effects of electronic voting on turnout involve fundamentally different theoretical problems than other questions associated with the Internet and politics. Internet voting is not a phenomenon of information abundance. Instead, it is a phenomenon of lowered transaction costs for voting itself. While Internet voting makes the singular act of voting easier and less "costly" in a Downsian sense, it does not necessarily contribute directly to changes in the informational context of politics. It therefore has more in common with mail balloting and registration requirements such as the "motor voter" provisions than with candidate web sites, new forms of collective action, or the new environment for news.

On that basis, efforts have been made to model the possible effects of Internet voting on turnout. R. Michael Alvarez and Jonathan Nagler analyzed registration requirements across states and also Oregon mail balloting, coming to several conclusions.[58] First, as the cost of registering to vote falls, the total number of voters rises, while the turnout rate among registered voters falls. Second, the number of people voting rises for both high socioeconomic status (SES) and low SES citizens. While the rate of increase is greater for high SES, the larger pool of low SES nonvoters means that in total numbers, more low-SES citizens are drawn to the ballot box by lowered registration requirements. In Oregon, reduced voting costs through mail balloting had little overall effect on voting rates, and exerted no stimulus to vote among disinterested citizens. The previously cited Arizona experiment confirmed the enormous SES bias in Internet access, although lack of individual-level data creates ecological inference problems and limits the opportunity to test who took advantage of Internet voting and who did not. Alvarez and Nagler suggest that people higher on the SES scale will likely have a disproportionately high propensity to take advantage of Internet voting, even were it made universally available to all citizens. On the other hand, the larger pool of low SES citizens among nonvoters means that on balance, Internet voting could in the long run reduce the SES gap, were it to become universally available. However, in the short run, they conclude that Internet voting is an exclusive activity for the highly engaged.

It will likely be several years before sufficient data from "Internet elections" exist to test these hypotheses thoroughly. Certainly, we know more about how new information technology affects traditional voting than about the dynamics of voting through information technology. While it

[58] R. Michael Alvarez and Jonathan Nagler, "The Likely Consequences of Internet Voting for Political Representation," paper prepared for the Internet Voting and Democracy Symposium at Loyola Law School, Oct. 26, 2000, Los Angeles, Calif.

may one day become an integral part of the story of how information technology affected democracy in the early twenty-first century, Internet voting is best kept conceptually distinct from the parts of that story examined in this chapter, namely, how a changed information environment may affect individual-level political engagement.

Where that larger issue is concerned, the following conclusions can be drawn about changes in political engagement in information revolutions. By creating opportunities for national-scale flows of information, the first information revolution produced enormous increases in political engagement. The second and third revolutions had important effects on the structure of political engagement and on the nature of political intermediaries, but exerted no positive effect on levels of engagement; in fact, they likely contributed to the declines in political engagement, especially in the case of voting during the second half of the twentieth century. The fourth information revolution, which is still in its infancy, also appears to be exerting little influence on participation levels, although a few intriguing effects are visible that cannot yet be fully explained with available evidence.

6

Information, Equality, and Integration
in the Public Sphere

DRAWING CONCLUSIONS: A REVOLUTION IN THE MIDDLE

In what sense is the contemporary information revolution really revolutionary for democracy in the United States? Together the conclusions of the previous chapters suggest a set of important changes that are concentrated between the level of the mass public and institutions of the state itself – a revolution in the middle. The use of technologies associated with the Internet by political actors is making information and communication increasingly abundant: inexpensive, decentralized, and widely distributed. A central feature of this abundance is that information flows more readily within and between organizations than at any time in the past. The traditional boundaries, resources, and structures of organizations have less influence over who has facility with political information and communication and who does not. In this sense, information itself is becoming politically less institutionalized. As a result, processes of political intermediation, organizing, and mobilizing appear to be changing. Some traditional political organizations, such as Environmental Defense, the Libertarian Party, and members of the Save the E-Rate Coalition, are undergoing changes as they adapt to information abundance, while more flexible, ad hoc organizations, such as the Million Mom March, appear better able than ever before to have a voice in politics, if not necessarily to defeat richer organizations outright.

A second feature of information abundance is the reinforcement of patterns of political engagement and disengagement at the level of political individuals. Americans in the aggregate are not growing any more engaged in their political system as a result of new technology. On the whole, those who pay the most attention to the media of previous information revolutions are also paying the most attention to new media, and those most likely to be active in democratic processes in earlier information regimes are those engaged with the new organizational structures of the emergent information regime. Perhaps more clearly and directly than historical developments, contemporary technologies reveal the psychological phenomena that accompany organizational adaptations to new information conditions. These are highly contingent and biased learning and knowledge acquisition and a tendency for the best-informed to learn even more as information grows more accessible.

In the emergent postbureaucratic pluralism of the contemporary period, the number of elites and potentially viable mobilizers appears to be increasing, and competition for political attention growing more aggressive, against a background of largely unchanged habits of political knowledge and learning. This means that the terms and structures of collective action are more sensitive than ever before to the flow of events and information and are less reflective of the traditional organization of interests. The developments of this information revolution are therefore not wholly new, since elements of postbureaucratic political organization – as well as information abundance – extend well back into American political history. Without a doubt, though, rapid technological innovations of the last decade or so are dramatically broadening and accelerating these changes.

How far these developments will go cannot be known yet, certainly not from the assessments of these chapters. What the information regime that eventually emerges will look like must therefore remain something of a mystery. From today's perspective, at what is likely not even the midpoint of the fourth information revolution, it is possible only to identify limiting factors, conditions that make postbureaucratic pluralism maladaptive to aspects of the exercise of power. Some of these involve structure and process, such as the largely unaltered face of state institutions themselves and the electoral and policy-making processes associated with them. Others involve human needs and limits, including the social nature of political influence and trust and the cognitive capacities of humans to deal with information and communication, all of which are unchanged by new technology or new characteristics of communication and information.

The fourth information revolution, along with its predecessors, illuminates important pathways by which information influences democracy. It shows that the information citizens choose to learn is often less important than the information directed to them by elites and organizers. At the same time, it suggests that elites and organizations are themselves defined and constituted in large part by the information they possess and are able to command. In these ways at least, the flow of information is central to political structure and political behavior. Not only is information a tool and resource used by political actors in a strategic or psychological sense, its characteristics and qualities help define political actors themselves. This is how changes in information arising from technological development can bear so directly on the structure of politics.

A BRIEF COMPARISON WITH OTHER NATIONS

It is intriguing to inquire how well these conclusions might explain developments in other nations.[1] Seeing whether a country-specific theory is applicable in other nations would certainly be the next logical step in testing the theory. Since the information revolution is clearly global or nearly global in scope, one can reasonably expect that the theory of information revolutions described here might apply in Europe, Asia, or South America. At the same time, there is no reason to suspect that technological developments would exert precisely the same forces and result in precisely the same outcomes across nations. Indeed, one of the lessons of the history of information revolutions in the United States is that sociotechnological developments such as the postal–press system are partly the *product* of politics. For this reason alone, we should expect politically relevant technologies to evolve differently across nations. No less important is the fact that sociotechnological developments do not determine political outcomes, but instead simply alter the matrix of opportunities and costs associated with political intermediation, mobilization, and the organization of politics.

How altered opportunities and costs play out is a function of nontechnological factors: the state of political participation, the identity and forms of political intermediaries, the structure of institutions of the state, and so on. The fact that the postal–press system obviously contributed to the development of the party system in the United States does not mean that the press, post office, or combination of the two needs to have done so in other countries with different social structures and institutions, different geographies, different systems of franchise, and so on. Similarly, the powerful effects of television on American political evolution are attributable not only to inherent features of the technology but to features of American politics that differentiate it from that of other nations, in particular, the comparatively weak parties, the primary system,

---

[1] I leave aside questions of the effect of the information revolution on international relations.

and comparatively few restrictions on paid political advertising in the United States. The proper question is not whether specific developments in the United States have been replicated elsewhere, but whether the same basic relationship between information and political change seems also to be at work.

The first conclusion one draws from examining the contemporary state of information technology and politics globally is that the nation where the Internet was created in the late 1960s and 1970s is among the nations with the deepest incorporation of new technology into politics. In most other countries, the far slower rate of diffusion of technology to citizens limits the capacity of political systems to adopt new means for communication and information management. At the turn of the century, for example, Internet access across Eastern Europe, the Middle East, Asia, and South America was well under 10 percent, while it was three to five times higher across Western Europe, Scandinavia, and North America. According to one global survey, at a time when Internet access in the United States was about 40 percent, it was about 15 percent in Germany and Japan, and 1 percent in Mexico, Argentina, and Costa Rica.[2] A medium that was viable for political communication among a substantial fraction of the population in the United States was therefore below a critical mass of citizens in many other countries. And in no country, even those with higher rates of citizen access (such as Sweden), has the political system incorporated information technology more deeply than in the United States through its parties, interest groups, mass media, and state offices.

Pippa Norris has shown that several factors explain the varying national rates of incorporation of technology, including socioeconomics and level of economic development, the presence of technology-based industries, and culture.[3] The variation in extent of state control over communication systems also regulates the evolution of new information environments in politics. In China, Vietnam, Indonesia, and Thailand, for instance, comparatively strong state dominance of telecommunications has clearly slowed development of new technology as political media compared with the United States and other nations.[4]

---

[2] Pippa Norris, *Digital Divide: Civic Engagement, Information Poverty and the Internet Worldwide* (Cambridge, Eng.: Cambridge University Press, 2001).

[3] Ibid.

[4] Peter Lovelock, "The Asian NII Experience," paper presented at the INET Conference, Kuala Lampur, Malaysia, June 24–27, 1997, http://www.isoc.org/isoc/whatis/conferences/inet/97/proceedings/E3/E3_2.HTM.

In many countries, the evolution of new information technology follows closely the deregulation of broadcast media. One of the most common consequences of deregulation has been the kind of "channel" multiplication that also occurred in the United States. Increased opportunity for choice has in turn led media businesses to compete more intensely for viewers. European mass media, for example, underwent a transformation in the 1980s, as strong institutions of public ownership gave way to privatization. The commercialization of European media weakened their links to party organizations, and in many nations undermined the depth and extent of political information conveyed by print and broadcast media.[5] That competition has led media businesses away from traditional news formats and toward a greater entertainment orientation.[6] While the United States may lead the way in this more superficial format for news, the effect has also been found in many other countries. This means that information technology is arriving on the political scene at a time of increased competition and fragmentation of political communication. The undermining of the authority of traditional institutions and nation-state processes associated with globalization and postmodernization are now part and parcel of the international picture for information technology and politics. In a general sense, such large-scale trends represent global facets of the U.S. pattern of development of postbureaucratic forms of political organization.

In a number of nations, one finds examples of the new information environment undermining the dominance of traditional organizations and institutions over political information and communication. A small but growing literature has recently emerged to document such developments, which bear a number of similarities to the situation in the United States. In Germany, for example, new media have contributed to substantially greater involvement in local political communication by nongovernmental organizations (NGOs). The availability of nonlocal funding for local groups, along with decentralization and out-sourcing of services by local governments to private organizations, has fostered

---

[5] Paolo Mancini, "How to Combine Media Commercialization and Party Affiliation: The Italian Experience," *Political Communication* 17, no. 4 (2000): 319–324; Jay Blumler and Michael Gurevitch, *The Crisis of Public Communication* (New York: Routledge, 1995); Jay Blumler, *Television and the Public Interest* (Newbury Park, Calif.: Sage Publications, 1992).

[6] Anthony Mughan and Richard Gunther, "The Media in Democratic and Nondemocratic Regimes: A Multilevel Perspective," in Richard Gunther and Anthony Mughan, eds., *Democracy and the Media: A Comparative Perspective* (Cambridge, Eng.: Cambridge University Press, 2000), pp. 1–27.

the development of new organizations, which have been more effective because of their capacity to use new information technologies to function flexibly and interact and coordinate with one another.[7]

New German NGOs have less of an ad hoc character than most of the novel American political groups and practices described in this book. They behave in many ways more like traditional American interest groups, and their story has as much in common with the second information revolution in the United States as with the fourth. According to Sabine Lang, new German NGOs are contributing to political complexity by multiplying the number of participants in politics, opening up corporatist political processes to additional voices. At the same time, technology facilitates new coalitions among local, national, and international groups. Still, more established, resource-rich NGOs are among the most effective exploiters of new information technology. The greater success of established groups in conveying information and mobilizing citizens through the Internet has to a large degree simply reinforced traditional patterns of power.

Among German parties, use of new information technology has produced substantially less organizational change, but has nonetheless produced some intriguing developments. All major parties in Germany operate virtual offices as a means for communicating with citizens, and many of these systems have become very successful in attracting citizen involvement. According to Christoph Bieber, some of these new communication systems have engaged so many citizens that party officials and politicians have had little choice but to respond by participating in Internet-based forums and discussions with their "virtual" party members.[8] The surge of interest in Internet interaction by parties in Germany comes at a time when traditional party membership has been declining, and when many believe that parties have stagnated as organizations. It would be premature, to say the very least, to predict that information technology will revitalize or reorient German parties, as it has organizations in the United States like Environmental Defense. But the new information environment is indeed offering new modes of affiliation and interaction, and it hints at prospects for altering organizational structures.

[7] Sabine Lang, "NGOs, Local Governance, and Political Communication Processes in Germany," *Political Communication* 17, no. 4 (2000): 383–387.
[8] Christoph Bieber, "Revitalizing the Party System or Zeitgeist on-line? Virtual Party Headquarters and Virtual Party Branches in Germany," in Peter Ferdinand, ed., *The Internet, Democracy, and Democratization* (London: Frank Cass, 2000), pp. 59–75.

Some of the most important examples of how information technology affects politics involve marginalized groups overcoming resource limitations and other more serious barriers to gain political power, as the Libertarian Party did in the Know Your Customer case. The successful overthrow of the Suharto government in Indonesia is perhaps the most dramatic and clear-cut case available so far.[9] Despite a weak telecommunications infrastructure and very low levels of citizen access to the Internet in the mid-1990s, networks of anti-Suharto students and activists used the Internet aggressively to circumvent state domination of political information and news. From as early as the late 1980s, antigovernment organizing had a strong orientation toward information dissemination because of state control of broadcast media, bans on antigovernment print publications, and the jailing of journalists. One of the groups that would eventually be important in the Internet-based struggle in the mid-1990s was formed in 1989 as the Center for Information and Reform Action Network, with the acronym PIJAR. The rise of information technology provided the perfect means for PIJAR and other groups to advance their cause. They could employ computer servers outside Indonesia and beyond the reach of the state, and through them distribute and coordinate information back into the country. These networks provided the means for activists to disseminate news about the regime, solicit international support, and organize protests, including the eventual occupation of the Parliament building. What scholarly analysis is available so far largely confirms the claim of a summer 1998 headline in the *Jakarta Post* that compares the overthrow of Suharto with the fight for independence from the Dutch: "Internet Replaces Bamboo Spears in Fight for Freedom."[10]

Another comparable example has been called "the Zapatista Effect." Since 1994, revolutionaries opposing the Mexican government in the state of Chiapas benefited substantially from the decentralized, inexpensive, and self-organizing nature of communication facilitated through new information technology. The geographic isolation of Chiapas, in combination with limited coverage by the Mexican media and efforts by Mexican military forces to contain the movement, meant that the rebels faced large obstacles to attracting support and political attention. New information technology provided a quite successful means for waging

[9] The role of the Internet in Indonesian politics has been analyzed by David Hill and Krishna Sen, and my account is based on theirs. See David Hill and Krishna Sen, "The Internet in Indonesia's New Democracy," in Ferdinand, ed., *The Internet, Democracy, and Democratization*, pp. 119–136.

[10] Cited in ibid.

a war of propaganda and public relations to counter a lopsided military conflict. Messages carried out of Chiapas, sometimes by hand, were distributed globally by supporters with Internet access. This method of communication rapidly evolved into an international network of information about the Chiapas struggle, as observations by international visitors and delegations, along with stories and coverage from traditional media inside and outside Mexico, were added to the network. This created substantial political pressure on the Mexican government, which was unable to dominate this new form of communication to the extent it could traditional communication – Mexico has historically had one of the most highly monopolized broadcast media systems in the world, one where private control of media was tightly connected to the structure of political power.[11] As early as 1995, the government recognized the effectiveness of decentralized, inexpensive communication networks for the Zapatistas. In that year, the Secretary of State described the movement as "a war of ink, of the written word, and of the Internet."[12] Several scholars have reached the conclusion that without the Internet the Zapatista movement would have failed.[13] The closest analogue among the U.S. cases may be the Million Mom March, in which adept use of the Internet was instrumental in gaining a marginal group attention from traditional media and sources of political influence.

The consequences of new technology may have gone beyond simply facilitating new organizational forms. As Sidney Tarrow writes in *Power in Movement*, overcoming collective action problems requires "shared understandings and identities" because these are the foundation of trust and cooperation.[14] Building of such identities and understandings works best in face-to-face communities and networks, of course, but absent physical proximity, communication systems that bring people into contact with the circumstances and plights of others can on occasion serve as a viable alternative. The Zapatista Effect may rest in part on the power of pervasive communication opportunities to foster shared identity and

[11] Daniel C. Hallin, "Media, Political Power, and Democratization in Mexico," in James Curran and Myung-Jin Park, eds., *De-Westernizing Media Studies* (New York: Routledge, 2000), pp. 97–110.

[12] Cited in Harry Cleaver, "The Zapatistas and the Electronic Fabric of Struggle," paper presented at the INET Conference, Montreal, Dec. 23, 1996, http://www.isoc.org/isoc/conferences/inet/96/proceedings/e1/e1.htm.

[13] See Peter Ferdinand, "The Internet, Democracy, and Democratization," in Ferdinand, *The Internet, Democracy, and Democratization*, pp. 1–19.

[14] Sidney Tarrow, *Power in Movement: Social Movements and Contentious Politics*, 2nd ed. (Cambridge, Eng.: Cambridge University Press, 1998), p. 21.

understanding as well as to coordinate more directly the behavioral elements of collective action.

Even more so than in the United States, empirical conclusions about the relationship around the world between changes in the properties of information and political processes or structure must be drawn carefully, because of the early stage of the evidence. This is true for both individual-level effects and organizational effects. At the individual level in particular, it is yet unclear to what extent the U.S. pattern exists elsewhere. It is likely that the relationship between changes in the information environment and participation rates that is so weak in the United States may prove stronger in other political systems.[15] The strength of this relationship is likely to be a function of the constraints on opportunities for political participation in prior information regimes and of the extent of state dominance of political communication. In systems similar to those of the United States that have long traditions of opportunities for civic engagement of various kinds, reasonably transparent government processes connected to competitive private media, and a reasonably long history of universal or near-universal suffrage, contemporary developments in information technology may lead to little in the way of expanded individual-level participation. In systems with weaker traditional infrastructure for political organization and more highly constrained traditional media systems, individual-level effects may be greater. In nations that remain media-poor and which have had fewer opportunities for engagement, the best comparison with the United States may be the first information revolution rather than the contemporary one.

For these reasons, fewer individual-level effects may emerge in Australia, Great Britain, Germany, and Canada than in former Soviet republics and parts of Southeast Asia and the Middle East. However, the effects of new, more open media in many countries will be regulated to a large degree by the success of their states to control communication in new technological environments. China provides one of the best examples of formidable state efforts to prevent new communication channels and flows of political information from providing novel opportunities for political organization, but many other nations are also attempting to exert as much control over new media as old. In Laos, for example, the government issued an "Internet Decree" in 1997, aimed at preventing market-based organization or citizen-driven political activity using new

---

[15] Dana Ott and Melissa Rosser, "The Electronic Republic? The Role of the Internet in Promoting Democracy in Africa," in Ferdinand, ed., *The Internet, Democracy, and Democratization*, pp. 137–156.

information technology. The Lao Prime Minister's statement about the need for state control over the Internet reveals the belief inside the government that new information technology holds the potential for facilitating new kinds of political action. In the Prime Minister's words, state regulation of the Internet was intended "to ensure peace and safety and to protect Lao culture, society, and economy from the destructive elements."[16]

One important theme in emergent scholarship on new media and comparative political communication involves the question of whether information technology is inherently democratizing. This is an old question, dating back to the early development of personal computers. In the 1970s and 1980s, many pondered the conundrum that in highly democratized societies like the United States, one of the chief political concerns of observers of technology was the power computers apparently gave governments to monitor the activities of citizens; at the same time, one of the chief concerns of observers in nondemocratic countries such as the Soviet Union was the power computers apparently gave individuals to disseminate information beyond government control. The Internet is giving this question new life. A number of examples exist worldwide of how groups with nondemocratic aims have taken advantage of the new information environment. In Afghanistan, the Taliban and Al Qaeda were enthusiastic employers of information technology in a nation with little traditional media infrastructure. The Internet appears to have been key in the ability of leaders to communicate readily with one another and to disseminate messages outside Afghanistan to supporters worldwide. Far-right groups in Europe, especially German neo-Nazis, have also been energetic users of information technology for internal communication and for disseminating information externally. As Peter Chroust argues, both the Taliban and neo-Nazis have used inexpensive information infrastructure to build network-based organizations in the face of substantial structural, legal, and financial obstacles to the formation of traditional, bureaucratic organizations.[17] The general principle in these examples is Tocqueville's and not Madison's: Richer information environments facilitate collective action by all sorts of groups, whether democratic or nondemocratic in their aims.

---

[16] Cited in Paula Uimonen, "Connecting Laos: Notes from the Peripheries of Cyberspace," paper presented at the INET Conference, San Jose, June 22–25, 1999, http://www.isoc.org/isoc/conferences/inet/99/proceedings/3a/3a_2.htm.

[17] Peter Chroust, "Neo Nazis and Taliban On-Line: Anti-Modern Political Movements and Modern Media," in Ferdinand, ed., *The Internet, Democracy, and Democratization*, pp. 102–118.

DAHL'S EQUALITY PROPOSITION

If information abundance tends to facilitate collective action, then important normative questions arise, especially regarding political equality. In *Democracy and Its Critics*, published in 1989, Robert Dahl concludes his evaluation of democracy with an intriguing argument that anticipates questions about the Internet and equality. For Dahl, the pursuit of political equality is not simply a political end in itself, but rather a means to freedom and self-determination, which are the ultimate objectives of democracy. He rejects the view that advances in equality must be paid for in freedom. Instead, he justifies a set of democratic arrangements that advance equality because they serve "freedom, human development, and human worth."[18]

Dahl approaches inequality as the product of the uneven distribution of political resources of three major kinds: those that permit violent coercion, those stemming from economic position, and those involving knowledge, information, and cognitive skills. As to the first of these, Dahl prescribes arrangements needed for civilian governance of military and police. As to the second, he defends a conception of market democracy, rejecting the assumption that citizens in the market are simply producers or consumers of goods, freely entering into economic contracts absent relations of power or authority. He would require economic arrangements to be "instrumental not merely to the production and distribution of goods and services but to a much larger range of values, including democratic values."[19]

It is the third and last category of unevenly distributed resources that concerns us here: knowledge and information. This obstacle to equality Dahl views as the most formidable of all.[20] Even more than the political power that derives from economic position, the political power of unevenly distributed knowledge and information constrains the achievement of equality, he argues. "For I am inclined to think that the long-run prospects for democracy are more seriously endangered by inequalities in resources, strategic positions, and bargaining strength that are derived not from wealth or economic position but from special knowledge."[21] The locus of informational inequality lies in two interconnected phenomena: (1) the increasing complexity of public policy and government action; and (2) the rise of institutionalized policy elites and

---

[18] Robert A. Dahl, *Democracy and Its Critics* (New Haven: Yale University Press, 1989), p. 323.
[19] Ibid., p. 324.   [20] Ibid., p. 333.   [21] Ibid.

239

specialists housed in legislatures, parties, interest groups, executive agencies, the media, and universities. Throughout the political system, democracy depends on the labor of many individuals whose chief political qualification is knowledge and the possession of information. During the twentieth century, Dahl observers, these "policy specialists" exerted enormous if indirect effects on democracy through their influence on agendas, attitudes and beliefs, the system of education, and the content of policies.

The key point is that by itself the existence of policy specialists in a political system does not necessarily lead to inequality. The reason is that specialized knowledge and the possession of information are not sufficient to create a class interest that might work in concert against less privileged groups. Policy experts are not, in the Marxian sense, a "class" because their interests are divergent and frequently at odds with one another. However, as complexity in a political system increases, opportunities for experts and the well informed to exploit their informational advantage become widespread. Historically, complexity has been the product of increasing scope of government: a greater number of public policies and decreasing transparency in means–ends relationships. Complexity undermines the capacity of the public to participate in the formation of political agendas, engage in the policy process, and monitor and ultimately control democratic institutions. Under such conditions, experts derive a natural advantage over the public at large from their command of information. Moreover, experts tend to be housed in organizations and institutions of various sorts, since the mobilization of specialized knowledge and information is a resource-intensive task. Political organizations and institutions therefore become a locus of information-based political inequality between the mass public and information elites, who can function as if they constituted a traditional class. This makes democracy vulnerable to drift toward a state of Platonic guardianship, in which the judgment of citizens is severed from the decisions of elites. For Dahl, this is an equality problem of the highest order: the more complex a polity, the greater the contribution of information asymmetries to political inequality. In this view, the developments in information and political organization since the second information revolution described in Chapter 2 have created increasingly important threats to political equality.

Dahl concludes *Democracy and Its Critics* by suggesting remedies. For those who do not know the eminent philosopher to be an observer of technology, his conclusions may come as a surprise. He believes the most promising remedy, with which he concludes the book, is "telecommuni-cations."[22] Dahl argues that information technology offers several means to reduce political inequality. The evolution of information technology increases accessibility to information about the political agenda, which in turn facilitates public participation. New technology also expands the means for citizens to contribute to political processes. It makes obser-vation and monitoring of public officials easier for the public at large. As telecommunication technology expands the flow of information and communication, it makes government more transparent, and the more transparent government is, the smaller the advantage information elites enjoy with respect to the public at large. One general consequence of technological development, then, may be to diminish the third class of resource-based obstacles to political equality.

This argument does not depend on the simplistic view that all citi-zens will avail themselves of new possibilities for political learning and engagement in a polity increasingly rich with information technology – or even that most citizens will do so. Dahl's claim is in general agreement with Anthony Downs's assertion that "any concept of democracy based on an electorate of equally well-informed citizens presupposes that men behave irrationally."[23] Rational citizens choose to delegate some infor-mation acquisition tasks as long as information is not free; therefore, information will be asymmetrically distributed among perfectly ratio-nal citizens. Dahl suggests that, in practice, only a subset of citizens will likely take advantage of the information richness made possible by new technology. But this engaged and informed subset of citizens can form an adequate check and counterbalance against the power of professional, institutionalized information elites.

This argument echoes the old debate between Federalists and Anti-Federalists over political complexity and institutional arrangements. The late eighteenth century provided for American political thinkers no ready examples of complex, highly articulated Weberian bureaucracy vested with policy-making power, nor examples of a policy intelligentsia. At the time of the founding, the colonies had no mass media, policy think tanks, parties, interest groups, nor tradition of professional staff in legislatures, and only a few institutions of higher education. The protoclass of policy specialists of concern to Dahl could not have been a consideration in the calculus of constitutional engineering at the time of the founding. For

[22] Ibid., p. 339.
[23] Anthony Downs, *An Economic Theory of Democracy* (New York: Harper and Brothers, 1957), p. 221.

Anti-Federalists, informational complexity was indeed a threat, as we saw in Chapter 2, but complexity arose simply from the country's size and diversity of interests. For the Federalists, complexity could be remedied by intermediation and the layered aggregation of information through the states. To Publius, more information was indeed better, and a larger scope of government superior at judicious decision-making.

History has endorsed the Federalists' position on information in the most basic sense, as well as their positions on a number of other matters. At the same time, the Anti-Federalists' concern with threats to representation and public control arising from complexity have grown more pertinent over time, as Dahl's argument suggests. The original American question of political complexity concerned the survival of central government in the face of heterogeneous citizen interests, and for that time and place the Anti-Federalists misjudged how political communication could work. Yet, as Dahl points out, by a century later, institution building and increasing scope of public policy have returned us to matters of complexity and lack of transparency in government. The contemporary complexity question concerns the capacity of citizens to retain control of political processes in the face of institutionalized policy elites whose power derives from dominance over information.

That Dahl would approach this problem with a technological remedy is provocative. Serious political thinkers are rightly dismissive of technological solutions to political problems. Yet the conclusions of Chapters 3 and 4 of this book about new structures for collective action and mobilization are supportive of Dahl's technology-centric proposition. The mechanisms of postbureaucratic organization are precisely those that Dahl claims might diminish the influence of institutionalized elites in politics. As information grows more abundant and decentralized, and as it moves more readily across the boundaries of organizations, the capacity of a narrow class of elites to exploit information asymmetries to their advantage decays. The capacity of the Libertarian Party to inform and mobilize large numbers of citizens about an obscure but relevant policy change constructed by the banking industry and its regulators is among the best examples one might imagine. So too is the new capacity of environmental organizations to distribute highly specific and timely political information to citizens with a particular policy concern but who are not otherwise "members" of a political organization. Such cases, as well as the brief illustrations above from other nations, endorse the idea that the contemporary information revolution is undermining one form of political inequality.

On the other hand, the findings from Chapter 5 suggest another path by which contemporary developments are exacerbating political inequality. Access to the new information environment is unequal in ways that reinforce traditional societal inequalities. As of the early 2000s, access to the Internet in the United States is still strongly biased toward those with more education and income, and use of the Internet as a political resource is unequal across an even wider range of demographic categories. The situation is similar in other nations and across countries.[24]

To be sure, the size of the digital divide is changing for the better, and at the same time the consequences of being "offline" are changing in complex ways. Recall that in 1996, about a quarter of adults reported having access to the Internet in the United States, and about one in eight used the Internet in a political way. Five years later, over half had access and a quarter used it politically. In 1996, nearly half of the people who used the Internet regularly had a four-year college degree, and five years later the figure was down to about a third. The pool of Americans excluded from the new information environment is indisputably shrinking. Yet at the same time, the political resources available to a citizen through information technology have grown in importance. Being "offline" in 1996 meant little and conferred few disadvantages politically and economically; being so after the turn of the century can be far more consequential insofar as direct access to political information is concerned. So, information abundance produced by new technology is widening certain inequalities associated with economic class, even while narrowing other inequalities between institution-based elites and the citizenry at large.

Beyond matters of political equality, the contemporary information revolution raises many important normative questions about the health of democracy. These concern the nature of the liberal self in civil society, the processes by which the public and the private are defined and differentiated, the constitution of community and the construction of values associated with sense of belonging, the processes by which culture is embodied and preserved by institutions, and the capacity of citizens to deliberate adequately on public matters. It is beyond the scope of this book to assess these aspects of postmodernity or to mount a cultural critique of new technology, but one set of normative problems is especially relevant to the findings of this book, and they provide a concluding set of considerations.

This set of problems might be labeled deintegration of the public sphere. I take as a model for the public sphere roughly that sketched by

---

[24] Norris, *Digital Divide.*

Jürgen Habermas in *The Structural Transformation of the Public Sphere.* Habermas's term is *Offentlichkeit,* which can be interpreted into common English as "the public" or "publicity" and into academic English as "public sphere."[25] The public sphere is the domain of perception and conversation about public issues that produces and sustains public as opposed to private opinion. Thomas McCarthy defines Habermas's conception as the realm "in which public opinion can be formed through unrestricted discussion of matters of general interest."[26] In this formulation, the concept of general interest is of greatest concern here. It is vital to the concept of a public sphere and the conception of public opinion associated with it that communication occur about issues and interests that are general in nature across the polity. Peter Dahlgren sharpens the concept in terms of "questions of common concern."[27] The public sphere is therefore not merely civil society; rather, it is the realm of communication about commonly perceived questions or issues that integrate civil society and connect it to the state. In the public sphere, citizens hardly agree about what political choices are best, but they perceive in common what political choices are to be made. The public sphere is therefore a realm of integration of perceptions and understandings of common issues.

A central concern for Habermas and others such as Marcuse is the intrusion of the market into the public sphere and the collapse of the distinction between the public and the private.[28] For Jacques Ellul, market forces aided by science and technology intrude into the public sphere and thereby displace normative politics with mere administration – what Lewis Mumford calls "technics" and some Frankfurt School theorists the "totally administered society."[29] For Habermas, this constitutes the "refeudalization" of the public sphere.

---

[25] For a discussion of definitions and translations, see Thomas Burger's "Translator's Note" in Jurgen Habermas, *The Structural Transformation of the Public Sphere: An Inquiry into a Category of Bourgeois Society* (Cambridge, Mass.: MIT Press, 1989).

[26] Thomas McCarthy, *The Critical Theory of Jurgen Habermas* (Cambridge, Mass.: MIT Press, 1981), p. 15.

[27] Peter Dahlgren, *Television and the Public Sphere: Citizenship, Democracy, and the Media* (Thousand Oaks, Calif.: Sage Publications, 1995), p. 7.

[28] Herbert Marcuse, *One Dimensional Man* (New York: Beacon, 1964).

[29] Jacques Ellul, *The Technological Society* (New York: Vintage, 1964); Lewis Mumford, *Technics and Civilization* (New York, Harcourt, Brace and World, 1963); Lewis Mumford, *The Myth of the Machine,* vol. 1: *Technics and Human Development* (New York: Harcourt, Brace and World, 1967). For overviews of relevant Frankfurt School analysis, see McCarthy, *The Critical Theory of Jurgen Habermas;* and John Ehrenberg, *Civil Society: The Critical History of an Idea* (New York: New York University Press, 1999).

Postbureaucratic political organization and new structures for plural-ism threaten the public sphere in a different way. Aside from colonization of the public sphere by media giants, which is a phenomenon of the third information regime, the fourth information revolution threatens to pro-duce fragmentation and the loss of the common among what remains public. As traditionally well-institutionalized organizations yield some of their dominance over political gatekeeping and agenda-setting to a larger number of less well-institutionalized groups and postbureaucratic orga-nizations, the stability and predictability of the national political agenda can decay. To the extent that the fourth information revolution succeeds at undermining centralized, organization-based flows of information, it will tend to feed self-selection, polarization, and fragmentation. The capacity for increasingly individuated information environments pro-motes the autonomous, individually constructed liberal self, more free of the force of community values and agendas that come from living in a particular place and from interacting with others within the domain of various institutions. As Cass Sunstein argues, democracy is enriched by the multiplication of voices only when mechanisms for common atten-tion and deliberation are present.[30] In their absence, the heterogeneity of the newest information environment could contribute toward a soci-ety that is more divided rather than less. What Dahlgren calls universal "sense-making" and the building of shared conceptions is that much harder as the public sphere grows more diverse and fluid as a result of technological change.[31]

The collapse of the common has been the subject of commentary for a generation of scholars and cultural critics; contemporary infor-mation technology exacerbates many of their concerns. Previous work has attributed pathologies of the public sphere to the industrial and postindustrial workplace, the replacement of the rural community with the urban landscape, the collapse of associations in civil society, the de-cay of the family, the rise of racial and ethnic tensions, and the maturing of political pluralism. For Eric Åsard and Lance Bennett, technology is implicated in the failing organizational coherence of politics.[32] One of the consequences of more highly bureaucratized forms of political

---

[30] Cass Sunstein, *Republic.com* (Princeton, N.J.: Princeton University Press, 2001).
[31] Peter Dahlgren, "The Internet and the Democratization of Civic Culture," *Political Communication* 17, no. 4 (2000): 335–340.
[32] Eric Åsard and W. Lance Bennett, *Democracy and the Marketplace of Ideas: Communi-cation and Government in Sweden and the United States* (Cambridge, Eng.: Cambridge University Press, 1997).

intermediation is a tendency to stabilize and generalize political communication. John Ehrenberg writes that the deintegration of the public sphere is the result of the unraveling of public communication "into isolated acts of individual reception,"[33] while David Swanson sees "newly porous political systems struggle to maintain coherence in the face of new entrants into the policy arena."[34] For philosopher Philip Brey, it is a matter of increased "presence competition" as citizens disengage from an expanding and shifting body of elites seeking their attention.[35] Problems of deintegration of the public sphere can be found in the literature on political pluralism in the United States at least as far back as Theodore Lowi's classic polemic, *The End of Liberalism*. Lowi's blasting of pluralistic government for failing to address the truly public and for its commitment to bargaining about the private instead is a concern with the common and the integration of interests in a public realm.[36] For Lowi, writing decades before the rise of the Internet, the deintegration of the public sphere is a product not simply of economics or technology, but also of a political philosophy that privatizes what ought to be public and therefore validates fragmentation as a way of political life. The technologies of the fourth information revolution show every sign of accelerating and advancing such problems.

The lesson here is that the extent to which institutionalized elites can dominate the flow of information in a democracy regulates the extent of integration and coherence in the public sphere. A limited and stable body of organizations and elites provides order and clarity to the public sphere and helps to integrate interests into a common public opinion – whatever other effects they may also have. Technological change that multiplies elites and diminishes the bureaucratization of the public sphere may, as Dahl argues, enhance political equality, but it does so at the cost of political coherence. It is an unwelcome conclusion that information abundance creates possibilities for greater equality and for a less intelligible public sphere through the very same mechanisms.

Whether these developments constitute a secular decline in the health of the public sphere or simply a setting of the stage for a reconstitution of political order and publicness is not yet clear. Meaningful and productive

---

[33] Ehrenberg, *Civil Society*, p. 221.

[34] See Swanson, "The Homologous Evolution of Political Communication and Civic Engagement," *Political Communication* 17(2000): 410.

[35] Philip Brey, "New Media and the Quality of Life," *Philosophy and Technology* 3, no. 1 (1997): 1–23.

[36] Theodore J. Lowi, *The End of Liberalism: The Second Republic of the United States*, 2nd ed. (New York: Norton, 1979).

forms of public identity and opinion formation may well configure themselves around new patterns of communication and new postbureaucratic
structures. Two of the most important foundations of a coherent, integrated public sphere and the social order that goes with it have been in the
past geographic and institutional. Spatial proximity is the original basis
for political order, followed closely by the influence of institutions and
organizations on communication, ideas, and behavior. Throughout the
first, second, and third information regimes, these remained the foundation of the public sphere. The fourth information revolution makes
both space and some traditional institutional structures less important
in the constitution of political order and the public sphere. The question
is, What kind of public sphere can exist on such altered foundations?

Dahlgren is one hopeful observer who wonders whether the novel ways
of interacting through contemporary media are contributing to "new
ways of doing – and imagining – democracy."[37] Bennett hypothesizes
that affinity groups and new political networks that span the boundaries
of nations and traditional organizations and communities through new
technology – what I have called postbureaucratic organizations – may be
"filling the spaces in civil society created by the decline in traditional civic
organizations."[38] Francis Fukuyama makes a similar argument, suggesting that the coherence of public life follows a cyclical pattern of decay
and reconstitution rather than a trajectory of monotonic decline.[39] In
his view, the changing social order is attributable to the fall of Weberian
culture and norms not just inside organizations but across society: declining social structures rooted in centralized organizations, the crumbling
of highly institutionalized relationships, and the fading of hierarchically
organized social rules.[40]

The most important countertrend to fragmentation and individuation
of the public sphere involves media concentration. The concentration
of media ownership that emerged during the third information regime
is regrettable for many reasons, but it had the merit of contributing
toward common political communication and perceptions, at least in
comparison to the most extreme possibilities of decentralization and
fragmentation now visible. Concentration of ownership of mass media
clearly will persist in the emergent information regime. The fact that

---

[37] Dahlgren, "The Internet and the Democratization of Civic Culture," p. 339.
[38] Bennett, "Introduction," p. 310.
[39] Francis Fukuyama, *The Great Disruption: Human Nature and the Reconstitution of Social Order* (New York: Free Press, 1999).
[40] Ibid.

major traditional media outlets, from NBC and CNN to *USA Today*, provide the most highly subscribed news sites on the web would appear to be evidence of the sustained dominance of a few traditional firms over information and communication. This has led some observers to a conclusion that traditional patterns of political communication will simply reproduce themselves in the new information environment.[41]

Despite the obvious and continuing influences of a few media conglomerates, there are reasons to doubt that old patterns of power will map directly onto new media. It may be true that the most highly subscribed news sites are the products of major firms, but the vast number of alternatives to those sites simply has no parallel in history, especially during the period when three networks monopolized virtually all broadcast television, and also earlier when citizens in any particular city chose between just a few newspapers for their access to the public sphere. The direct and indirect effects of an effectively unlimited number of news and information sources, even if they share among them less than a majority of citizens as patrons, limit in new ways the capacity of a few elites to dominate the content and pace of news. The array of readily available electronic information sources sponsored by individuals, nonmedia organizations, and government offices has no comparable analogue in the world of traditional media. At the same time that the economic power of a few media businesses to control communication is indeed expanding, technological developments are making information and communication fundamentally less controllable by any narrow class of interests.

This confrontation between trends toward media concentration and fragmentation is a central feature of the modern public sphere. A decade ago, W. Russell Neuman argued correctly that the future of media would be driven by a tension between the increasing technological capacity of individual citizens to control their information environment and a set of economic and social forces that tend away from diversity, openness, and a free marketplace of ideas.[42] The tendency of contemporary information technology toward individualization and accelerated, fragmented pluralism is opposed by two forces. One is the political economy of the media business, which favors centralization, economies of scale, and the mass

---

[41] See Michael Margolis and David Resnick, *Politics as Usual: The Cyberspace "Revolution"* (Thousand Oaks, Calif.: Sage Publications, 2000); and Richard Davis, *The Web of Politics* (New York: Oxford University Press, 1998).

[42] W. Russell Neuman, *The Future of the Mass Audience* (Cambridge, Eng.: Cambridge University Press, 1991).

audience. The other is the political psychology of the individual, which is dominated by semiattentiveness and an orientation toward entertainment over information and learning. It is now more clear than ever that the power of these politicoeconomic and politicopsychological features of the previous information regime will limit fragmentation and development of individualized spheres of political information as the fourth information revolution develops. The tension between the dynamics of the third and fourth information regimes promises to be one of the major features of political communication for years to come.

These connections across time between the evolution of media technology and the structure of the public sphere endorse one of the basic claims of post–World War II sociology and philosophy of technology. The indisputably progressive nature of technology toward more speed, power, and efficiency does not in and of itself signal social or political progress. A society using technology that is technically "better" than what went before may or may not be a society that is itself better, judged against any particular normative conception of the good. Clearly, the contemporary information revolution is unleashing technology that is technically superior to that of prior regimes. This technology and its effects on the structure of information and political interests promise to enhance as well as undermine various features of American democracy, and only time will tell the outcome.

Select Bibliography

The most important scholarly works consulted in the preparation of this book are listed here. For primary source material, government documents, and the complete set of citations to all sources, see the footnotes.

Abramson, Jeffrey B., F. Christopher Arterton, and Gary R. Orren. *The Electronic Commonwealth.* Cambridge, Mass.: Harvard University Press, 1988.

Aldrich, John. *Why Parties? The Origin and Transformation of Political Parties in America.* Chicago: University of Chicago Press, 1995.

Alexander, Cynthia J., and Leslie A. Pal. *Digital Democracy: Policy and Politics in the Modern World.* New York: Oxford University Press, 1998.

Althaus, Scott L., and David Tewksbury. "Agenda Setting and the 'New' News." Paper prepared for the annual meeting of the American Political Science Association, Washington, D.C., Aug. 31–Sept. 3, 2000.

————. "Patterns of Internet and Traditional News Media Use in a Networked Community." *Political Communication* 17, no. 1 (2000): 21–45.

Altheide, David L., and Robert P. Snow. *Media Logic.* Thousand Oaks, Calif.: Sage Publications, 1979.

Altschuler, Glenn C. and Stuart M. Blumin. *Rude Republic: Americans and Their Politics in the Nineteenth Century.* Princeton: Princeton University Press, 2000.

Alvarez, R. Michael, and Jonathan Nagler. "The Likely Consequences of Internet Voting for Political Representation." Paper prepared for the Internet Voting and Democracy Symposium at Loyola Law School, Oct. 26, 2000, Los Angeles, Calif.

Ansolabehere, Stephen, and Shanto Iyengar. *Going Negative: How Attack Ads Shrink and Polarize the Electorate.* New York: Free Press, 1995.

Arnold, R. Douglas *The Logic of Congressional Action.* New Haven: Yale University Press, 1990.

Åsard, Eric, and W. Lance Bennett. *Democracy and the Marketplace of Ideas: Communication and Government in Sweden and the United States.* Cambridge, Eng.: Cambridge University Press, 1997.

Banks, Jeffrey. *Signaling Games in Political Science.* New York: Harwood Academic, 1991.

Barber, Benjamin R. "The New Telecommunications Technology: Endless Frontier or End of Democracy." In *A Communications Cornucopia*, edited by Roger G. Noll and Monroe E. Price. Washington, D.C.: Brookings, 1998. Pp. 72–98.

———. *Strong Democracy*. Berkeley: University of California Press, 1984.

Barber, Lucy Grace. "Marches on Washington, 1894–1963: National Political Demonstrations and American Political Culture." Ph.D. diss., Brown University, May 1996.

Baumgartner, Frank R., and Beth L. Leech. *Basic Interests: The Importance of Groups in Politics and Political Science*. Princeton: Princeton University Press, 1998.

Beard, Charles A. *An Economic Interpretation of the Constitution*. New York: Macmillan, 1913.

Beniger, James R. *The Control Revolution: Technological and Economic Origins of the Information Society*. Cambridge, Mass.: Harvard University Press, 1986.

Bennett, Daniel, and Pam Fielding. *The Net Effect: How Cyberadvocacy is Changing the Political Landscape*. Merrifield, Va.: E-Advocates Press, 1997.

Bennett, W. Lance. "Introduction: Communication and Civic Engagement in Comparative Perspective." *Political Communication* 17, no. 4 (2000): 307–312.

———. "The UnCivic Culture: Communication, Identity, and the Rise of Lifestyle Politics." *PS: Political Science and Politics* 31, no. 4 (1998): 741–761.

Berry, Jeffrey M. *The Interest Group Society*. Boston: Little, Brown, 1984.

Bessette, Joseph M. *Toward a More Perfect Union: Writings of Herbert J. Storing*. Washington, D.C.: American Enterprise Institute, 1995.

Best, Michael. *The New Competition: Institutions of Industrial Restructuring*. Cambridge, Mass.: Harvard University Press, 1990.

Bieber, Christoph. "Revitalizing the Party System or Zeitgeist On-Line? Virtual Party Headquarters and Virtual Party Branches in Germany." In *The Internet, Democracy, and Democratization*, edited by Peter Ferdinand. London: Frank Cass, 2000. Pp. 59–75.

Bimber, Bruce. "Information and Civic Engagement in America: The Search for Political Effects of the Internet." *Political Research Quarterly* 54, no. 1 (2001): 53–67.

———. "The Internet and Citizen Communication with Government: Does the Medium Matter?" *Political Communication* 16, no. 4 (1999): 409–428.

———. "The Internet and Political Mobilization: Research Note on the 1996 Election Season," *Social Science Computer Review* 16, no. 4 (1998): 391–401.

———. "The Internet and Political Transformation: Populism, Community, and Accelerated Pluralism," *Polity* 31 no. 1 (1998): 133–160.

———. "Measuring the Gender Gap on the Internet," *Social Science Quarterly* 81, no. 3 (2000): 868–876.

———. "The Study of Information Technology and Civic Engagement." *Political Communication* 17, no. 4 (2000): 239–333.

Blocker, Jack S., Jr. *American Temperance Movements: Cycles of Reform*. Boston: Twayne Publishers, 1989.

Blumler, Jay. *Television and the Public Interest*. Newbury Park, Calif.: Sage Publications, 1992.

Blumler, Jay, and Michael Gurevitch. *The Crisis of Public Communication*. New York: Routledge, 1995.

Blumler, Jay, and Dennis Kavanaugh, "The Third Age of Political Communication: Influences and Features," *Political Communication* 16 (1999): 209–230.

Borden, Morton, ed. *The Antifederalist Papers.* N.p.: Michigan State University Press, 1965.

Borgmann, Albert. *Holding on to Reality: The Nature of Information at the Turn of the Millennium.* Chicago: University of Chicago, 1999.

Bosso, Christopher J. "Seizing Back the Day: The Challenge to Environmental Activism in the 1990s." In *Environmental Policy in the 1990s*, 3rd ed., edited by Norman J. Vig and Michael E. Kraft. Washington, D.C.: CQ Press, 1997. Pp. 31–50.

Brainard, Lori A., and Patricia D. Siplon. "Activism for the Future: Using the Internet to Reshape Grassroots Victims Organizations." Paper presented at the annual meeting of the American Political Science Association, Boston, Sept. 4–7, 1998.

Brey, Philip. "New Media and the Quality of Life." *Philosophy and Technology* 3, no. 1 (1997): 1–23.

Bruce, John M., and Clyde Wilcox, eds. *The Changing Politics of Gun Control.* Lanham, Md.: Rowman and Littlefield, 1998.

Burger, Thomas. Translator's Note to *The Structural Transformation of the Public Sphere: An Inquiry into a Category of Bourgeois Society*, by Jurgen Habermas. Cambridge, Mass.: MIT Press, 1989.

Burrows, James G. *AMA: Voice of American Medicine.* Baltimore: Johns Hopkins University Press, 1963.

California Internet Voting Task Force. *A Report on the Feasibility of Internet Voting, Executive Summary.* Sacramento: Office of California Secretary of State, January, 2000. http://www.ss.ca.gov/executive/ivote/final_report.htm#final-1.

Carey, George W. *The Federalist: Design for a Constitutional Republic.* Urbana: University of Illinois Press, 1989.

Carter, Gregg Lee. *The Gun Control Movement.* New York: Twayne Publishers, 1997.

Castells, Manuel. *The Rise of the Network Society.* Malden, Mass.: Blackwell, 1996.

Chaffee, Steven H., and Stacey Frank Kanihan. "Learning about Politics from the Mass Media." *Political Communication* 14, no. 4 (1997): 421–430.

Chaffee, Steven H., and Donna G. Wilson. "Media Rich, Media Poor: Two Studies of Diversity in Agenda Holding." *Journalism Quarterly* 54 (Autumn 1977): 466–476.

Chroust, Peter. "Neo Nazis and Taliban On-Line: Anti-Modern Political Movements and Modern Media." In *The Internet, Democracy, and Democratization*, edited by Peter Ferdinand. London: Frank Cass, 2000. Pp. 102–118.

Cigler, Allan J., and Burdett A. Loomis, eds. *Interest Group Politics*, 5th ed. Washington, D.C.: Congressional Quarterly, 1998.

Clemens, Elizabeth Stephanie. *The People's Lobby: Organizational Innovation and the Rise of Interest Group Politics in the United States.* Chicago: University of Chicago Press, 1997.

Coase, R. H. "The Nature of the Firm." *Economica* 6, no. 4 (1937): 423–435.

Congressional Quarterly, Inc. *Congressional Quarterly's Guide to U.S. Elections*, 3rd ed. Washington, D.C.: CQ Press, 1994.

Converse, Philip E. "Change in the American Electorate." In *The Human Meaning of Social Change*, edited by Angus Campbell and Philip E. Converse. New York: Russell Sage Foundation, 1972. Pp. 263–337.

Cook, Timothy E. *Governing with the News: The News Media as a Political Institution.* Chicago: University of Chicago Press, 1998.

Cooke, Jacob E., ed. *The Federalist.* Middletown, Conn.: Wesleyan University Press, 1961.

Corrado, Anthony, and Charles M. Firestone, eds. *Elections in Cyberspace: Toward a New Era in American Politics.* Washington, D.C.: Aspen Institute, 1996.

Curran, James and Myung-Jin Park, eds. *De-Westernizing Media Studies.* New York: Routledge, 2000.

Dahl, Robert A. *Democracy and Its Critics.* New Haven: Yale University Press, 1989.

―――. *A Preface to Democratic Theory.* Chicago: University of Chicago Press, 1956.

Dahlgren, Peter. "The Internet and the Democratization of Civic Culture." *Political Communication* 17, no. 4 (2000): 335–340.

―――. *Television and the Public Sphere: Citizenship, Democracy, and the Media.* Thousand Oaks, Calif.: Sage Publications, 1995.

Davidson, Roger, and Walter Oleszek. *Congress and Its Members,* 7th ed. Washington, D.C.: Congressional Quarterly, 2000.

Davis, Richard. *The Web of Politics.* London: Oxford University Press, 1998.

Davis, Richard, and Diana Owen. *New Media in American Politics.* London: Oxford University Press, 1998.

Delli Carpini, Michael X. "Gen.com: Youth, Civic Engagement, and the New Information Environment." *Political Communication* 17, no. 4 (2000): 341–349.

Scott Keeter and Delli Carpini, Michael X., "The Internet and Informed Citizenry." In *The Civic Web: Online Politics and Democratic Values,* edited by David M. Anderson and Michael Cornfield. Lanham, Md.: Rowman and Littlefield, forthcoming.

―――. *What Americans Know about Politics and Why It Matters.* New Haven: Yale University Press, 1996.

Delli Carpini, Michael X., Scott Keeter, and J. David Kennamer. "Effects of the News Media Environment on Citizen Knowledge of State Politics and Government." *Journalism Quarterly* 71, no. 2 (1994): 443–456.

Dertouzos, Michael. *What Will Be: How the New Information Marketplace Will Change Our Lives.* San Francisco: Harper Edge, 1997.

Downs, Anthony. *An Economic Theory of Democracy.* New York: Harper, 1957.

Dulio, David A., Donald L. Goff, and James A. Thurber. "Untangled Web: Internet Use during the 1998 Election." *PS: Political Science and Politics* 32, no. 1 (1999): 53–59.

Durkheim, Emile. *The Division of Labor in Society.* New York: Free Press, 1933.

Dye, Thomas. *Understanding Public Policy,* 7th ed. Englewood Cliffs: Prentice Hall, 1997.

Ehrenberg, John. *Civil Society: The Critical History of an Idea.* New York: New York University Press, 1999.

Ellul, Jacques. *The Technological Society.* New York: Vintage, 1964.

Epstein, David F. *The Political Theory of "The Federalist."* Chicago: University of Chicago Press, 1984.

Etzioni, Amitai. *The Spirit of Community: Rights, Responsibilities, and the Communitarian Agenda.* New York: Crown Publishers, 1993.

Fang, Irving. *A History of Mass Communication: Six Information Revolutions.* Boston: Focal Press, 1997.

Fishbein, Morris. *A History of the American Medical Association, 1847–1947.* New York: Kraus Reprint, 1969.

Flanagin, William H., and Nancy Zingale, eds. *Political Behavior of the American Electorate*, 8th ed. Washington, D.C.: Congressional Quarterly, 1994.

Formisano, Ronald P. "Federalists and Republicans: Parties, Yes – System, No." In *The Evolution of American Electoral Systems*, edited by Paul Kleppner, Walter Dean Burnham, Ronald P. Formisano, Samuel P. Hays, Richard Jensen, and William G. Shade. Westport, Conn.: Greenwood, 1981. Pp. 33–76.

Frantzich, Stephen. *Write Your Congressman: Citizen Communications and Representation*. New York: Praeger, 1986.

Fritz, Sara, and Dwight Morris. *Handbook of Campaign Spending: Money in the 1990 Congressional Races*. Washington, D.C.: CQ Press, 1992.

Fukuyama, Francis. *The Great Disruption: Human Nature and the Reconstitution of Social Order*. New York: Free Press, 1999.

Gerth, H. H., and C. Wright Mills. *From Max Weber: Essays in Sociology*. New York: Oxford University Press, 1958.

Gilbert, Norman T. "The Mass Protest Phenomenon: An Examination of Marches on Washington." Ph.D. diss., Northern Illinois University, 1971.

Goldschmidt, Kathy. "E-Mail Overload in Congress: Managing a Communications Crisis." The Congress Online Project, a joint project of the George Washington University and the Congressional Management Foundation, March 19, 2001.

Goldstein, Kenneth M. *Interest Groups, Lobbying, and Participation in America*. Cambridge, Eng.: Cambridge University Press, 1999.

Goodman, Paul. "The First American Party System." In *The American Party Systems: Stages of Political Development*, edited by William Nisbet Chambers and Walter Dean Burnham. New York: Oxford University Press, 1967. Pp. 56–90.

Graber, Doris A. *Mass Media and American Politics*, 5th ed. Washington, D.C.: CQ Press, 1997.

Grossman, Lawrence K. *The Electronic Republic: Reshaping Democracy in America*. New York: Viking, 1995.

Gurak, Laura. *Persuasion and Privacy in Cyberspace: The Online Protests over Lotus Marketplace and the Clipper Chip*. New Haven: Yale University Press, 1997.

Hagen, Inguun. "Communicating to an Ideal Audience: News and the Notion of an 'Informed Citizen.'" *Political Communication* 14, no. 4 (1997): 405–419.

Hague, Barry N., and Brian D. Loader, eds. *Digital Democracy: Discourse and Decision Making in the Information Age*. London: Routledge, 1999.

Hallin, Daniel C. "Media, Political Power, and Democratization in Mexico." In James Curran and Myung-Jin Park, eds., *De-Westernizing Media Studies*. New York: Routledge, 2000. Pp. 97–110.

Hart, David M. *Forged Consensus: Science, Technology and Economic Policy in the United States, 1921–1953*. Princeton: Princeton University Press, 1998.

Hays, Samuel P. *A History of Environmental Politics since 1945*. Pittsburgh: University of Pittsburgh Press, 2000.

———. "Political Parties and the Community-Society Continuum." In *The American Party Systems: Stages of Political Development*, edited by William Nisbet Chambers and Walter Dean Burnham. New York: Oxford University Press, 1967. Pp. 152–181.

———. *The Response to Industrialism 1885–1914*, 2nd ed. Chicago: University of Chicago Press, 1995.

Heckscher, Charles. "Defining the Post-Bureaucratic Type." In *The Post-Bureaucratic Organization: New Perspectives on Organizational Change*, edited by Charles Heckscher and Anne Donnellon. Thousand Oaks, Calif.: Sage Publications, 1994. Pp. 14–62.

Heckscher, Charles, and Lynda M. Applegate. Introduction to *The Post-Bureaucratic Organization: New Perspectives on Organizational Change*, edited by Charles Heckscher and Anne Donnellon. Thousand Oaks, Calif.: Sage Publications, 1994. Pp. 1–13.

Heckscher, Charles, and Anne Donnellon, eds. *The Post-Bureaucratic Organization: New Perspectives on Organizational Change*. Thousand Oaks, Calif.: Sage Publications, 1994.

Heilbroner, Robert. "Do Machines Make History?" *Technology and Culture* 8, no. 3 (1967): 335–345.

Heinz, John P., et al. *Private Interests in National Policy Making*. Cambridge, Mass.: Harvard University Press, 1993.

Herring, Pendleton. *Group Representation before Congress*. Baltimore: Johns Hopkins University Press, 1929.

Hill, David, and Krishna Sen. "The Internet in Indonesia's New Democracy." In *The Internet, Democracy, and Democratization*, 3rd ed., edited by Peter Ferdinand. London: Frank Cass, 2000. Pp. 119–136.

Hill, Kevin A., and John E. Hughes. *Cyberpolitics: Citizen Activism in the Age of the Internet*. New York: Rowman and Littlefield, 1998.

Huckfeldt, Robert, and John Sprague. *Citizens, Politicism and Social Communication: Information and Influence in an Election Campaign*. Cambridge, Eng.: Cambridge University Press, 1995.

Hughes, Thomas P. *Rescuing Prometheus*. New York: Pantheon, 1998.

Hula, Kevin. *Lobbying Together: Interest Group Coalitions in Legislative Politics*. Washington, D.C.: Georgetown University Press, 1999.

Internet Policy Institute. *Report of the National Workshop on Internet Voting: Issues and Research Agenda*. Sponsored by the National Science Foundation, conducted in Cooperation with the University of Maryland, and hosted by the Freedom Forum, March 2001. http://www.netvoting.org/Resources/E-Voting%20Report_3_05.pdf.

James, Karen, and Jeffrey D. Sadow. "Utilization of the World Wide Web as a Communicator of Campaign Information." Paper presented at the annual meeting of the American Political Science Association, Washington, D.C., Aug. 27–31, 1997.

Jasanoff, Sheila, Gerald E. Markle, James C. Petersen, and Trevor Pinch, eds. *Handbook of Science and Technology Studies*. Thousand Oaks, Calif.: Sage Publications, 1995.

John, Richard R. *Spreading the News: The American Postal System from Franklin to Morse*. Cambridge, Mass.: Harvard University Press, 1995.

Johnson, Paul E. "Interest Group Recruiting: Finding Members and Keeping Them." In *Interest Group Politics*, 5th ed., edited by Allan J. Cigler and Burdett A. Loomis. Washington, D.C.: CQ Press, 1998. Pp. 35–62.

Jones, Steven G., ed. *Cybersociety: Computer-Mediated Communication and Community*. Thousand Oaks, Calif.: Sage Publications, 1995.

Kahn, Kim Fridkin, and Patrick J. Kenney. "Do Negative Campaigns Mobilize or Suppress Turnout? Clarifying the Relationship between Negativity and Participation." *American Political Science Review* 93, no. 4 (1999): 877–889.

Kamarck, Elaine Civlla, and Joseph S. Nye, Jr. *Democracy.com: Governance in a Networked World*. Hollis, N.H.: Hollis Publishers, 1999.

Kernell, Samuel. *Going Public: New Strategies of Presidential Leadership*, 3rd ed. Washington, D.C.: Congressional Quarterly, 1997.

Kingdon, John. *Congressmen's Voting Decisions*, 3rd ed. Ann Arbor: University of Michigan Press, 1989.

Klein, Hans K. "Tocqueville in Cyberspace: Using the Internet for Citizen Associations." *The Information Society* 15, no. 4 (1999): 213–220.

Klotz, Robert. "Virtual Criticism: Negative Advertising on the Internet in the 1996 Races." *Political Communication* 15, no. 3 (1998): 347–365.

Kollman, Ken. *Outside Lobbying: Public Opinion and Interest Group Strategies.* Princeton: Princeton University Press, 1998.

Koppes, Clayton R. "The Social Destiny of the Radio: Hope and Disillusionment in the 1920s." *South Atlantic Quarterly* 68, no. 3 (1969): 363–376.

Kraditor, Aileen S. *The Ideas of the Woman Suffrage Movement, 1890–1920.* New York: Columbia University Press, 1965.

Kuklinski, James H., Robert C. Luskin, and John Bolland. "Where Is the Schema? Going Beyond the 'S' Word in Political Psychology." *American Political Science Review* 85, no. 4 (1991): 1341–1356.

Lang, Sabine. "NGOs, Local Governance, and Political Communication Processes in Germany." *Political Communication* 17, no. 4 (2000): 383–387.

Langbein, Laura I. "PACs, Lobbies, and Political Conflict: The Case of Gun Control." *Public Choice* 77, no. 3 (1993): 551–572.

Langbein, Laura I., and Mark A. Lotwis. "The Political Efficacy of Lobbying and Money: Gun Control in the U.S. House, 1986." *Legislative Studies Quarterly* 15, no. 3 (1986): 413–440.

Lawrence, Regina G., and W. Lance Bennett. "Civic Engagement in the Era of Big Stories." *Political Communication* 17, no. 4 (2000): 377–382.

Leighley, Jan. "Group Membership and the Mobilization of Political Participation." *Journal of Politics* 58, no. 2 (1996): 447–463.

Levy, Pierre. *Collective Intelligence: Mankind's Emerging World in Cyberspace.* Cambridge, Mass.: Perseus, 1997.

Lewis, John D. *Anti-Federalists versus Federalists: Selected Documents.* San Francisco: Chandler Publishing, 1967.

Lippmann, Walter. *Drift and Mastery.* New York: Mitchell Mennerly, 1914.

Locke, John. *An Essay Concerning Human Understanding,* Book 3, Ch. 10. Public domain version [1690] 1995, available at http://www.ilt.Columbia.edu/digitexts/locke/understanding/chapter0310.html.

Lodge, Milton, Charles Tabor, and Aron Chase Galonsky. "The Political Consequences of Motivated Reasoning: Partisan Bias in Information Processing." Paper prepared for the Annual Meeting of the American Political Science Association, Atlanta, Ga. Sept. 2–5, 1999.

Lohmann, Susan. "An Information Rationale for the Power of Special Interests." *American Political Science Review* 92, no. 4 (1998): 809–827.

Lord, Charles G., Lee Ross, and Mark R. Lepper. "Biased Assimilation and Attitude Polarization: The Effects of Prior Theories on Subsequently Considered Evidence." *Journal of Personality and Social Psychology* 37, no. 11 (1979): 2098–2109.

Lowi, Theodore J. *The End of Liberalism: The Second Republic of the United States,* 2nd ed. New York: Norton, 1979.

Luskin, Robert C. "Explaining Political Sophistication." In *Controversies in Voting Behavior*, 3rd ed., edited by Richard G. Niemi and Herbert F. Weisberg. Washington, D.C.: CQ Press, 1993. Pp. 114–136.

Malone, Thomas W., Joanne Yates, and Robert I. Benjamin. "Electronic Markets and Electronic Hierarchies." *Communications of the ACM* 30, no. 6 (1987): 484–497.

Mancini, Paolo. "How to Combine Media Commercialization and Party Affiliation: The Italian Experience." *Political Communication* 17, no. 4 (2000): 319–324.

Mann, Thomas E., and Norman J. Ornstein, eds. *The New Congress*. Washington, D.C.: American Enterprise Institute, 1981.

Marcuse, Herbert. *One Dimensional Man*. New York: Beacon, 1964.

Margolis, Michael, and David Resnick. *Politics as Usual: The Cyberspace "Revolution."* Thousand Oaks, Calif.: Sage Publications, 2000.

Marx, Leo. *The Machine in the Garden: Technology and the Pastoral Idea in America*. London: Oxford University Press, 1964.

McCarthy, Thomas. *The Critical Theory of Jürgen Habermas*. Cambridge, Mass.: MIT Press, 1981.

McCormick, Richard P. "Political Development and the Second Party System." In *The American Party Systems: Stages of Political Development*, edited by William Nisbet Chambers and Walter Dean Burnham. New York: Oxford University Press, 1967.

McCormick, Richard P. *The Second American Party System: Party Formation in the Jacksonian Era*. Chapel Hill: University of North Carolina Press, 1966.

McKee, Samuel Jr., ed. *Alexander Hamilton's Papers on Public Credit, Commerce, and Finance*. New York: Liberal Arts Press, 1957.

McLeod, Douglas M., and Elizabeth M. Perse. "Direct and Indirect Effects of Socioeconomic Status on Public Affairs Knowledge." *Journalism Quarterly* 71, no. 2 (1994): 433–442.

McVeigh, Rory, and Christian Smith. "Who Protests in America: An Analysis of Three Political Alternatives – Inaction, Institutionalized Politics, or Protest." *Sociological Forum* 14, no. 4 (1999): 685–702.

Millican, Edward J. *One United People: The Federalist Papers and the National Idea*. Lexington: University of Kentucky Press, 1990.

Mitchell, William J. *City of Bits: Space, Place, and the Infobahn*. Cambridge, Mass.: MIT Press, 1995.

Moe, Terry M. *The Organization of Interests*. Chicago: University of Chicago Press, 1980.

Mott, Frank Luther. *American Journalism – A History of Newspapers in the United States through 260 Years: 1690 to 1950*. New York: Macmillan, 1950.

Mowrey, David C., and Nathan Rosenberg. *Paths of Innovation: Technological Change in 20th Century America*. Cambridge, Eng.: Cambridge University Press, 1998.

Mughan, Anthony, and Richard Gunther. "The Media in Democratic and Nondemocratic Regimes: A Multilevel Perspective." In *Democracy and the Media: A Comparative Perspective*, edited by Anthony Mughan and Richard Gunther. Cambridge, Eng.: Cambridge University Press, 2000. Pp. 1–27.

Mumford, Lewis. *The Myth of the Machine*, vol. 1: *Technics and Human Development*. New York: Harcourt, Brace and World, 1967.

————. *The Myth of the Machine*, vol. 2: *The Pentagon of Power*. New York: Harcourt, Brace and World, 1970.

———. *Technics and Civilization.* New York: Harcourt, Brace and World, 1963.

Neuman, W. Russell. *The Future of the Mass Audience.* Cambridge, Eng.: Cambridge University Press, 1991.

———. *The Paradox of Mass Politics: Knowledge and Opinion in the American Electorate.* Cambridge, Mass.: Harvard University Press, 1986.

Neuman, W. Russell, Ann N. Crigler, and Marion R. Just. *Common Knowledge: News and the Construction of Political Meaning.* Chicago: University of Chicago Press, 1992.

Norris, Pippa. *Digital Divide: Civic Engagement, Information Poverty, and the Internet Worldwide.* Cambridge, Eng.: Cambridge University Press, 2001.

Olson, Mancur. *The Logic of Collective Action: Public Goods and the Theory of Groups.* Cambridge, Mass.: Harvard University Press, 1971.

Ott, Dana, and Melissa Rosser. "The Electronic Republic? The Role of the Internet in Promoting Democracy in Africa." In *The Internet, Democracy, and Democratization,* 3rd ed., edited by Peter Ferdinand. London: Frank Cass, 2000. Pp. 137–156.

Owen, Bruce M. *The Internet Challenge to Television.* Cambridge, Mass.: Harvard University Press, 1999.

Patterson, Thomas E. *The Mass Media Election: How Americans Choose Their President.* New York: Praeger, 1980.

Petracca, Mark. *The Politics of Interests.* Boulder: Westview, 1992.

Popkin, Samuel L. *The Reasoning Voter: Communication and Persuasion in Presidential Campaigns.* Chicago: University of Chicago Press, 1991.

Poster, Mark. *The Second Media Age.* Cambridge, Mass.: Polity Press, 1995.

Powell, Walter W. "Neither Market nor Heirarchy: Network Forms of Organization." *Research in Organizational Behavior* 12 (1990): 295–336.

Price, Vincent, and John Zaller. "Who Gets the News? Alternative Measures of News Reception and their Implications for Research." *Public Opinion Quarterly* 57, no. 2 (1993): 133–164.

Putnam, Robert D. *Bowling Alone: The Collapse and Revival of American Community.* New York: Simon and Schuster, 2000.

Quade, Quentin L. *Financing School Education: The Struggle between Government Monopoly and Parental Control.* New Brunswick, N.J.: Transaction Press, 1996.

Rabe, Barry G. "Power to the States: The Promise and Pitfalls of Decentralization." In *Environmental Policy in the 1990s,* 3rd ed., edited by Norman J. Vig and Michael E. Kraft. Washington, D.C.: Congressional Quarterly, 1997. Pp. 31–52.

Rogers, Everett. *Diffusion of Innovations.* New York: Free Press, 1962.

Rosenbaum, Walter A. *Environmental Politics and Policy,* 3rd ed. Washington, D.C.: CQ Press, 1995.

Rosenstone, Steven J., and John Mark Hansen. *Mobilization, Participation, and Democracy in America.* New York: Macmillan, 1993.

Rosenstone, Steven J., Roy Behr, and Edward Lazarus. *Third Parties in America: Citizen Response to Major Party Failure.* Princeton: Princeton University Press, 1984.

Scammon, Richard M., Alice V. McGillivray, and Rhodes Cook, eds. *America Votes: A Handbook of Contemporary Election Statistics.* Washington, D.C.: CQ Press, 1996.

Schattschneider, E. E. *The Semisovereign People: A Realist's View of Democracy in America.* New York: Holt, Rinehart and Winston, 1960.

Schier, Steven E. *By Invitation Only: The Rise of Exclusive Politics in the United States.* Pittsburgh: University of Pittsburgh Press, 2000.

Schlesinger, Arthur M., Jr. *The Age of Jackson*. Boston: Little, Brown, 1946.

Schlozman, Kay Lehman, and John Tierney. *Organized Interests and American Democracy*. New York: Harper and Row, 1986.

Schudson, Michael. *Discovering the News: A Social History of American Newspapers*. New York: Basic Books, 1978.

————. *The Good Citizen: A History of American Civic Life*. New York: Martin Kessler Books, 1998.

Schwartz, Evan. "Looking for Community on the Internet." *The Responsive Community* 5, no. 1 (1995): 54–58.

Shade, William G. "Political Pluralism and Party Development: The Creation of a Modern Party System, 1815–1852." In *The Evolution of American Electoral Systems*, edited by Paul Kleppner, Walter Dean Burnham, Ronald Formisano, Samuel P. Hays, Richard Jensen, and William G. Shade. Westport, Conn.: Greenwood, 1981. Pp. 77–112.

Shaiko, Ronald G. *Voices and Echoes for the Environment: Public Interest Representation in the 1990s and Beyond*. New York: Columbia University Press, 1999.

Shannon, C. E. "A Mathematical Theory of Communication." *Bell System Technical Journal* 27 (July 1948): 379–423; (October 1948): 623–656.

Simon, Herbert A. *Models of Man: Social and Rational*. New York: Wiley, 1957.

Singh, Robert. "Gun Control in America." *Political Quarterly* 69, no. 3 (1998): 288–296.

Skocpol, Theda. "How Americans Became Civic." In *Civic Engagement in American Democracy*, edited by Theda Skocpol and Morris P. Fiorina. Washington, D.C.: Brookings Institution and Russell Sage Foundation, 1999. Pp. 27–80.

Skolnick, Jerome, ed. *The Politics of Protest and Confrontation: A Staff Report to the National Commission on the Causes and Prevention of Violence*. Washington, D.C.: Government Printing Office, 1969.

Skowronek, Stephen. *Building a New American State: The Expansion of National Administrative Capacities 1877–1920*. Cambridge, Eng.: Cambridge University Press, 1982.

Smith, Bruce L. R. *American Science Policy since World War II*. Washington, D.C.: Brookings Institution, 1990.

Smith, James Allen. *The Spirit of American Government*. New York: Macmillan, 1907.

Smith, Merritt Roe, and Leo Marx, eds. *Does Technology Drive History? The Dilemma of Technological Determinism*. Cambridge, Mass.: MIT Press, 1994.

Smith, Raymond Arthur. "Overcoming the Collective Action Dilemma: Political Participation in Lesbian-Gay-Bisexual Pride Marches." Ph.D. diss., Columbia University, 1999.

Sniderman, Paul M., Richard A. Brody, and Philip E. Tetlock. *Reasoning and Choice: Explorations in Political Psychology*. Cambridge, Eng.: Cambridge University Press, 1991.

Solop, Fred. "Digital Democracy Comes of Age in Arizona: Participation and Politics in the First Binding Internet Election." Paper prepared for the annual meeting of the American Political Science Association, Washington, D.C., Aug. 31–Sept. 3, 2000.

Spitzer, Robert J. *The Politics of Gun Control*. New York: Chatham House, 1995.

Standage, Tom. *The Victorian Internet: The Remarkable Story of the Telegraph and the Nineteenth Century's On-Line Pioneers*. New York: Walker and Company, 1998.

Stanley, Harold W., and Richard G. Niemi. *Vital Statistics on American Politics, 1997–1998*. Washington, D.C.: Congressional Quarterly, 1998.

Stinchcombe, Arthur L. *Information and Organizations*. Berkeley: University of California Press, 1990.

Sundquist, James L. *Dynamics of the Party System: Alignment and Realignment of Political Parties in the United States*, rev. ed. Washington, D.C.: Brookings Institution, 1983.

Sunstein, Cass. *Republic.com*. Princeton, N.J.: Princeton University Press, 2001.

Swanson, David. "The Homologous Evolution of Political Communication and Civic Engagement: Good News, Bad News, and No News." *Political Communication* 17, no. 4 (2000): 409–414.

Switzer, Jacqueline Vaughn. *Environmental Politics: Domestic and Global Dimensions*. New York: St. Martins, 1994.

Tarrow, Sidney. *Power in Movement: Social Movements and Contentious Politics*, 2nd ed. Cambridge, Eng.: Cambridge University Press, 1998.

Taylor, Frederick W. *The Principles of Scientific Management*. 1911. Reprint, New York: W. W. Norton, 1967.

Thompson, Margaret Susan. *The "Spider Web": Congress and Lobbying in the Age of Grant*. Ithaca: Cornell University Press, 1985.

Tiedt, Sidney W. *The Role of the Federal Government in Education*. New York: Oxford University Press, 1966.

Tocqueville, Alexis de. *Democracy in America*, vol. 2. 1840. Reprint, New York: Vintage Books, 1945.

Truman, David. *The Governmental Process: Political Interest and Public Opinion*. New York: Alfred E. Knopf, 1965.

Verba, Sidney, Kay Lehman Schlozman, and Henry E. Brady. *Voice and Equality: Civic Voluntarism in American Politics*. Cambridge, Mass.: Harvard University Press, 1995.

Walker, Jack L. *Mobilizing Interest Groups in America: Patrons, Professions, and Social Movements*. Ann Arbor: University of Michigan Press, 1991.

Weare, Christopher, Juliet A. Musso, and Matthew L. Hale, "The Political Economy of Electronic Democratic Forums: The Design of California Municipal Web Sites." Paper presented at the annual meeting of the American Political Science Association, Atlanta, Ga., Sept. 2–5, 1999.

West, Darrell. *Air Wars: Television Advertising in Election Campaigns, 1952–1996*. Washington, D.C.: CQ Press, 1997.

Wiebe, Robert H. *The Search for Order, 1877–1920*. New York: Hill and Wang, 1967.

Wilhelm, Anthony G. *Democracy in the Digital Age: Challenges to Political Life in Cyberspace*. New York: Routledge, 2000.

Williams, Bruce A., and Michael X. Delli Carpini. "Unchained Reaction: The Collapse of Media Gatekeeping and the Lewinsky-Clinton Scandal." *Journalism: Theory, Practice and Criticism* 1, no. 1 (2001): 61–85.

Williamson, O. E. *Markets and Hierarchies*. New York: Free Press, 1975.

Wills, Gary. *Explaining America: The Federalist*. Garden City, N.Y.: Doubleday, 1981.

Wirt, Frederick M., and Michael W. Kirst. *The Political Dynamics of American Education*. Berkeley: McCutchan Publishing, 1997.

Wolfinger, Raymond E., and Steven J. Rosenstone. *Who Votes?* New Haven: Yale University Press, 1980.

Wolpert, Robin M., and James G. Gimpel. "Self-Interest, Symbolic Politics, and Public Attitudes toward Gun Control." *Political Behavior* 20, no. 3 (1998): 241–262.

World Almanac and Book of Facts. Mahwah, N.J.: Funk and Wagnalls, 1994.

Yoho, James. "Madison on the Beneficial Effects of Interest Groups: What Was Left Unsaid in *Federalist 10*." *Polity* 27, no. 4 (1995): 587–605.

Young, James Sterling. *The Washington Community 1800–1828*. New York: Columbia University Press, 1966.

Zaller, John. *The Nature and Origins of Mass Opinion*. Cambridge, Eng.: Cambridge University Press, 1992.

Zaret, David. *Origins of Democratic Culture: Printing, Petitions, and the Public Sphere in Early-Modern England*. Princeton, N.J.: Princeton University Press, 2000.

Zillman, Dolf, and Jennings Bryant, eds. *Selective Exposure to Communication*. Hillsdale, N.J.: Lawrence Erlbaum Associates, 1985.

Index

Food and Drug Administration (FDA), 66
framing, 75, 87, 131, 145, 154, 161, 164

General Federation of Women's Clubs, 73
General Social Survey (GSS), 223, 224
Gilded Age, 62–63, 69, 72
Girl Scouts, 67
Gore, Albert, Jr., 123, 154, 155, 172, 185,
    186, 187, 193, 194
Great Depression, 62, 212
Green, Ben, 186, 187
Greenpeace, 135, 136, 140
gun control: American Bar Association,
    Coordinating Committee on Gun
    Violence and, 161; American Jewish
    Congress and, 161; Citizens
    Committee for the Right to Keep and
    Bear Arms and, 161; Gun Owners of
    America and, 161; politics of, 161–173;
    Second Amendment Sisters and,
    169–171; survey data and, 162
Gutenberg bible, 9

Hamilton, Alexander, 34–35, 39–40,
    43–44, 50, 106
Handgun Control, Inc., see Brady
    Campaign to Prevent Gun Violence
Harding, Warren G., 78
Harrison, Benjamin, 46
Health Insurance Association of America,
    83
Hoover, Herbert, 78, 79

industrial revolution, 13, 19, 20, 21, 62–76
information: abundance, 28, 29, 31,
    89–95, 97–109, 112, 125, 143, 188, 190,
    192, 197, 200, 203, 205, 227, 229–231,
    239–243, 246; campaign advertising
    and, 101; citizenship and, 35–38;
    conflicting sources of, 205; cost of,
    8, 21, 22, 24–26, 45, 46, 74, 87, 89–90,
    95–102, 107, 132, 146, 182, 188–194,
    196, 201, 205, 210, 231, 240–242;
    environmental knowledge culture and,
    137; factions and, 41–47; formation of
    groups and, 92; Hotelling effect and,
    204; instrumental approach to, 200,

205; marginal returns and, 205, 206;
    mediation of, 39–41, 45; penny papers
    and, 52; policy development and, 17;
    political change and, 12; political size
    and, 36–38, 39; recording and archiving
    of, 91; relationship to structural
    features of society, 95–96; relationship
    to technology, 8, 230–231; responsible
    citizen and, 197; role of state
    governments, 39; sources of inequality,
    239–240; unitary government and, 38.
    See also information regimes;
    information revolutions; information
    technology
information regimes: broadcast television
    and, 86; general theory of, 18–21,
    25–27, 33, 62, 65, 69, 75, 89, 91,
    119–120, 196, 199–200, 209, 217, 228,
    230, 245–249; information specialists
    and, 85; political influence and, 22;
    specialized groups and, 74;
    technological developments and,
    59–60. See also information revolutions
information revolutions: broadcasting
    and, 19; characteristics of, 91–92;
    collective action and, 18; definition of,
    15, 20; general theory of, 13, 17–18,
    21–22, 25, 26–27, 33, 50, 87, 89, 91, 92,
    119, 196, 197–200, 203, 217, 229–231,
    237, 240, 242, 245–247;
    industrialization and, 62; mass
    audience and, 75–78; pluralism and,
    19; political parties and, 71–72,
    174–175, 185; postal service and, 19;
    voting behavior and, 199, 200. See also
    information regimes
information technology: acceleration of
    political processes and, 191–192;
    bulletin boards and, 28; Center for
    Information and Reform Action
    Network (PIJAR) and, 235; changes in
    characteristics of information and, 96;
    cheap talk problem and, 107–108,
    194–195; citizen engagement and, 197,
    198; competition for engagement and,
    191; contemporary characteristics of,
    204–205; cost of, 158, 172, 180, 187,

priming, 75, 106
Progressive Era, 69, 71, 72, 76, 198
psychological approach to political
  learning, 205–210, 217, 224, 230–231,
  249
public sphere, 1, 7

radio, 75, 78–84, 150, 186, 203, 211,
  213
railroads, 46, 59–60, 62, 65, 94
rational choice theory, 14, 24, 25,
  200–202, 205–207, 241
Reagan, Ronald, 134–135, 162
Reed, Lynn, 181, 187, 189
Roosevelt, Franklin D., 79, 80
Roosevelt, Theodore, 71

Save Our Environment Coalition,
  147–149
Second Amendment, 161, 163, 164,
  169
Second Amendment Sisters, 169–171
Seventeenth Amendment, 67
Shakespeare, William, 9
Sierra Club, 133–136, 140, 147

Taft, William H., 73
Telecommunications Act of 1996,
  150–151, 156
telegraph, 46, 60–62, 77, 94
telephone, 28, 29, 46, 74, 75, 90, 108, 116,
  150, 179, 194, 196, 212, 213
television, 1, 20, 28–30, 61, 75–77, 80–86,
  90–91, 101–102, 106, 150, 176–177,
  181, 186–188, 199, 204, 207–208, 211,
  217–219, 231, 248
Time magazine, 155
Tocqueville, Alexander de, 16–17, 64, 90,
  92–94, 98, 104, 116, 139, 238
Truman, Harry S, 80
Twenty-second Amendment, 198
Tyler, John, 46

United States Constitution, 21, 26, 35, 42,
  106
United States Department of Agriculture,
  66; Forest Service, 66, 134, 146
United States Department of Commerce,
  66
United States Department of Education,
  159
United States Department of Energy, 134
United States Department of Labor, 66
United States Department of State, 59
United States Department of
  Transportation, 134
United States Department of the
  Treasury, 59, 127
United States Navy, 59, 116–117
United States Postal Service, 19, 47,
  50–55, 60, 66, 74, 116, 231

Vance, Stephanie, 195
Violent and Repeat Juvenile Offender
  Accountability and Rehabilitation
  Act of 1999 (Juvenile Crime bill), 172,
  173
Votenet, 174, 195
voter turnout: Australian ballot and, 67,
  76; cost of information and, 200,
  201–202; decline of, 22, 24; historical
  changes in, 198–200; information
  technology and, 200, 204; rationalized
  citizen and, 199; surveys and 210, 224,
  228
voting, 198, 199, 200, 227

Weber, Max, 17, 64, 94–99, 102, 109, 196,
  241, 247
Wilderness Society, 135, 138
Wilson, Woodrow, 71
World Trade Organization, 117
World War II, 79, 96, 249
World Wildlife Fund, 133, 141, 144–147,
  191